HORTUS
Revisited

A Twenty-first Birthday Anthology

HORTUS
Revisited
A Twenty-first Birthday Anthology

Editor DAVID WHEELER

F

FRANCES LINCOLN LIMITED
PUBLISHERS

DEDICATION.

For Lis Robinson, who twitched the colons... and more.

Frances Lincoln Limited
4 Torriano Mews
Torriano Avenue
London NW5 2RZ
www.franceslincoln.com

Hortus Revisited: A 21st Birthday Anthology
Copyright © Frances Lincoln Limited 2008
Copyright in each of the individual articles rests in the
contributor indicated at the head of the article

British Library Cataloguing in Publication Data
A catalogue record for this book is available from the British
Library

ISBN 978-0-7112-2738-5

Designed by Ian Hunt

Printed in Singapore

9 8 7 6 5 4 3 2 1

Contents

From the Editor's Desk

Twenty-one is a significant number. It's a yardstick for humans reaching their majority (to use an old-fashioned term) and it's a landmark in the life of any small business. And twenty-one years of HORTUS offers a delightful opportunity to look back along a tunnel of time and savour once more a few of the high points along the way. This anthology is both a sampler (if you like this book, you'll like reading HORTUS every quarter) and a modest celebration of some 10,000 pages of original garden writing so far published in HORTUS.

As far as I know, HORTUS is the world's only privately published gardening periodical. Why, I'm often asked, did I start it? It all began on the kitchen table of my Farnham (Surrey) cottage in 1987. I had for several years run the RSPCA's then-new animal welfare campaigns department, following a decade in Fleet Street, where I worked for both the *Observer* and the *Spectator*. When, after a short while and because of financial problems, the RSPCA abandoned their bold new venture I was left to decide my future: should I return to London and try my hand again in the 'street of shame', or should I strike out alone and find something remunerative that would also chime with my freshly rekindled childhood love of gardening? The latter triumphed. By working as a jobbing gardener five days a week I was able to pay the bills – but a potent whiff of printers' ink lingered in my nostrils, as potent as the fragrance of my newly rediscovered roses. It overcame me at a time when magazine gardening articles were getting shorter (to allow for ever more photographs) and as a seemingly endless crop of highly illustrated books was published to provide the quick fix that rookie gardeners are said to crave. The victim was the printed word. Yes, there were magazines issued by various horticultural societies, and the weekend broadsheets began to expand their garden coverage, but there seemed no natural home for the well-turned garden essay, writing that favoured aesthetics over practicalities, and was a pleasure to read for its own sake. Enter HORTUS, deliberately modelled on interwar private press production values almost as important as the words themselves.

In my Introduction to HORTUS 81, the issue which marked the beginning of our twenty-first year, I said:

> The title HORTUS was suggested to me by garden designer John Brookes when I expounded my crazy notion to set up as a publisher.

After all, I was untrained as a gardener and what I knew about publishing was distinctly second-hand. John was nevertheless encouraging; he contributed to the first issue, but thought, I'm sure, that I'd bankrupt myself within a year. That hasn't happened, but nor has the magazine provided the comfortable living I once imagined it might. Asked if HORTUS makes a profit I'm fond of saying 'it breaks even elegantly' or, put more graphically: it pays for the tonic, not the gin.

In preparing this anthology I have relived some poignant and stimulating moments. I have been especially proud of the lighter, in some cases comic self-deprecating, pieces – for gardening provides an enormous measure of fun and entertainment, unaccountably little of which has translated comfortably to the printed page. To publish the likes of John Kelly, John Francis and Derek Toms – to name but three distinctive writers, each one called in far too soon by the Grim Reaper – has given me the chance to leaven a broad range of styles with wit and humour. I could have filled this book with their jocose deliberations, although it is comforting to know that they are preserved for all time in a long string of back numbers now, happily, considered by many readers to be indispensable.

With so many pages of original garden writing to choose from, my job of selecting a representative collection has not been easy. So much of value must for now remain between the covers of those indispensables (almost all in print, by the way, so don't needlessly deprive yourself) and – who knows? – another landmark anniversary, or another generation may spawn further collections. In the end I decided to let the chosen authors speak through just one typical piece. Regrettably, this means passing over – for example – many deep and penetrating interviews by Diana Ross with such present-day luminaries as Beth Chatto, Roy Lancaster, Richard Mabey and the Marchioness of Salisbury. Portraits of Christopher Lloyd (through a series of reverent and irreverent tributes by a group of his close friends), Valerie Finnis and Graham Stuart Thomas must also wait for another occasion.

I have been able to find room for only one piece (about Henry James's *The Aspern Papers*) to exemplify our long-running look at gardens in fiction. Many writers have contributed to this series, revealing the myriad horticultural pleasures to be found in novels by E. F. Benson, Dickens, Ronald Firbank, Elizabeth Bowen, Guiseppe di Lampedusa, Barbara Pym, Molly Keane, Angus Wilson, Nancy Mitford, Jocelyn Brooke – the list goes on . . .

It is such components of HORTUS, I believe, that led Anne Raver to say in the *New York Times*: 'What a relief to read lean, sturdy sentences. To leap free of prose gushing with advertising-driven enthusiasm for the perennial-of-the-year. To see gardening as part of civilization, bound up in commerce, science, art and literature.'

The HORTUS mini-monographs of genera including *Papaver*, *Primula* and *Salvia* can only be represented here by Audrey le Lièvere's delvings into the world of tulips. At a sprint rather than the long haul, HORTUS has also included innumerable shorter pieces about garden plants by a diversity of writers: gardeners, nurserymen, landscapers, botanists. Roses, quite rightly, have featured throughout, culminating on one occasion with a whole issue to themselves, with specially commissioned articles from several countries, including Saudi Arabia, India and China.

Nor have we overlooked the United States, whose inhabitants in our early years seemed to want only to hear about British gardens. My attempts to return the compliment have resulted in numerous articles on American gardening, garden-making and garden history.

Adventure plays its part, too: here, Tony Schilling's yarns from Annapurna must suffice as a taster for HORTUS's many tales of plant-hunters ancient and modern.

For many readers it is stories of garden-makers and the gardens themselves that take centre stage in HORTUS. The list seems unending, with writers young and old, British and foreign, chronicling great gardens – from the grandest National Trust establishment to the obscure, enclosed, private world of one individual. Tim Longville has been a veritable Sherlock Holmes in seeking out (and sharing the joys of) many hitherto little-known gardens in the north of England. Others have brought to the journal's pages the heroic, eccentric and sometimes downright mad goings-on of men and women chasing their own particular gardening dreams.

HORTUS owes a tremendous debt to these numerous writers – and to a legion of wood-engravers (notably Yvonne Skargon), illustrators and photographers – who have helped furnish its pages for sums of money far less than they deserve, or could have earned elsewhere.

Well-known names are only part of the story: HORTUS has published many new and previously unheard-of writers, frequently giving a helping hand where one was needed. In 2003 our concern for the encouragement of new writing talent led to a competition held in conjunction with the *Times* newspaper – an initiative that generated more than 700 entries.

Although put together by a very small team, HORTUS is the work of many hands. Let me therefore award a few laurels, heartfelt thanks and much appreciation to copy-editor Liz Robinson, who nagged me from the very beginning to let her twitch the colons and put the commas in the right place; to Simon Dorrell, who 'joined' HORTUS for the winter 1988 issue and who has since contributed countless fine drawings (dammit, he still doesn't wear glasses) which have won a special place in subscribers' hearts. (Simon, by the way, is rather more than our Art Editor: he somehow manages separate careers as successful landscape painter, with a trail of one-man shows to his credit; garden designer; 'master' of the HORTUS garden(s); expert bookcase builder; and – when asked – tireless 'gopher' and great encourager.) And, not least, thanks to Barbara Lancett, for eight years our subscriptions supremo, and to her husband Tony, who somehow copes with my imbecile computering and makes sure the wretched machines tick along as best they can. Stan Lane at Gloucester Typesetting slaved over his hot-metal machines for many years until improved technology made it both quicker and more economical for us – reluctantly – to give up hot-metal typography in favour of photo-typesetting. For those interested in such matters, by the way, the new technology has allowed us to continue with the distinctive Van Dijck typeface based on that used in the great Dutch gardening books of the mid-seventeenth century and recut for the Monotype system in 1937 – chosen for HORTUS by John Commander in our first year. (Incidentally, any inconsistency in the type size in this book simply reflects the various point sizes used during the past twenty-one years.) Finally, thanks to Smith Settle, Yorkshire-based printers, binders and sometime typesetters, who, despite our variable schedules have managed to produce a long succession of handsome-looking Horti. Many others have helped from time to time (Pete, Alison, Martin, Liz, Max, Cathy, Antonia . . .) with extra proofreading and the all-important mailing of subscribers' copies – still packed and stamped four times a year on the kitchen table. To everyone, again, thanks indeed. Oh, and I almost forgot . . . our loudest 'thank you' of all is to our subscribers, to those who have 'kept the faith' and – most importantly – continued to renew their HORTUS subscriptions (hooray, more tonic!) every year.

David Wheeler
Founder and Editor of HORTUS
www.hortus.co.uk
Herefordshire, June 2007

Scent Gardening

STEPHEN LACEY

Of all the ingredients we employ in the creation of a garden, scent is probably the most potent and the least understood. Its effects can be either direct and immediate, drowning our senses in a surge of sugary vapour, or they can be subtle and delayed, slowly wafting into our consciousness, stirring our emotions and colouring our thoughts. Sometimes a scent will linger in the air for days, filtering through open windows and engulfing armchairs and dinner tables; at other times a fragrance will evaporate almost the moment it arrives, leaving only a tantalising taste in the nostrils. Plants themselves play tricks with their scents, exuding perfume one day and not the next, chemically altering their fragrance from sweetness to putrefaction, and even, in one notorious case (that of the musk plant, *Mimulus moschatus*), abandoning their scent altogether.

Faced with all this uncertainty and unpredictability, gardeners tend to shy away from any attempt to manage scent in the garden in any coherent way. Fragrance becomes very much an afterthought, an addition to a carefully composed planting scheme. Only after deciding that your border should consist of silver foliage and yellow flowers, for example, and after organising a pleasing arrangement of tiered heights and contrasting leaf forms, will you stop for a moment to consider whether you have incorporated any items to please your nose. To a large extent this sort of approach to planting is inevitable. This visual impact is after all crucial. But I wonder whether you have ever thought of attempting the process in reverse in one or two parts of the garden, and taken up the challenge of allowing scent to dictate the entire composition.

The best place to construct a scented scheme is somewhere sunny and sheltered, ideally against a warm wall where the air is still and where heat is radiated on cool evenings, somewhere you are inclined to sit and ruminate, where you will be most receptive to a fragrant siege. A seat is a most important component for, apart from encouraging relaxation, it enables you to enjoy many different scents simultaneously. Not only can you position aromatic foliage around your feet, scented perennials at your elbow and fragrant shrubs near your nose, but you can construct the seat out of scent as well by making a raised bed of chamomile and prostrate thymes and giving it arms and a back rest.

The next stage is to decide on a theme. Do you want, perhaps, an assortment of fruity scents, a blend of apple and plum, orange and pineapple, lemon and banana? Or an Indian bouquet of herbs and incense and hot spices? Or a pot pourri of rose petals with the perfume of violet and honey sharpened with mint or musk? Your choice of theme is obviously governed by the scents available in the plant world, but you will be surprised how many distinct fragrances you discover once you begin noting them down for future reference. Some readers may like to know that even the smell of bubblegum is available through the slightly tender but beautiful climber, *Trachelospermum asiaticum*.

Often a particular scented plant will be the inspiration for the entire scheme, but where the theme comes first you will probably need to use your notebook to jog your memory. In the above examples we could use, for our basket of fruit, the leaves of *Rosa eglanteria* (apple), *R. soulieana* (banana), *Lippia citriodora* (lemon), and *Ruta graveolens* (orange) and the flowers of *Iris graminea* (plum) and *Cytisus battandieri* (pineapple); for our Indian bouquet, a host of herbs including sage, rosemary, fennel and marjoram, curry-scented *Helichrysum angustifolium*, *Rosa primula* for incense, and viburnums and pinks for clove; and for our old-fashioned pot pourri, the flowers of rugosa, alba, bourbon, and hybrid musk roses blended with honeysuckle and the leaves of peppermint and *Pelargonium tomentosum*.

The visual appearance of your scented scheme is the next matter to consider. If all your ingredients are wild and wispy, untidy in foliage and dreary after flowering, then you have to introduce some strong architectural forms as a counterbalance. Box is ideal, especially when clipped into cones, for its leaves are scented of summer; meat-scented *Iris foetidissima* is also valuable as is the silver foliage of artemisias, and, if you are desperate, you can always turn to the resinous leaves of conifers. Where there is an interestingly leafed variant of a scented plant that you want to include, it may be wise to plump for that instead of the ordinary variety – the golden and variegated forms of *Philadelphus coronarius*, the variegated forms of applemint, thyme and lemon balm, and maybe the new golden form of *Choisya ternata* called 'Sundance' (though I have been told the leaf colour is at the expense of flowers) would be examples.

The most rewarding approach to gardening with scent is to pursue a strong visual theme in conjunction with your fragrant theme. Colour is the obvious visual medium to choose because it has a clear relationship with scent. While it is not true to say that similarly coloured flowers have similar scents, scientists have demonstrated that flowers in certain colour ranges are more likely to be scented than others: white, cream, pink and pale yellow are fruitful areas of the spectrum for scented flowers while purple, blue, gold, and red are relatively poorly endowed.

It is particularly amusing to devise schemes in which the colours and scents present are so well matched that they unite to give you one really potent sensuous encounter; the teaming up of lemon flowers and citrus scents, for instance, or sumptuous wine crimsons with rich French perfumes. Many flowers have exactly the fragrance that their appearance suggests – think of *Cosmos atrosanguineus* with its dark velvety blood red petals and its mysterious scent of hot bitter chocolate, or *Buddleia × weyeriana* with its soft orange yellow balls of flower and its warm fragrance of honey, or *Salvia discolor* with its hooded blooms of blackish purple and its sticky scent of blackcurrant. The most fabulous example is perhaps *Hedychium gardnerianum* whose curiously exotic heads of amber yellow and spiky orange are matched by an equally strange perfume, a mixture (unless my nose deceives me) of cloves and mothballs.

Sir Cedric Morris, Artist-Gardener

BETH CHATTO

I first met Cedric Morris about thirty-five years ago, when I was half his age, and he was the age I am now. This is how it came about. Staying with us one summer weekend was a family friend, Nigel Scott, an impulsive, exciting person, gifted with a charm that made him friends wherever he went. He was also an enthusiastic plantsman. He did not know Cedric, but knew of his famous garden. Why shouldn't we go over and see it? It would not have occurred to Andrew and me to invite ourselves, but Nigel had no such qualms. He rang Benton End, and off we went, winding through narrow Suffolk lanes between drifts of Queen Anne's lace, innocent of what lay ahead, unaware that this day was a turning point in the lives of us all.

We arrived, walked across the gravel yard, knocked at the old wooden door and entered a large barn of a room, the like of which we had never seen before. Pale pink-washed walls rising high above us were hung with dramatic paintings of birds, landscapes, flowers and vegetables whose colours, textures and shapes hit me as though I were seeing them all for the first time. Bunches of drying herbs and ropes of garlic hung from hooks on a door, while shelves were crammed with coloured glass, vases, jugs, plates with mottoes – a curious hotch-potch, remnants from travels in years past. Filling the centre of the room was a long, well-scrubbed refectory table, and round it a rim of heads turned towards us. From the far end of the table a tall lean figure rose immediately, hand outstretched, informal and courteous. This was Sir Cedric Morris, artist and famous gardener, elegant in crumpled corduroys, a soft silk scarf around his long neck upon which was a fine head crowned with short-cut waving hair. His tanned face creased into a mischievous grin. Without fuss, a space was made, chairs were shuffled round on the bare yellow brick floor, three more mugs were found, Cedric poured tea and the conversation resumed. I took a deep breath, and listened, feeling incapable of any worthwhile contribution. I was the wife of Andrew Chatto, fruit farmer and grandson of the publisher. Andrew's real interest and life-long study was finding the origins and natural associations of garden plants so that we might know better how to grow them. I was also the mother of two small daughters: much of my time was spent teaching myself the art and

crafts of home-making. I was already influenced by Andrew to appreciate species plants as well as cultivars, but my knowledge was much
more limited than Andrew's who knew and recognised plants through
his studies.

Tea finished, the party broke up. Nigel, Andrew and I were invited
into the garden. It was not a conventionally designed garden with
carefully selected groups of trees and shrubs leading the eye to some
premeditated feature or walk. There were surprisingly few trees or
shrubs. Before Cedric's time it was probably a kitchen garden, and was
surrounded by still sound brick walls, the enclosed area divided into
rectangles by straight and narrow paths. Low box hedges had been
planted along the path edges. Some years later I was pleased to see these
disappear and better use made of the space and time required to keep
box in good condition. A few ancient fruit trees were dotted around.
Among them a tall cherry made the principal feature, wreathed with
ropes of wisteria; sadly, it all collapsed one night in a wild storm. The
other remarkable feature was a vast, spreading medlar (*Mespilus ger-
manica*) whose umbrella-like head covered a wide area, valued by
Cedric for those precious plants requiring shade and shelter from the
drying winds.

Dotted here and there were pillars of old-fashioned roses and several
huge clumps of sword-leafed *Yucca gloriosa*. The rest was a bewildering,
mind-stretching, eye-widening canvas of colour, textures and shapes,
created primarily with bulbous and herbaceous plants. Later I came to
realise it was probably the finest collection of such plants in the
country. But that first afternoon there were far too many unknown
plants for me to see, let alone recognise. You may look, but you will
not see, without knowledge to direct your mind. As you become
familiar with more plants and plant families your eye will pick out the
unfamiliar ones and so add to your pleasure and knowledge. Walking
behind the three men, pricking up my ears (I knew perhaps one Latin
name in ten) I felt like a child in a sweet shop, wanting everything I
saw. Ecstatic, I knew I must grow such plants in my own garden.

It is no exaggeration to say that at Benton End not only the plants,
but the people too were 'characters'. Larger, more intimidating, more
intriguing than any, was Arthur Lett-Haines, always called Lett. An
inventive, introspective painter, he and Cedric had lived together
since the end of the First World War. He ran the household. I doubt if
Cedric could boil an egg; he rarely wrote a letter. Lett organised and

taught in the East Anglian School of Painting and Drawing, which he and Cedric founded, and of which Cedric was Principal. He practically gave up his own work during the latter years of his life to foster Cedric's talents and promote his work. He cooked for the students, who were of all ages and from all walks of life, and for numerous visitors, complaining eloquently as he stirred the pot with one hand, a glass of wine in the other, producing at the end of it memorable dishes.

Lett introduced me to Elizabeth David's books (the three of them had been friends for many years). He sent me into the garden to find wild strawberries beneath the rose bushes, he showed me how to make salad on a chill March evening with blanched pink and cream leaves of sea kale. But it was Cedric who gave me a little type-written catalogue, produced by Kathleen Hunter, who supplied seed of unusual vegetables long before they appeared, in colour, in much grander catalogues. Most of them were not new; in fact they could all be found in *The Vegetable Garden*, published in 1885, written by Messieurs Vilmorin-Andrieux, of Paris, beautifully illustrated with fine line drawings describing all the different kinds of vegetables and salads grown in the latter half of the nineteenth century when gardeners were expected to know how to provide a wide variety of fresh food for the kitchen all the year round. In a way, my interest in unusual plants began in my kitchen garden. Growing unusual vegetables and salads was good training when eventually I came to organise a tidy nursery.

A few months after that first visit we were not surprised when Nigel went to live at Benton End. He looked like a Viking, with his narrow face, handsome hooked nose and sharply jutting eyebrows. By nature a pacifist, Nigel volunteered to fight in Finland in the last war, arriving there without proper clothing or equipment to deal with the terrible conditions. Eventually he escaped back to England via Norway and spent the rest of the war in a minesweeper in the Mediterranean, occasionally being dropped off to spend a few days climbing in the southern Alps, where his interest in species plants began. When peace came he attempted to settle down in a West Country nursery, but he was not equipped for organised routine. The atmosphere at Benton End was, by comparison, relaxed. Nigel added his own aura and fitted into the scheme of things as they were. During his time there the garden expanded and blossomed to the peak of its

Drawing of Sir Cedric Morris by Glyn Morgan

development and fame. This takes nothing away from Cedric as its creator; in Nigel he found a companion who shared his enthusiasm for plants to its fullest extent. They worked together, often from dawn till dusk.

It was about this time, the early fifties, that Cedric's work as a breeder of bearded iris was at its peak. He was the first person in this country to produce a pink iris. One of these was first shown in 1948, on the Gold Medal stand at Chelsea of Messrs Wallace, then of Tunbridge Wells. It was admired by Queen Elizabeth, now the Queen Mother, and she allowed it to be called 'Strathmore', after her own home. The names of Cedric's irises were usually preceded by Benton. I have an old Wallace catalogue containing Cedric Morris introductions in 1951 and '52 with romantic names like 'Benton Damozel', 'Benton Ophelia', 'Benton Fandango'. This last-named variety was a plicata type, meaning the pale silk-textured petals were lightly 'stitched' with fine veins, deepening in tone towards the ruffled edges.

On a few rare occasions, when the iris season was at its best, Cedric and Nigel prepared some of the newest varieties to take to one of the Iris Society shows in London. Can you imagine the performance involved for them to arrive with flowers intact? They had no car, so someone would offer to drive them to the station in Ipswich. Cedric would have hated every minute. He loved to have his plants admired and appreciated but he was not competitive and had no time for pot hunters.

It would be a pity if the records show Cedric only as a famous breeder of iris. Those of us who knew him and his garden over the last thirty years cannot adequately express our debt to him for introducing to us such an amazing collection of unusual plants, primarily species plants rather than cultivars. Today the National Council for the Conservation of Plants and Gardens is doing valuable work, with many specific genera being cared for individually in separate gardens. To us, Cedric's garden appeared to contain them all! An exaggeration, perhaps, but over the span of a long lifetime he collected, preserved and increased a wealth of plants never before seen together in one place. It was practically impossible to take him a plant he did not already possess, although it was tempting to try to do so.

One winter evening after dinner, sitting alone at the table with Cedric and Nigel, I was stunned to hear Cedric say I would never make a good garden where we were living, in our first married home. My heart dropped to the brick floor while my mind struggled to assess what this meant. We had been pouring ourselves into this garden, battling with chalky boulder clay, while I taught myself to propagate plants from the precious screws of paper full of seed, berries or cuttings I had been given by Cedric as well as generous earthy bundles of roots, tubers and bulbs. We were still far away from the ideal we admired in Cedric's garden, where no season was boring, where each time we visited we found fresh plants we had not noticed before. Several years were to pass before circumstances opened our eyes to the inevitability of building a new home and starting a new garden, but the seed had been planted in the dark of that winter night.

Today the great majority of plants established in our garden at White Barn came originally from Benton End. Certain ones in

Irises at Benton End, 1946. Photograph © *Country Life*

particular bring Cedric vividly to life in my mind: the many kinds of
Allium, in flower and seed; the lime-green heads of euphorbia, in particular *Euphorbia wulfenii*, which billowed at the base of a deep Suffolk
pink wall; fritillaries, large and small, plum-purple, soft chestnut, or
pale lemon-yellow, with speckled or netted insides, looking as if they
had been flung into sweeps and drifts among other plants whose
season was yet to come! 'How do you get so many?', I would ask
when I was still cosseting only two or three of these rare bulbs.
'Scatter the seed', he would say. So I did. But I had to learn, as he
had done before me, to nurse the young seedlings for some years before they appeared 'like weeds' in my borders. Old fashioned roses,
hellebores, old double primroses, and lace-edged primulas; alas I have
almost lost those. There could be pages more.

Cedric abominated salmon-pink: 'Knicker pink!', he would snort.
But he loved soft, 'off-beat' shades where the pink was sometimes
greyed with tiny purple veins. His interest in breeding, never far
beneath the surface, led him to produce an oriental poppy far removed from the bright scarlet and crimson of the species. Its flounc-
ing petals were ashen-pink, with a central velvet knob deep in a pool of
dark purple-black blotches. We always called it 'Cedric's Pink', but
now it has become officially known as *Papaver orientale* 'Cedric Morris'.

Another poppy which seeded all over the place at Benton End, with
magic effect, was Cedric's selection taken from the wild scarlet poppy
of the fields. I think he was aiming to get a lavender-coloured poppy;
occasionally he succeeded. Translucent, crumpled petals reflected the
soft dove-grey of rain clouds, faintly suffused with pink. Others, in
shades of pink, were heavily veined with crimson. Or again, shadowed,
shell-pink overlapping petals were edged with a thin dark rim.

Recently I was brought a pan crammed with seedlings of these
poppies, preserved by Mary Grierson, whose minutely observed
paintings I greatly admire. We sat and indulged in nostalgic memories
while she told me how much she owed to Cedric and his garden. It
was he who set her on her career as a famous botanical illustrator.

It was not always dream-like. Meal times could be electrified by
sudden squalls and conflicts, but the roof never fell in. We sat and
waited, suffering with our idols, seeing them as human beings, our
bonds of shyness shattered by the storm.

Sometimes there were nightmares. Nigel died, suddenly and tragic-
ally. Would summer ever be as bright again? Not long after Nigel's

death Millie Hayes found refuge at Benton End. Slender as a flower on a stem, with huge dark eyes and expressive hands, she devoted twenty years of her life, helping to run the household, caring for the two handsome, naughty, darling old men who coloured our lives until eventually the light of each was blown out.

English Bones, American Flesh

ROBERT DASH

My garden is at the far eastern end of Long Island, in New York State, in a town settled in 1656. It is set amidst fields continually farmed since that time and one would need a maul and sledgehammer in order to separate it from its profoundly English influences. Yet a wedge struck with equal force might be needed to pry it from its continuous involvement with the patterns of Abstract Expressionism, a largely American form of painting.

Painting is closely related to gardening but closer still is poetry. I frame poems like canvases and daily see work by Douglas Crase, John Koethe, Marjorie Welish, Donald Britton, Peter Schjeldahl, John Ashbery, Barbara Guest, Gerrit Henry and many others. Winter, for me, has now become the 'sure season' when 'sounds skip long distances' and 'the outside light contracts, the inside one expands /Out of necessity' (Douglas Crase: *The Sure Season*). Autumn is, very definitely, when 'Canada geese zoom in to land and /sleep, a murmurous, feathered herd' (James Schuyler: *To a Watercolorist*).

Further, there is much else that went towards the making of my garden: a love of Indian paths, rather like the secret walks small children think to make, (which counts a lot for how one moves through my garden); an admiration of the roan beauties of abandoned farmland pierced by red cedars and laced and tied by dog roses, honeysuckle and brown, dry grass; the memory of a meadow of a single species of short, grey-leaved, flat-topped, open-flowered Golden rod whose October display was feathered by hundreds of monarch butterflies. I have a stubborn Calvinist belief in utility which causes me to plant vegetables among flowers, use herbs as borders and berrybushes as ornamentals. This brutish littoral, continental climate leads me to choose only such plant material which has infinite stamina. There are recollections of an ancestress who planted hollyhocks at the gate and lilacs out back – but all gardens are a form of autobiography. Moreover, as a painter, I am predelicted towards shape, mass and form and have learned that the predominate colour of all gardens is green and all the rest rather secondary bedeckment. Finally, there is something else, too: a sign on my gate which reads No Callers. (A fierce addiction to privacy, in a democracy, is no small sin, which is why my wind-break is thicker than it need be.)

Madoo, which in an old Scots dialect means My Dove, is the name of my garden of 1.91 acres and I have been at it now for twenty years. I have gone about it as I would a painting, searching for form rather than prefiguring it, putting it through a process more intuitive than intellectual. The blunders are there to learn from; the successes, more often than not, are the result of bold throws. I started from the house and went out towards the edges, often revising solid achievements until they seemed made of finer matter, like marks and erasures of work on paper which sometimes may be torn and fitted again in collage. Black pine, privet and Russian olive form the windbreak, pruned to show their fine trunks and branches, husbanded at their base by a carefully controlled invasion of Golden rod, chicory, Joe Pye weed and milkweed among which I have planted a variety of thalictrum, rhododendron and kalmia. *Lonicera flava* go up white birch. Pebbled areas, through which soar *Lilium canadense*, have brick setts for easier walking and small trickles of santolina, rue, and grasses. I am particularly fond of *Molinia* 'Windspiel'.

Although I like white on white (the Duchess of Edinburgh clematis on a white fence over *Rosa* 'Blanc Double de Coubert' and I like to whiten white by throwing *Clematis paniculata* over yew and holly), the major push is for green on green. I have never cared much for all grey gardens or all blue gardens, indeed I am not certain that they are ever successful, colour being too quixotic to control in that fashion, full of lurking betrayals so that sky blue becomes sea-blue or slate blue and then not blue at all. The air over my garden from whose several points I can see the Atlantic surf is full of a most peculiar double light, rising and falling, and is itself one of the heroes of my landscape, kinder to foliage and bark than to flowers at any rate. Wild air will always do the painting. I have increased the atmosphere's multiple shimmer by putting in four small ponds above whose surfaces small mists sometimes gather. In contrast I have made darkness with a copse of twisted, pruned Arctic willows and another of a spinney of Black pines, the former underplanted with a mix of epemedium, woodruff, Japanese wood anemones and ferns and both washed with the littlest of spring bulbs. Paths are of brick, pebbles or setts or grass and alternate

curves with strict, straight geometries the better to bound, heighten
and confine the predominantly relaxed, semi-wild, superabundant
atmosphere I like.

A meadow garden has been quite successful. Formerly it was
lawn giving a rather dull view from the dining table, made duller
by summer heat and inevitable drought. America is no climate
for lawns. I did not starve the soil to make the meadow but plunged
in robust, thrusty perennials through the grass in pits carefully
nourished with well-rotted manure and much moss peat: monardas,
peonies, Scotch broom, *Rosa rugosa*, Michaelmas daisy, buddleia,
globe thistle, daylilies (of course), sewn tightly into the now,
mostly timothy and volunteered milkweed, Queen Anne's lace,
chicory and Golden rod. It is roughly oval with a backing of Nootka
cycpress, cryptomeria and rhododendron, whose darks perfectly
outline the brighter foil of the foliage.

To my way of seeing, a garden is not a succession of small rooms
or little effects but is one large tableau whose elements are inextricably linked to the accomplishment of the entire garden just as in
painting all passages conduce to the effect of the whole. Lack of
keyed strength in any one of them may lower the pitch and thrift
of the finished canvas.

A muting of a too perfect area is often in order, no matter how
lovely it might be. Just so I have found those recent silvery clematises
are too huge a cynosure to be acceptable to the general garden and
I have taken them out. One can very definitely have too much of a
good thing unless it be some grand ground cover like *Lamium*
'Nancy' whose very modest performance excludes it from the
egregious. The subtle is more alluring. The quieter painting enters
the heart and stays there while those of tremendous, immediate
impact have long since dwindled away.

I do not paint in the way that I garden or garden as I would
employ the brush although the process is often the same. Both
are arts of the wrist, the broadest, largest sort of signature, if you
will, highly idiosyncratic, the result of much doing, much stumbling,
and highly intuited turns and twists before everything fits and
adheres to the scale of one's intention. A good tree must often
be moved to a more reticent spot when it begins to dominate and
thus ruin the total orchestration. Beautiful tunes don't end up as
symphonies nor do witticisms write books. Certain flowers may

emblazon a room but be abusive to a fine garden. For that reason and that of stamina and the ability to take the brunt of the climate (I am in Zone 7, whose average lowest temperature is 0° to —10° F). I choose older varieties of the plant kingdom whose foliage and blossom are, more often than not, circumspect and discreet.

I am now becoming more geometric. In front of the Winter House and Winter Studio I have just installed a brick path I call a view-swiper. It's 120 feet long, (flying out to the potato fields and to the ocean, bringing all that fine view inside the purview of the garden as if it were mine), eight feet wide at the near end, six at the far, with eighty roses ('Frau Dagmar Hartopp') on the sides. The far border will have other, taller rugosas and daylilies mixed with teasels. The site is but a narrow spur attached to my property, surrounded by changing crops whose patterns of growth and tilling are overwhelmingly seductive, requiring but the simplest sort of anchor to moor the peninsula. My canvases now have changed, too, and are rather like foliant form held very close to the eye. Both gestures, then, are new for me, and the feeling from both is a bit scary, akin to someone in the middle of a new high-wire act performing over a slowly withdrawing net. The air of gardens and paintings now seems to me to be filled with a wild, deliciously cold oxygen through which I can still see the first plain view of the working barns I converted, twenty years ago, grey above a blowing field of grass. That verdure, it seems to me, was the very soul of the place 'working backwards, year by year' until it 'reached the center of a landscape'. (John Koethe: *The Near Future*.)

The English bones with which I began now seem entirely covered by what I have done, but that is the way of flesh.

Gardens in Fiction

The Aspern Papers

NANCY-MARY GOODALL

Henry James set this story in Venice. What follows is no more than is relevant to the garden. Two shy, mysterious American ladies, the Misses Bordereau, aunt and niece, live in a 'sequestered and dilapidated old palace' on a quiet canal. They possess a garden behind a high blank wall 'figured over with the patches that please a painter' and also some jealously-guarded secret papers which the hero intends to obtain. Seeing 'a few thin trees and the poles of certain rickety trellises' over the wall, he decides to use the garden as a pretext and to get himself taken in as a lodger.

He gains admission, meets the niece, 'a long pale person' of uncertain age, sees the garden from an upper window and decides that, though shabby, it has 'great capabilities'. He tells her he is doing literary work, *must* have a garden, must be in the open air and cannot live without flowers. It is already April, but he says: 'I'll put in a gardener. You shall have the sweetest flowers in Venice'; and that he would 'undertake that before another month was over the dear old house would be smothered with flowers.' The ancient aunt is rightly suspicious but needs money, so she offers him some empty rooms on the second floor at an extortionate rent. He takes them. Has he not already said that his tastes and habits are of the simplest, and added the irritating words: 'I live on flowers'?

Anyone with a knowledge of gardening may feel that Henry James has prepared a horticultural time-bomb here. His hero will never be able to supply enough flowers from a neglected garden to smother a large Venetian palace in the space of one month; indeed, he is already running two weeks behind schedule when 'Six weeks later, towards the middle of June' – so his first visit must have been at the end of April – he has furnished his rooms, moved in with a manservant and started to spend part of every day in the garden. The ladies will have nothing to do with him, he never sees them, but he had told himself that he would 'succeed by big nosegays. I would batter the old women with lilies – I would bombard their citadel with roses. Their door would have to yield to the pressure when a mound of fragrance should be heaped against it' – a tall order for any gardener. We sit back to watch him come unstuck.

Let us try to follow the timing. As soon as his rooms are arranged – and as this involves engaging his servant as well as the ordering and delivering of a boat-load of furniture, it must have taken at least a week – he 'surveyed the place with a clever expert and made terms' for having the garden put in order. But the 'Venetian capacity for dawdling is of the largest, and for a good many days unlimited litter was all my gardener had to show for his ministrations. There was a great digging of holes and carting about of earth.' After a while our schemer grows so impatient that he thinks of buying flowers – but he suspects the ladies will be watching through their shutters and contains himself. 'Finally, though the delay was long,' he 'perceived some appearances of bloom', he had 'had an arbour arranged' and, in it, worked and 'waited serenely enough till they multiplied.'

By July he was no nearer to obtaining the papers or even seeing the ladies, but as he sat in his arbour 'the bees droned in the flowers', though which he does not say, and he was spending the hot evenings floating in his gondola or at Florian's eating ices. Then, one evening, he comes back early, enters the garden's 'fragrant darkness' and finds the younger Miss Bordereau 'seated in one of the bowers'.

Now comes the bombshell, and it is not for the hero but for us. He says: 'I asked her why, since she thought the garden nice, she had never thanked me . . . for the flowers I had been sending up in such quantities for *the previous three weeks* . . . there had been *a daily armful*' and he would have liked 'a word of recognition'.

Gardeners may well ask how this was possible. Even if work on the garden started immediately, although this seems unlikely among 'Venetians with their capacity for dawdling', if, say, the 'clever expert' was able to find an unemployed gardener by the middle of May, the process of taming a wilderness can take weeks, and we have been told that the garden was 'a tangled enclosure' and had been 'brutally neglected'. We are not told how big it was nor what plants had survived from earlier days, although Miss Bordereau had said 'we've a few but they're very common', while the reference to rickety trellises leads us to suppose that there were at least some climbing roses and jasmine. There was only one gardener to clear the 'unlimited litter', dig his holes, 'cart earth about' and get his plants established – and he may also have had to 'arrange' the arbour. How on earth had he done it?

With his orders to provide 'big nosegays' we can imagine him, by the end of May, working from dawn to dusk, feverishly preparing the soil and sowing annuals – work that should have been done in March or April – and planting anything he could find that would produce flowers suitable for cutting. What would he choose? 'Digging holes' suggests that he put in a number of shrubs, but which? So many shrubs that are useful for flower arranging have finished blooming by July: lilacs, philadelphus and so on, likewise wisteria and blossoming trees – and few shrubs produce much in their first year anyway. Would oleanders or hibiscus have fitted the bill? The irises which grow so well in Italy would also be over, with the peonies, oriental poppies, lupins and the rest of the first flush of perennial flowers. He must have relied heavily on whatever was supplied in pots by the local shops and stalls or perhaps by nurserymen in the Veneto. But we are speaking of late Victorian Venice, not England, today. Did they sell bedding plants in boxes? Could he, at this late stage, obtain sweet peas, carnations, stocks, lilies, potted or boxed and ready to flower? In England sweet peas should be sown, and gladiolus corms planted, in March. Would these be available in Venice as late as May? Sweet Williams should have been planted the previous autumn, and are hardly Italian flowers.

Classic Italian gardens are not known for masses of flower colour but for architectural design, topiary, stonework, ironwork and water, the contrast of light and shade, for cypresses, yew, bay, box and marble, and while Venice has many pots and window boxes these are mainly of small plants, trailing geraniums, marigolds and the like. Such colour as there is in Italian gardens seems, at least in these days, to come, apart from roses, mainly from such things as azaleas, fuchsias, geraniums, Paris daisies and petunias grown in containers that are set out at strategic points as they come into bloom. You could not pick armfuls of flowers from them, and if you did they would take weeks to recover, while a gladiolus or lily, having bloomed, has shot its bolt and can be picked no more.

More is to come. After a talk with the younger lady during which they 'wandered two or three times round the garden' he dares to mention the all-important papers. She takes fright, hurries away and does not reappear, and after four or five days he tells the gardener 'to

stop the floral tributes'. The cutting of armfuls of flowers has lasted
for very nearly *four weeks*. In a later scene, between our hero and the
ancient aunt, she thanks him for the flowers: 'You sent so many . . .'
'I suppose you know you could sell them – the ones you don't use.'
And he replies: 'My gardener disposes of them and I ask no questions.'
It is quite a jolt to realise that Henry James saw flowers as something
to be used or disposed of, and that he imagined that once a supply of
flowers – the only ones he names are lilies and roses – has been turned
on, it flows like a fountain that cannot be turned off. His hero even
turns to the younger Miss Bordereau and invites her to 'come into
the garden and pick them, come as often as you like: come every day.
The flowers are all for you.'

Even if the garden were fairly large – and he says at one point that
he 'wandered about the alleys smoking cigar after cigar' – it must
have been remarkable. This is a famous novel, written by a master,
and the plot takes many fascinating turns: but we are amazed to find
the niece still picking flowers weeks later, her hands full of 'admirable
roses'. Surely most of the roses grown at that time bloomed in June
and early July only. What repeat-flowering roses would we have
found in Venice then?

Could it have been done? Or, and I may well be wrong, are there
only two possible explanations: either that gardener, whose name is
never mentioned, and who was never given a word of praise, was an
unsung hero of horticultural literature, a genius who given an acre in
England could have supplied Covent Garden; or – dare I suggest it?
– fear it may be the case – Henry James, that legend, that great
wordsmith and story teller, was as horrid as his hero who, in all the
long days that the novel records, never touches a flower, never lends
a hand by so much as dead-heading one rose, and, like his hero who
pretended to love flowers so much but knew only two by name, was
a townee and a beast, and unworthy to write about flowers?

Phyllis Reiss at Tintinhull

PENELOPE HOBHOUSE

Phyllis Reiss, a quarter of a century after her death in 1961, would undoubtedly be surprised to find that her strongly individual gardening tastes merit a thorough analysis. She was the sixth child of Colonel and Mrs Alfred Lucas of Hobland Hall near Great Yarmouth in Norfolk. In the family there was a keen tradition of gardening interest. A grandfather, Alfred, and his brother Charlie were both notable gardeners, the latter at Warnham Court near Horsham in Sussex. Colonel Lucas grew prize fruit and his wife was a gardener and beekeeper. According to the family Phyllis was an original child with individual tastes – ready to have a go at anything – and with a sense of humour which she retained all her life. A devoted aunt and a warm and welcoming hostess to people from every walk of life, at both Dowdeswell in Gloucestershire and later at Tintinhull House in Somerset, she and Captain Reiss were childless. This may be significant in that much of her emotional energy could be devoted to developing a gardening taste and style. Characterised by a natural modesty, Mrs Reiss never sought publicity – indeed, like her mentor Lawrence Johnston at Hidcote, she thoroughly disliked having her photograph taken – and if she were alive today might well disclaim her influence on garden styles.

What are the qualities that make her garden planning at Tintinhull memorable? A gifted amateur, she certainly had no formal horticultural training. She came from a family with a gardening tradition, but from a background that would have accepted the innate amateurism of her class and time. Most people of her background would have been expected to have absorbed a fair aesthetic sense, which would find expression in both their house decoration and their garden arrangements. It seems, although nothing is known of her schooling, that she travelled widely, and in Italy would have seen some of the great Renaissance layouts where interconnected garden 'rooms', extensions of the villa, reflected its scale and architecture. Lawrence Johnston when he first envisaged his garden framework at Hidcote must also have drawn on a similar experience. When Mrs Reiss discovered Tintinhull in 1933 she must have recognised not only the classical proportions of its compartmentalised garden areas, but also its almost uncanny similarity, on a reduced scale, to Johnston's inspired composition.

What made her different from many of her contemporaries was her architectural approach to garden layout, to plants and to the colour schemes she prepared for her borders. She went beyond the conception of beds and borders as pictorial compositions; instead she interpreted the garden in terms of spatial relationships, and saw plants as playing a structural part in the overall layout, as fundamental to the framework as walls, paving areas or ancillary buildings. By her, leaf and flower associations were not only considered from the point of view of colour harmony or contrast, but were also judged for weight and density to give balance to a whole or a part of any scheme. Thus, like an architect simplifying the materials with which he would work and which were appropriate to a particular site, she often chose to repeat a particular planting theme in another garden area, refusing to allow additional colours or types of plants to distract from overall unity of purpose. Her contemporaries, especially woman gardeners such as Vita Sackville-West, used pictorial rather than architectural compositions. The latter, the framework of whose own garden at Sissinghurst was created by her husband Harold Nicolson, originally planned the forecourt borders at Montacute House (a few miles from Tintinhull) with pale grey and silver foliage plants and pale flower colours. In the 1950s the National Trust invited Mrs Reiss to replace this planting with stronger, brighter colour blocks to anchor the towering Elizabethan mansion to its site. Margery Fish, a close neighbour at East Lambrook, collected hardy plants which she arranged to emphasise each specimen's particular beauty, rather than seeking any unity of garden design. With her, Mrs Reiss studied plants and their needs. They remained true gardening colleagues, but their gardening ethic was totally different.

Good gardens set an aesthetic standard and, if they survive, become inspirational to future generations. Mrs Reiss was not in any sense a professional designer yet her gardening style, as developed in her own garden at Tintinhull during nearly thirty years, has a simplicity and lack of fuss which make it memorable. Although colour schemes at Tintinhull are strict and many individual harmonies or contrasts are striking, and indeed often daring, the essence of her work lies in the way she used certain plants as architectural features to link the more pictorial and ephemeral seasonal colours. There is another salient

Tintinhull House, the west front

point which is worth making. The garden at Tintinhull is not large – perhaps hardly two acres if the kitchen area is included – and Mrs Reiss had only one gardener and limited resources. Its modest size – and the fact that within the whole garden each of the six geometric compartments could be a prototype for a self-contained garden – ensures that many of today's garden visitors who have small modern gardens, maintained without any outside assistance, can feel that Mrs Reiss's teaching has relevance to their own circumstances.

After the First World War every proper garden had an herbaceous border, some more successful than others, where hardy deciduous perennials were arranged to give pictorial effects as if on a painter's flat canvas. The effects of these compositions were revealed to the appreciative garden visitor as a series of images, sometimes glimpsed across a lawn from afar, at other times unfolding in progression during a garden walk. For the garden *cognoscenti* the Robinson–Jekyll school was firmly established; hardy exotic and native plants grew beside each other in natural-looking clumps and the bedding-out of annuals in ribbons or concentric colour circles had become unfashionable. In gardens such as Hidcote made by Lawrence Johnston between 1907 and the outbreak of war in 1914, cottage-type gardening was on a grand scale. A formal layout of garden 'rooms' with walls of yew, beech, and pleached hornbeam and lime provided a framework and

Tintinhull. Looking west from the house

background for tightly packed informal planting. Captain and Mrs Reiss were neighbours living not far away at Dowdeswell through the 1920s. Undoubtedly the Hidcote style helped form Phyllis Reiss's own tastes. In 1933 they moved to Tintinhull House, near Yeovil.

Tintinhull, where the original Jacobean farmhouse was added to in 1700 and a classical Queen Anne façade faces on to the garden, is as firmly balanced by its garden compartments as any architectural purist could desire. A series of garden 'rooms' is laid out to the west and north in such a way that a garden tour follows a logical route. A long axial stone path links three distinct garden areas. Off this to the north three larger rectangular areas at slightly descending levels are divided by tall yew hedges. In addition mature trees balance with the mass of the house and frame the skyline. Basically Tintinhull was a Hidcote in miniature: two acres instead of ten made it possible to follow the Hidcote theme with only one gardener. When Captain and Mrs Reiss came the basic layout was already established, although the final embellishment, the centrally placed pool garden, was still a tennis court until after the war ended in 1945. Then wide borders were designed in contrasting colour schemes to face each other over lawns and a central water canal.

Mrs Reiss read Gertrude Jekyll's books and may even have visited

Montacute. Mrs Reiss replanted the borders in stronger colours

her garden at Munstead Wood before her death in 1933. Nevertheless her own planting schemes, which often incorporated plants and plant associations taken directly from Miss Jekyll's teaching, remained simpler and therefore easier to follow and interpret. Where Miss Jekyll recommended complicated and sophisticated drifts of colour sequences which blended in the eye, Mrs Reiss kept each plant and colour group in sufficiently large blocks so that each colour remained distinct. She used pure hues such as reds and yellows in strong contrasting blocks which she linked by deliberately repetitive foreground planting of grey and silvery foliage. At the back arching grasses (*Miscanthus sinensis* in various forms) performed the same unifying function. 'Frensham' roses, spires of yellow verbascum, scarlet dahlias and *Achillea* 'Coronation Gold' were set in front of a hedge of dark yew. Elsewhere low-growing blue-flowered plants were massed effectively to make a carpet to frame pale pink shrub roses and magenta-flowered *Geranium psilostemon*. Perhaps the most frequently copied scheme at Tintinhull is a wide border where purple and golden foliage plants make a tapestry background for crimson roses and bright blue *Veronica teucrium*. Purple-leaved plum (*Prunus cerasifera* 'Pissardii') and *Berberis* × *ottawensis* 'Purpurea' with *B. thunbergii atropurpurea* contrast with gold variegated dogwood (*Cornus alba* 'Spaethii'). In search of continuity and to link the different garden 'rooms' together she planted the purple-leaved smoke bush (various cultivars of *Cotinus coggygria*) in more than one place but with different companions; similarly, groups of *regale* lilies were distributed in pots and beds to create different yet repetitive effects, and grey-leaved hostas and alchemillas edged beds and marked corners.

Perhaps fortunately, no detailed Reiss planting plans exist; instead comprehensive plant lists (made by Graham Stuart Thomas in 1954 in conjunction with Mrs Reiss) indicate plant and colour schemes while allowing a certain freedom of arrangement to those in charge today. At Tintinhull and Montacute all planting is 'mixed' in form. Every gardener knows or soon learns that this sort of gardening cannot depend on a blue-print. In mixed beds and borders small trees and shrubs with spreading canopies give height and architecture as well as seasonal flowers and foliage; beneath and between them, covering the ground, bulbs and perennials and drifts of annuals (or tender bedding plants) complete the composition. Almost yearly adjustments keep planting relationships in satisfying proportions. A gardener such as Mrs Reiss, having chosen and placed her foundation planting of trees and shrubs which structured the garden, composed and recomposed her less permanent planting schemes around them.

Some might call it luck that when she came in 1933 she found an almost perfect garden framework within which she could manipulate plants in their design roles. It seems equally fortunate for posterity that she could garden here for nearly thirty years and give the house and garden into the care of the National Trust, ensuring its future. Dame Sylvia Crowe, who took her first job after Swanley Horticultural College with Mrs Reiss's father Colonel Lucas at Hobland, first met her in 1922, when she was already married. They remained firm and affectionate friends. In *Garden Design* (published in 1958 and now reprinted) Sylvia Crowe discusses the qualities of Tintinhull and Mrs Reiss's use of plants. More recently she writes, 'One of Phyllis's strengths was that she knew just what plant was right in a particular place, and would not be seduced by novelty or extra colour'. Perhaps the secret of Mrs Reiss's garden planning lay not only in her capacity to see plants and plant colours in architectural roles, but more simply in her capacity for a limiting self-discipline – most gardens suffer from too many diverse plants placed in too many diverse schemes. Yet how many other gardeners could practice such restraint and not have a tedious garden? Tintinhull was restful but never dull.

Lawrence Johnston, Creator of Hidcote Garden

ALVILDE LEES-MILNE

To thousands of gardeners and horticulturists both professional and amateur in Western Europe, and even to some in Australia, the USA, Canada and Africa, the word Hidcote means only one thing. It means one of the most beautiful, interesting, haunting gardens in existence. Yet how many of these thousands of visitors, who go there year after year, ever give a thought to its creator?

Who was Lawrence Johnston? Where did he come from? Why did he choose a remote and cold Cotswold hilltop on which to make this remarkable garden? How, anyway, did he know so much about gardens? In fact, how could any one man in his lifetime create something so perfect? Perhaps it is time he was brought out a little into the limelight which he so much disliked.

Lawrence Waterbury Johnston was born in Paris on 12 October 1871. His father, Elliott Johnston, came from Baltimore, Maryland, USA, and must have died before 1887, for in that year Lawrence's mother, born Gertrude Cleveland, married Charles Francis Winthrop, son of a prominent New York family. Winthrop died in Paris in 1898. The Johnstons, who had Scottish connections, came from the north of Ireland. Lawrence Johnston's early life was spent in France. His parents evidently belonged to that cultured group of rather well-to-do Americans who in the late nineteenth and early twentieth centuries felt drawn to Europe, where they found more to satisfy their interests and where they often settled for good. In fact, they were what are often loosely termed 'Henry James Americans'.

So Lawrence must from an early age have been accustomed to being surrounded by beauty and culture. Walks in the streets of Paris, visits to museums, visits to *châteaux* and *manoirs* with exquisite gardens, all this and a great deal more must have made a lasting impression upon the small boy. Being in a foreign country he was educated at home by a tutor. He was always very close to his mother; when they went to Hidcote, she lived with him for nearly twenty years and was buried nearby. She seems to have been quite a character, and inevitably somewhat dominated her son.

There is no clear picture to be drawn of him in his early years, and there are a great many gaps in our knowledge of his life. When quite young he became a Roman Catholic, possibly through the influence of his French tutor. It is not known when he first came to England, but it was certainly before he was twenty. The first definite date in his life is 1894 when, after cramming at Shelford, he matriculated at Trinity College, Cambridge. He was then twenty-three. He received an ordinary second class degree in history in 1897, and left the university that year. The next landmark is 1900, when he became a naturalised British subject. In that same year he joined the Imperial Yeomanry as a trooper, and went off to the Boer War. What drew him into that mesh remains a mystery. A longing for adventure, perhaps, coupled with a way of seeing a new continent.

In 1902 he returned, and went to live in Northumberland. The reason for this was twofold. Firstly, when in South Africa he made friends with a young man called Savile Clayton, whose home was near Humshaugh. Secondly, he was suffering from weak lungs, and the bracing north country air was considered healthy. In Northumberland he became a student farmer, lodging with a landowner called George Ray.

Next comes the important date 1907. Lawrence was then thirty-six years old, and had presumably made up his mind where his real interests lay. It was in this year that his mother, Mrs Winthrop, bought for him a property in the heart of the Cotswolds, called Hidcote Bartrim. It consisted of about 280 acres of farmland, a tiny hamlet of thatched cottages, and a small stone farmhouse. There was a wonderful view from the escarpment over the Vale of Evesham away to the Malvern Hills. But the great attraction was a huge and ancient cedar of Lebanon and a clump of fine beech trees.

It was a strange choice, as in those days Hidcote was really remote, and one which could only have been made by someone with considerable vision and imagination. There is no doubt that his active interest in farming was a contributory factor to the acquisition of Hidcote, and perhaps the fact that this hilltop site was considered beneficial for his health. A friend who lived nearby remembered often seeing him ploughing. However, by then gardening had already become his chosen hobby. His interest in, and knowledge of, horticulture must have grown rapidly. Unfortunately, apart from a few very early photographs, there are no records to tell us how he planned the garden at Hidcote. Luckily Mrs Winthrop had a considerable fortune to draw on, and her son knew how best to spend it.

A wing for Mrs Winthrop was added to the little farmhouse, today known as the Manor, and other parts of the house were structurally altered with various embellishments. The farmyard was turned into a respectable courtyard and the cottages were renovated. Later Lawrence designed and built one or two more. He also converted a small barn in the courtyard into a chapel where sometimes he would have Low Mass said, or what the French call a *messe de chasse*.

Life in the country must have been very agreeable in the pre-Great War years, and from this point of view Hidcote was in an auspicious situation geographically. A few miles away at the foot of the escarpment lay Broadway. This lovely little town, as yet undiscovered by tourists, was in its intellectual heyday. A beautiful and famous American actress, Mary Anderson, had come to live there with her Spanish husband, Antonio de Navarro. They had a wide circle of interesting friends. Among others, Elgar, Sargent, William Morris and Burne-Jones were frequent visitors. The Navarros, too, were planning and planting a garden which today is of considerable interest and beauty. Writing in 1936 in her book, *A Few More Memories*, Madame de Navarro said: 'My Italian friends regard Hidcote as the most beautiful garden they have seen in England. Its wonderful blending of colours and its somewhat formal architectural character please them particularly.' Later she wrote of seeing Reginald Farrer's incomparable gentian blooming at Hidcote in November: 'It seemed too good to be true.' But of course this was sixteen years later.

Most of Lawrence Johnston's friends were passionate and knowledgeable gardeners. Here again he was fortunate in having several in the vicinity – Major Mark Fenwick at Abbotswood, the great alpine grower Clarence Elliott near Moreton-in-Marsh, Lord Barrington then living at Armscote and later at Nether Lypiatt where he emulated the tapestry hedges at Hidcote, Charles Wade, then at Snowshill, and George Lees-Milne at Wickhamford. Later the Jack Muirs came to Kiftsgate, which is at the end of the Hidcote drive. Here they created a garden which was to become a rival to Hidcote, though entirely different in character, and which to this day is still very spectacular, and of course immortalised by the great climbing rose that bears its name. Mrs Muir and Lawrence Johnston were able to help each other, and enjoyed many years of close gardening partnership. Then there was Norah Lindsay. Mrs Lindsay was probably Lawrence Johnston's closest woman friend, and though she did not live nearby was a constant visitor. She herself was no mean garden architect, and among her achievements is the parterre which she re-designed on the south side of Blickling Hall in Norfolk. She was gay, witty, amusing, and indeed wonderfully stimulating. Another, geo-graphically distant, friend was 'Bobbie' James (the Hon. Robert James), creator of a great garden, St Nicholas, near Richmond, Yorkshire and, like Lawrence Johnston, an avid collector of rare plants. In fact his friends were legion, each perhaps contributing an idea here and there towards the eventual form of the Hidcote which we know today.

Little by little the garden grew, and the acres of rough pasture were turned into acres of botanical and horticultural interest. Law-rence Johnston's planting was entirely original. It was the very opposite of the conventional herbaceous border setting, so popular among his contemporaries. His blending of sophistication and sim-plicity was unique. Nowhere else, except perhaps at Sissinghurst, are unusual plants found growing in cottage garden-like settings. This conception of little gardens within a large garden was entirely novel, as were the tapestry hedges and many other schemes. There are no fewer than twenty-two separate enclosures within the garden at Hidcote, excluding the Beech Allée, the Lime Avenue and the Holly Avenue.

I have been told that a trainful of lime-free soil arrived from Surrey for the camellias, rhododendrons and other lime-hating plants. This was mixed with rotted sawdust and peat. Those extraordinary lines of hornbeams, looking like hedges on stilts, a *palissade à l'italienne*, appeared later, as did the two little brick and stone pavilions with their pointed, ogival roofs, each side the centre walk. They are said to be copied from something Lawrence Johnston saw in France. But who knows? Some think they have a Dutch influence. The great avenue of Huntingdon elms by the north approach, devastated by the catastrophic elm disease and now replaced by *Quercus cerris* and horn-beam, was a truly bold planting, as was the Holly Avenue leading to the courtyard entrance. One could cover pages eulogising the endless and enthralling innovations at Hidcote, but that is not the purpose of this article. Many people have described the garden, but perhaps no one better than Vita Sackville-West in an article for the Royal Horticultural Society's *Journal* of November 1949. Anyone who has read it can be left in no doubt as to the genius of Lawrence Johnston.

The Fuchsia Garden in spring is a mass of *Scilla sibirica*.
The beds are edged with box. The topiary peacocks at the
entrance to the Pool Garden can be seen in the background

The truth is that in spite of, or because of, its simplicity and bold
planting Hidcote has a sophisticated, continental flavour, which in a
way puts one in mind of gardens in the Isle-de-France.

Like all dedicated gardeners Johnston was both acquisitive and
generous. Yet he allowed no room for poor specimens and failures.
He believed in cramming his beds and borders with what he most
wanted so that there was less space for what he did not want, that is,
weeds. Therefore in each category of plant at Hidcote you will find
only the best. People began to send him plants from far and wide, and
as his knowledge grew, so did his collection.

In his day there was a large winter plant house for the more tender things, a place for the cultivation of lush, sub-tropical species of rare plants, which he had collected on his travels or had been sent by other connoisseurs. Unfortunately, when the National Trust took over the garden this house, proving too costly to run, was demolished and the collection dispersed.

For seven quiet years the garden grew, and Lawrence Johnston worked alongside his gardeners. For he was no onlooker. He dug, and planted, and pruned as much as they did. Then came 1914 and the Great War. All thoughts of gardening had to be laid aside. Johnston, who had never retired from the Army, was promoted a Major and immediately sent off to France. Owing to his friendship with Savile Clayton, his commission was in the Northumberland Fusiliers. Nothing much is known about his military career except that he was wounded at the very beginning of the War, and again later. At one point he was laid out with a lot of other bodies awaiting burial. By chance an old friend from Broadway, Colonel Henry Sidney, had been detailed to see to the burial ceremony, and as he passed Major Johnston, he not only recognised him but saw him move.

When Johnston returned from the War there was much to be done at Hidcote. Four years' neglect in a garden can alter it drastically. As things gradually returned to normal he began to think of going off plant collecting, and in 1927 and 1931 he undertook two enthralling expeditions. The first was with Major Collingwood (Cherry) Ingram on a four-months' trip from Cape Town to the Victoria Falls, during which time he climbed the Drakensburg Mountains. George Taylor (later Sir George Taylor, and Director of Kew Gardens) and Reginald Cory made up the party. The expedition has been splendidly recorded by Major Ingram in his book, *A Garden of Memories*. Lawrence Johnston, who liked his comforts, brought along his Italian cook and chauffeur valet. Major Ingram described Johnston as a typical bachelor, wholly dedicated to gardening, and says that of the four of them he was by far the most catholic in his choice of plants. He would collect members of any genus if they had the slightest claim to beauty. The result was a vast accumulation which he sent for the most part to Edinburgh Botanic Gardens. Many of these plants were later to go to Mentone where he had acquired a property and was making another garden. The second expedition was much longer, more remote and tougher. Johnston accompanied George Forrest on what was to be

Forrest's last journey to Yunnan in China. But unfortunately it proved too arduous for him; he fell ill and had to come home before the expedition was completed. Among other plants which he brought back was that lovely, tender creeper, *Jasminum polyanthum*, which he grew in his south of France garden. Later he gave a plant of it to Major Warre at the Villa Roquebrune and he, in 1938, sent a cutting to England. *The Botanical Magazine* featured it in an article that year. Although it was already known to Kew from seeds which Forrest had collected in 1925, this was the first published reference, and from then on every plant-lover wanted it. Johnston also collected the seeds of *Mahonia siamensis*, and *M. lomariifolia*. The former is tender but it grew very well in his Mentone garden where, just before his death in 1958, it was still looking superb. He also gave it to the Botanic Garden at Cambridge. *Mahonia lomariifolia* is less tender and does well in sheltered positions in this country. It is a spectacular plant with its whorls of golden flowers in the winter. It is thought that, among other species, the seeds of *Hypericum patulum* 'Hidcote' may also have been collected by him, but this is uncertain. Johnston also made several less adventurous journeys in pursuit of rarities for his gardens. The list of plants sent from his Mentone garden to Cambridge after his death is staggering. Unfortunately, few have survived.

He bought the Serre de la Madone, as his French property was called, in the early twenties, with a view to creating a garden which he might enjoy in the winter months. It lies in one of the hidden valleys running up behind Mentone to the foothills of the Alpes Maritimes, right on the Italian frontier. It is a perfect natural setting for a sub-tropical garden, and was already well planted with olive and citrus trees, and sheltered from every wind. Johnston became increasingly absorbed in this Mediterranean paradise, which he crammed with all the plants that could not grow in the cold Cotswolds. He had many gardening friends along the Riviera. Mrs Warre and her husband lived nearby at the Villa Roquebrune. They shared his tastes and had also created a magnificent garden on terraces overhanging the Mediterranean.

Much further west at Hyères lived in those days that renowned French gardener, the Vicomte de Noailles. His property adjoined that of another of Johnston's close friends, Edith Wharton. He often visited them both. Mrs Wharton, writing to Louis Bromfield in 1935, asked, 'Do you know a Spanish rose called Apelles Mestres? Lawrence

Johnston tells me it is the most beautiful rose in the world.' And again later she wrote for the address of a nurseryman near Mortefontaine, 'where we all went one day last summer, and Lawrence Johnston who was staying with me, very kindly ordered for me a very big and splendid magnolia, to be *mis en bac* and delivered in the spring. Neither he nor I seem to have noted the address, and Johnnie wants to be sure the *mis en bac* has been done'.

With the Vicomte de Noailles he planned a journey to Burma for 1938 but owing to the menace of another war it never took place. The Noailles had a squash court where Johnston spent many hours playing. He was also a keen tennis player and liked to get professionals to come and play with him both at Hidcote and in France. He was at the Serre de la Madone when the Germans invaded France, and was evacuated on that terrifyingly overcrowded ship which brought thousands of stranded Britons home in 1940.

During the war he remained at Hidcote, struggling to keep things going, and had some Americans billeted on him. Later his memory began to fail and he found the effort of managing the garden increasingly difficult. Also, he wanted to make suitable arrangements for its preservation after his death. An old friend, Lady Colefax, persuaded him he could not do better than give it to the National Trust. After many months of negotiation the deeds were finally signed, and in 1948 Hidcote Bartrim Garden became the first property the Trust acquired under the new gardens scheme. Johnston retained the use of the house for his life. Partly for tax and partly for climatic reasons he planned to spend most of the year in France, with three months at Hidcote. Although the arrangement was a great weight off his mind, it was a sad one for, as he remarked to an old friend, 'Hidcote is not my baby any more'.

Norah Lindsay died but her daughter Nancy, herself a keen plantswoman, adopted Johnnie, as his friends called him, giving everyone to understand that she was his 'seeing eye', and that she knew just what his wishes were. This assumption led to difficulties, and in 1949 the Trust decided to form a small committee of his local friends, capable of managing the garden in his absence. It consisted of Colonel Shennan, who was the chairman and whose son was Johnston's godson, Mrs Muir from Kiftsgate, Mr de Navarro, the son of Mary Anderson de Navarro, who had inherited his parents' house in Broadway, and, inevitably, Nancy Lindsay. At that time there were four gardeners. Three of them received £1 a week, and Hawkins the head gardener £4 10s. until he asked for a rise, and got £5. In 1949 Hawkins was allowed to exhibit some geraniums at the Chelsea Flower Show and won the Banksian Medal, but that seems to have been the only time Johnston bothered to exhibit anything and perhaps it was really to please Hawkins. In those early days of opening to the public, attendance was very small. Admission was only from 2 till 5 p.m. on three days a week, at a shilling a head. On an August afternoon in 1949 someone counted seven visitors. In June 1950 the admission charge was raised to 1s. 6d. and it was thought very splendid that one day in May a hundred people came. The story is very different today. In 1986 there were approximately 90,000 visitors.

What more do we know about the creator of this truly great and unique garden? He was a small man with fair hair and very blue eyes. One of his old friends described him as blithe. He was shy and modest. He was scrupulous. When visiting the Vatican garden on one occasion he could not resist picking a piece of water ranunculus. Whereupon, turning to a friend, he said, 'Excuse me, I must now go and light a candle.' He also hated publicity. Of the many plants for which we are indebted to him today only one or two bear his name, but many that of Hidcote. He endeared himself to all who knew him well, especially his staff. He was an avid reader of all horticultural literature, and his library contained a fine collection of books on this subject. He enjoyed painting and did a frieze for one of the rooms at Hidcote, as well as decorating the two little garden pavilions. He also decorated a room in the Florentine style for the Muirs at Kiftsgate. He collected old glazed tiles on his travels, which he used very effectively in the bathrooms, kitchens and garden rooms of his two houses. He had a number of French eighteenth-century lead watering-cans, which he would group in strategic corners of his gardens. His choice of garden furniture was faultless and included some lovely reeded iron seats and terracotta urns. He was inseparable from his pack of little dachshunds who went with him to France when he finally decided to leave England. He never married. Above all he loved his gardens. He died at the Serre de la Madone in 1958, and is buried beside his mother in Mickleton churchyard, a mile or two from his beloved Hidcote.

A Gentle Plea for Chaos

MIRABEL OSLER

Looking round gardens, how many of them lack that quality which adds an extra sensory dimension for the sake of orderliness? There is an antiseptic tidiness which characterizes a well-controlled gardener. And I'd go further and say that usually the gardener is male. Men seem more obsessed with order in the garden than women. They are pre-occupied with flower bed edges cut with the precision of a pre-war hair cut. Using a lethal curved blade, they chop along the grass to make it conform to their schoolboy set squares, and with a dustpan and brush they collect 1 cm. of wanton grass. Or, once they hold a hedge-trimmer, within seconds they have guillotined all those tender little growths on hawthorn or honeysuckle hedges that add to the blurring and enchantment of a garden in early June.

The very soul of a garden is shrivelled by zealous regimentation. Off with their heads go the ferns, ladies' mantles or crane's bill. A mania for neatness, a lust for conformity and away goes atmosphere and sensuality. What is left? Earth between plants; the dreaded tedium of clumps of colour with earth between. So the garden is reduced to merely a place of plants. Step – one, two. Stop – one, two; look down (no need ever to look up for there is no mystery ahead to draw you on), look down at each plant. Individually each is sublime undoubtedly. For a plantsman this is heaven. But where is lure? And where, alas, is seduction and gooseflesh on the arms?

There is a place for precision, naturally. Architectural lines such as those from hedges, walls, paths or topiary are the bones of a garden. But it is the artist who then allows for dishelvement and abandonment to evolve. People say gardening is the one occupation over which they have control. Fine. But why over-indulge? Control is vital for the original design and form; and a ruthless strength of mind is essential when you have planted some hideous thing you lack the courage to demolish. But there is a point when your steadying hand should be lifted and a bit of native vitality can be allowed to take over.

One of the small delights of gardening, undramatic but recurring, is when phlox or columbines seed themselves in unplanned places. When trickles of creeping jenny soften stony outlines or Welsh poppies cram a corner with their brilliant cadmium yellow alongside the deep blue spires of Jacob's ladder all arbitrarily seeding themselves like coloured smells about the place.

Cottage gardens used to have this quality. By their naturally evolved planting, brought about by the necessity of growing herbs and fruit trees, cabbages and gooseberries, amongst them there would be hollyhocks and honesty, campanulas and pinks. How rare now to see a real cottage garden. It is far more difficult to achieve than a contrived garden. It requires intuition, a genius for letting things have their heads.

In the Mediterranean areas this can still be seen. Discarded cans once used for fetta cheese, olives or salt fish, are painted blue or white and stuffed to overflowing with geraniums placed with unaffected artlessness on steps or walls, under trees or on a window

sill. Old tins are planted with basil, they stand on the threshold of a house, not for culinary use because basil is a sacred plant, but for the aromatic pleasure when a sprig is picked for a departing traveller. Under a vine shading the well, are aubergines, melons, courgettes and a scatter of gaudy zinnias. An uncatalogued rose is grown for its scent near a seat where a fig tree provides shade and fruit. Common sense and unselfconsciousness have brought this about. A

natural instinct inspired by practical necessity. We are too clever
by half. We read too many books, we make too many notes. We lie
too long in the bath planning gardens. Have we lost our impulsive
faculties? Have we lost that intuitive feel for the flow and rightness
of things; our awareness of the dynamics of a garden where things
scatter where they please?

And this brings me to another observation which I think goes
with my original longing for a little shambles here and there. For it
seems that proper gardeners never sit in their gardens. Dedicated
and single-minded the garden draws them into its embrace where
their passions are never assuaged unless they are on their knees.
But for us, the unserious, the improper people, who plant and drift,
who prune and amble, we fritter away little dollops of time in sitting
about our gardens. Benches for sunrise, seats for contemplation,
resting perches for the pure sublimity of smelling the evening air
or merely ruminating about a distant shrub. We are the unorthodox
gardeners who don't feel compulsion to pull out campion among the
delphiniums; we can idle away vacantly small chunks of time
without fretting about an outcrop of buttercups groping at the
pulsatillas. Freedom to loll goes with random gardening, it goes
with the modicum of chaos which I long to see here and there in
more gardens.

Not all gardens fail, of course. There are two for instance which
have this enchantment from the moment you enter. One belongs to
people I know who live on the Welsh borders, where all the cottage
garden attributes such as mulberry, quince and damson trees grow
amongst a profusion of valerian and chives, marjoram and sedums.
The whole lush effect is immediate and soothing; it gives you a
feeling of coming home, it reminds you of what life ought to be like.

In complete contrast is Rosemary Verey's garden at Barnsley
House, near Cirencester in Gloucestershire. Here amongst the
strong lines of design, parterres and walks, classical temple and knot
garden, it is as if the owner had washed over the whole layout with
soft, diffused colours so that hard lines are blurred. Sweet rocket and
violas, rock roses and species tulips beguile, flow and confuse. It
may not be chaos, it certainly isn't, but it is as if this truly cohesive
effect happened while the owner had turned away her head. She
hasn't, we know, for a garden like this has been painstakingly
achieved from the brilliance of deliberation. Knowing when not to

do things as vitally as knowing when to. There isn't a dandelion unaccounted for.

So when I make a plea for havoc, what would be lost? Merely the pristine appearance of a garden kept highly manicured which could be squandered for amiable disorder. Just in some places. Just to give a pull at our primeval senses. A mild desire for amorphous confusion which will gently infiltrate and, given time, one day will set the garden singing.

Wood engravings by Yvonne Skargon

An Essayist in the Garden:
Spring

RONALD BLYTHE

One can only be selective. As the sap rises, the ink flows. So it has ever been. The writer, penned up in his stuffy room all winter, feels himself as let out in the spring as the beasts, and naturally it is the garden which first catches his eye. There is much to put down. Never mind if it has all been said a thousand times before and a thousand springs ago. The writer doesn't care. Nature repeats its order and he repeats for the most part what generations of novelists, poets and stylish horticulturists have said on the subject. There are countless cultivated acres of spring-garden writing, most of it private, though open to view. The reader doesn't care. The same joyful clichés shoot up over the centuries and he himself would fill pages with them if only he had a moment to spare. 'Spring has returned,' wrote Rilke, 'and the earth is like a child that knows poems.'

This spring I return to two, never more contrasting, women whose gardening comment and philosophy have pleased me for years, Colette and Alison Uttley. I make them step forward from the multitude who dig and plant and tell, not because they are the best (no garden writer is this), but because each in her different way is so passionate – the only word – about spring flowers, spring air, spring's capriciousness. Their gardens are those of childhood, one at Castle Top Farm in Derbyshire, the other at Manor Farm in Saint-Sauveur-en-Puisaye, Burgundy, and they carried them with them, so to speak, for the rest of their long lives. Alison Uttley's garden is that of chilly early spring, Colette's of approaching summer heat – although she revels in a good unseasonal shock, such as snow on roses. Spring-cleaning in the shape of billowing linen, and spring livestock, snap and cry just beyond their stone walls. These farm gardens are for intelligent ladies to rear clever daughters in. Colette's mother, the incomparable Sido, has one overriding word. It is 'Look!' Alison Uttley, the little girl who will become a scientist, never requires this injunction. Her rural essays are brilliant with minutiae accurately retrieved, and especially the minor detail of old country gardens.

The spring gardener is at his most tolerant when·it comes to

'wildings', as Alison Uttley calls them. When one comes to consider
it, a lot of her garden writing is about finding the first coltsfoot,
white violets and cowslips. 'These flowers, the wild flowers and the
ordinary little garden blossoms, were part of our life . . . They were
brave immortals, who were always beautiful . . . We felt we were
immortals with them.' She says that few wildings were ever refused
a home – except the dandelion, *dens Leonis*, lion's tooth. It took me a
long time to put up with having a fine dandelion in a flower-bed,
making its space during spring and promising a great golden kingly
head. During my childhood in Suffolk its double function as a diuretic
and clock blinded me to its splendour, although I did have a faint
sense of rapine when made to collect whole basketfuls of its blooms
for wine. Alison Uttley is hopelessly indifferent to what ranks as a
garden flower in springtime. In fact there isn't much gardening done
in her books. Things just come up and are welcomed back. Like her,
they stood the fearful Derbyshire cold ('The word "December" was
like music to me.') and in February, March and April she would
receive them with a mixture of correct botany and frank lyricism.
But, it being a farm, the kitchen garden was quite another matter.
Although there flourished here 'a spectacular root of red cowslips,
which my father had propagated himself from a cowslip root . . .
There were no weeds, for somebody weeded it with great thorough-
ness, and it was not the children of the house.'

Colette, after walking home from school to Sido, on her knees in
that lovely, holy garden described in *Earthly Paradise*, is not set to
toil either. Children hate gardening, anyway. One has to give them
one to make them work. Alison Uttley was given a space to make a
rock garden, the object being to collect as many species of stone as
plants. Aged ten my first garden was a rockery made on a mound
beneath flowering greengage trees. It did not contain a single rock,
it being Suffolk, only big flints which had been dragged out of the
fields by the plough, and brick sunflowers and other entablature
from an abandoned brickworks nearby. Seeds from penny packets of
annuals were poured between their sharp edges in May after I had
scraped all the fallen blossom from where I wanted to set them. My
brother and I jealously guarded our brick and flint rockeries with
half hoops of willow which would sprout in the spring. I don't know
who told us about this kind of fencing but fresh graves in the churchyard would be willowed like this until they had settled. Colette's

Earthly Paradise is urgent with instruction for the child in the garden.
She wants everybody to hear her mother saying, 'Look!' A Burgun-
dian farm garden is where both of them, who were always beautiful,
who never grew old or grey, the exciting novelist to be, and the
Parisian widow carried off to the country by the dashing Captain
Colette, first fell in love with flowers.

> In her garden my mother had a habit of addressing to the four cardinal
> points not only direct remarks and replies that sounded, when heard
> from our sitting room, like brief inspired soliloquies; but the actual mani-
> festations of her courtesy, which generally took the form of plants and
> flowers. But in addition to these points – to Cebe and the rue des Vignes,
> to Mother Adolphe, and Maître de Fourolles – there was also a zone of
> collateral points, more distant and less defined, whose contact with us
> was by means of stifled sounds and signals. My childish pride and
> imagination saw our house as the central point of a mariner's chart of
> gardens, winds, and rays of light, no section of which lay quite beyond
> my mother's influence.
>   . . . 'I'm really very worried. I can't remember whether it was a family
> of crocus bulbs I planted there, or the chrysalis of an emperor moth.'
>   'We've only got to scratch to find out.'
>   A swift hand stopped mine. Why did no one ever model or paint or
> carve that hand of Sido's, tanned and wrinkled early by household tasks,
> gardening, cold water, and the sun . . .?

More garden looking goes on in the spring than at any other
season. Some years ago I was in the Yonne in May and very close to
where Sido made her garden, and peering through lilac-locked gates
like hers, while bells for the Ascension jangled from Vézelay. In Suffolk the lawn-mowers would have been in full swing. My farm garden
has few lawns as such, but many wide lawn paths, the widest alongside the orchard and cut against a swaying wilderness of blossom, cow
parsley, buttercup and fritillary. On 21 April 1787 Gilbert White
wrote, 'Mowed the grass-walks in part: they were crisp with hoar
frost. Cut some grass in the orchard for the horses.' In May 1793 he
was still being tidy. 'My weeding-woman swept-up on the grass-plot
a bushel-basket [he is very fond of hyphens] of blossoms from the
white apple-tree: and yet that tree seems still covered with bloom.'
On Sunday, 19 April 1942 James Lees-Milne noted, 'Francis has been
mowing the lawns round the house with the motor tractor, leaving
the dead grass lying, so that there is a heavenly amber-sweet smell of

hay, as in midsummer. I wish there were more wild flowers here besides the dandelions, which I love and others disdain. I lay on the grass
and peered closely into the head of one. It was like looking into the
inmost recesses of the sun, aswirl with petal flames alive and licking
each other. To think that each of the million dandelions in Buckinghamshire, which are taken for granted or ignored, is in fact a marvellous star of golden beauty. How blind human beings are to the best
around them . . .' In May 1918 Virginia Woolf was with her sister at
Charleston: 'I lay with my window open listening to a nightingale,
which beginning in the distance came very near the garden. Fishes
splashed in the pond. May in England is all they say – so teeming,
amorous, & creative.'

Geoffrey Grigson (I hope that every HORTUS reader has a copy
of his *The Englishman's Flora* on his/her shelf) grew very pessimistic
when it came to our national response to the passionate nature of the
seasons.

> I think in England we came somewhere near such seasonable observances
> as moon-viewing or viewing orchards in flower, such a classification, a
> ritualization, of sensual enjoyment, a hundred and twenty years ago, in
> the wake of our romanticism, only then it was too late.

Is it? I don't myself believe so. But should you, this spring, have
been too active to have seen and absorbed what has happened in your
garden, then obey Sido. Look closely at what usually escapes your
glance. Let it engage each sense.

Take me to your Hostas

After a season of opening to a mostly well-behaved public,
NIGEL COLBORN *bites back at those who fell a fraction short of
being model garden visitors*

One Sunday, in the days of my youth, I was 'volunteered' with my
younger brother to superintend the family garden which was
opening up for a Red Cross Sunday. We had been weeding all
morning, and at lunch time handed over to the various dignitaries
who set up card tables, arrows to the lavatory, the tea tent and so
on. Meanwhile, my brother and I lurked in the rhododendrons,
ready to tackle cuttings pinchers, retrieve lost children, banish
unwelcome dogs and generally see to the needs of the public. One
of the first to arrive was a famous local Brigadier (retd.) who had a
short fuse and tended to speak in telegrams. He obviously disliked
teenagers intensely, for he glared at my brother and shouted
'Hostas!'

'Sorry?' queried my brother, who didn't know a dahlia from a
damson.

'Where are your hostas?' The Brigadier's face was turning crimson.

" Where are your hostas? "

Clearly, with words at a premium he disliked having to repeat himself.

'They're not here, sir,' said my brother.

'Can see that! That's why I'm asking.'

'They've gone to India. They'll be back next week.'

'Good God!' said the Brigadier and strode off looking perplexed. I looked at my brother.

'What on earth did you say that for?' I asked.

'I thought "hosta" must be a military word for "parent".' He shuffled more deeply into the rhododendrons to hide his embarrassment. Inevitably, the military gent found the hostas and strode back to berate us.

'India be damned!' he roared. 'Down by pond! Hostas! Dozens! Pretty sight. Love kalmias too! Very pretty. That boy your gardener? Useless! No clue!'

That episode twenty-five years ago did little to prepare me for the consequences of throwing my own gates open to the public; the feeling of living in a goldfish bowl, threats of divorce from a harassed

Some of the extraordinary types who trudge round other people's gardens...

wife, neglected children, plants raided for cuttings or stolen in their entirety and, above all, a bruised ego. Now that the season is closed for a few months, there is time to reflect on some of the extraordinary types who trudge round other people's gardens. Why do they do it? One can understand the garden enthusiasts, but the others? Ought there to be a fully-illustrated beginners' guide entitled *Getting the Best Out of Garden Visits*? Nobody expects to be good at golf or squash without coaching, and yet, when it comes to foraging in a National Trust shrubbery or worshipping at the shrine of an elderly dame who, in Edwardian days, invented the perfect colour border, it is surprising how few people really know how to go about it.

Serious gardeners

Wearing the right duds is essential. You can always tell the serious gardeners from the rest by what they wear. The women don sensible skirts, flat-heeled shoes or black wellingtons – green wellies are distinctly *passé* these days – and little or no makeup. Men, more often than not, come in shapeless trousers and well-worn sports jackets or shirtsleeves. Anoraks or weatherproof jackets should always be the colour of cow dung and must not look new. When your old one finally falls to pieces and has to be replaced, drag the new one behind your car for sixty-three miles. (It is safer not to wear it while you are doing this.)

Incidentally, transport is extremely important. No true horti-culturist should drive a car until it is at least ten years old and rusting steadily. A 1976 Cortina would be perfect, for example, or a strange make from one of those indeterminate Iron Curtain countries, the names of whose capital cities always come up in quiz games. There is no time for washing, let alone polishing, the chrome and the boot should have accumulated a three-inch layer of potting compost and Great Dixter labels. Inexperienced persons, often of great dignity, tend to arrive at gardens in faultless BMWs or Rovers, emerging with miraculously uncrumpled suits and shiny shoes. Any plants they buy are carried at arm's length and laid reverently onto plastic sheeting, not in deference to them, however rare or special they may be, but to protect the pure wool carpet in the car.

Fractionally lower down the income scale, but still inappropriately dressed, is the Middle Manager. Speaking as one who has no control over his middle at all, I have deep admiration for this type. He or she – they come in both sexes these days, of course – will have a highly polished Audi or the top Ford Sierra and possibly a privately educated child in tow. Often, they wear tracksuits – not the floppy ones which are so useful to hide the flab, but *designer* ones – hers kingfisher blue with orange flashing, his bubble-gum pink and no flashing at all, let's hope. They usually set off at a jog, running on the spot as they admire the herbaceous borders and encourage the child to find freedom of expression by pulling flower buds off the plants and shoving them into the jets of the fountain, or throwing stones at the golden orfe. You can tell the little blighter to buzz orfe but the parents glare at you and discipline will not be re-imposed until they get back into the Sierra. They probably won't buy any plants because the car boot is already full of sports equipment and three crates of Perrier.

Then come the painted ladies. Not the butterflies but persons resplendent with lipstick, vermilion nails and black eyeliner. Your typical painted lady is usually on the brink of being over-weight and dresses as if she was just off to a cocktail party – patent leather, stiletto-heeled shoes in which she teeters dangerously as she clacks over the uneven paving, a skirt that fits a little too tightly over the buttocks, and full accessories – hand bag, gloves, cigarettes in one hand, powder compact in the other, just in case a quick repair job to the face is needed. Painted ladies' husbands are often small and subservient but frequently turn out to be immensely successful businessmen, who lead a life of unfettered tyranny at the office but metamorphose into spaniels on the way home each evening. All painted ladies abhor gardens which lack dahlias, summer bedding, modern bush roses and patio loungers.

In complete contrast, wildlife enthusiasts are, of necessity, scruffy. They often look at me with incredulity when I profess keenness on having natural species in the garden, because I don't wear a beard and recycled clothing – I don't even cycle myself. Some wildlifers are highly specialist. Bird men, for example, trample marsh helleborines and grass of parnassus into the ground to get a better view of the kingfishers. Botanists curse local badgers for ruining the pasque flowers and bee orchids. But they all look at my mixed borders of cultivars and exotic species with ill-concealed scorn, or crow with delight when they find a patch of nettles I may have missed during a recent bout of weeding. They can also alarm other visitors. In the picnic area where we once served teas, cries of 'Oh look, Damien, a grass snake – no – *two* of them. That one must be a

Oh look, Damien, a grass snake – no – TWO of them!

gravid female. What a size! It must be nearly four feet long!' caused a rapid exodus of the majority of tea drinkers and a sprinting to The Spot by the naturalist minority. The snakes themselves were frightened out of their wits by all the commotion, fled, and weren't seen again until October, just before hibernation – theirs and ours.

More infuriating than all the other visitors put together are the Yortas. Sometimes there are whole families of Yortas but, thankfully, they usually come singly, and if accompanied, embarrass the living daylights out of their partners. Conversation with a Yorta usually begins: 'Are you the owner?'

'Possibly' – you can try prevarication but it probably won't help.

'Yorta do something about them steps. Weed 'em or something.'

'But it took ages to get those little plants established. There are seven different types of thyme growing there. Some are quite rare.'

'Oh, they're plants, are they? Yorta label them then. I thought they were weeds. Can't stand weeds, me.'

'Ah.'

" Yorta do something about them steps. Weed 'em or something."

During May I was particularly pleased with one part of the garden because the graded lilacs and purples of the spring perennials – *Lunaria rediviva* and *Lathyrus vernus* among others – were looking especially harmonious. We had planted the marvellous mauve, lily-flowered tulip 'Maytime' sporadically among them and the results were, I felt, good enough for a *Homes and Gardens* photograph. But while I was admiring the show, one Sunday afternoon, a chap in a cloth cap sidled up and said: 'Not much colour, is there, mate? Yorta plant more toolips. All different colours. That'd liven it up a bit.'

The agony of parting with the entrance fee affects different people in different ways. Usually, the more expensive the car and sumptuous the clothes, the harder it is for the owner to cough up. There are those who are astounded that they are expected to pay at all, and when approached, their excuses are surprisingly lame.

'Would you like to go in?'

'Ooh! Yes please!'

'It's a pound per adult.'

'Oh. Well, I've got a bad leg, I wouldn't be able to walk.' Or downright rude: 'Well, if we have to pay we won't bother, then. I don't suppose you've got anything I don't grow myself!'

When business is slack, waiting for arrivals is incredibly boring, but leave the gate unattended for a split second and someone will get through. Even in driving rain, when nobody has come for hours, slip off to answer a call of nature, as the euphemists say, and within a trice there are thirty-one Townswomen's Guild Members fanning out in the rose garden. Organised parties are usually very well behaved and pay a lump sum in advance. Professional fee dodgers know this, and when you greet your coach load 54 members will disembark but by the time they are half-way through the gate, the number has swelled to 71 with lots of 'I'm with her' and 'we're in the group.'

The time visitors take to get round the garden indicates their level of keenness. Coach parties spend most of the time searching for and then queuing outside the lavatory. Plantspersons may spend several hours – sometimes a whole day – studying the borders. Non-gardeners, not necessarily Middle Managers, can get around two-and-a-half acres of intensely planted garden in a couple of minutes, without resorting to anabolic steroids. Should this be a new Olympic event?

Namedroppers can be entertaining: 'I've just spent the day with Rosemary Hobhouse,' they might say, or 'Such a nice visit to Tintinhydrock last week. Penny actually stopped writing for long enough to show us round. After the public had been excluded, of course.' Plants are usually 'far bigger at Little Dixter' or 'happier growing in the greensand at Loderslee,' or 'Christopher Elliot has a much better form than that.' It never does simply to *possess* a rarity. One must have obtained it from a famous source, or from nature:

'Have you *Meconopsis quintuplinerva*?'

'I'm afraid not, it doesn't like our climate. Too dry.'

'I *know*. When Rodney and I went hunting for it in Nepal, it rained cats and dogs the *whole* time. We didn't manage to find it.'

'I'm not surprised. It doesn't grow in Nepal!'

'But dear, kind Alfred Lloyd Venison gave me one of his plants when we got back.'

Living in a remote, rural spot where the only sounds are of RAF jets practising low level bombing, Intercity trains roaring between London and Edinburgh, and chain-saws altering the face of the countryside, we are sometimes surprised by animal intruders. An apprentice gardener once came to the house to say, 'There's a pig in the garden.' She was a very large Landrace sow (the pig, not the apprentice . . . but then again . . .) and, though quite unaggressive, was determined not to be moved until she had finished all the windfalls from our Bramley. Sheep are a constant threat. The neighbouring farmer's flock has its own Escape Committee. One holds up the bottom of the wire fence while the others all slip through. Having got in, they then lose their nerve and stampede the fence, damaging it beyond repair in their panic to get back to the security of their field. This always makes a worthwhile sideshow for the visitors however, because it only happens on open days.

But enough of this carping. Most visitors are a pleasure to welcome. Anyone who takes an interest is well worth the time of day, because one always learns as much from the questioners as they hope to learn from the answers. Queries are usually concerned with plant identification or culture techniques, but there are some delightful howlers: 'I want to get a plant of that double lady's smock. What's its proper name?'

'*Cardamine pratensis* 'Flore Pleno'.'

'No, no. I've got the plain one, what's the double called?'

Goodness knows what the person meant who asked, 'Will this plant produce seed if it hasn't been comminuted?' and most embarrassing, from an elderly lady, 'Why all these confusing Latin names? For instance, what does "Orchis" really mean?'

'Actually, I think that's Greek,' I replied.

Drawings by John Verney

A Rash of Endemics

RICHARD MABEY

Is gardening an art? If so, is it a romantic art, concerned with the expression of mood and the recapturing of 'moment'? Or essentially modernist, more properly attentive to pure colour and form and the intrinsic qualities of materials? There have been gardeners who have tried to work to both of these extreme models, but such single-mindedness is usually scuppered by plants themselves, which have a habit of being simultaneously awash with symbolism *and* wilfully themselves. William Robinson understood this paradox over a hundred and fifty years ago when he wrote: 'Foolish old "laws" laid down by landscape-gardeners perpetuate the notion that a garden is a "work of art, and therefore we must not attempt in it to imitate nature!" the true garden differing from all other arts in that it gives us the living things themselves not merely representations of them in paint or wood or stone.'

This principle underlay all Robinson's thinking about the virtues of the 'wild garden'. He believed that plants deserved to have their natural vitality preserved in gardens, and that respecting the ways in which they lived, spread and associated could encourage that 'mystery and indefiniteness which constitute beauty of vegetation in its highest sense.'

Yet, at the risk of playing with words, I think there is something oversimplified about Robinson's distinction between 'the living things themselves' and their representations. Plants in gardens are, by definition, re-presentations, re-stagings of the small dramas of growth. They are taken from one context and re-set in another – and all along it was often the context itself we wanted, conjured up romantically in the border.

These rather unearthly philosophisings were prompted by a first visit to Crete in the spring. So many familiar garden plants grow there in such dramatic settings that the whole island is a re-education in plant associations. Plane trees (*Platanus orientalis*) seem quite transformed when growing as whole woods, as they do in some of the western valleys. So do the chionodoxas that grow underneath them. *Phlomis fruticosa*, too, though not that widespread in Crete, grows in emphatic masses on some rocky foothills. I've always found this a rather stiff and cardboardy shrub in gardens, but here, with its flowers a fierce chrome yellow in the Mediterranean glare, and the sweeps of white-felted leaves billowing over the limestone, it is altogether a different plant.

But it is Crete's endemics that bring the subject of context into sharp focus. The island (three small islands, to begin with) has been cut off from the mainland for at least eight million years, and in that time its flora has evolved an extraordinary array of indigenous specialities. There are about 140 of them, or close on ten per cent of the flora. Some are no more than slight local variations of more widespread Mediterranean species – for instance, the Cretan bee orchid, *Ophrys cretica*, and the pure white cyclamen, *C. creticum*, which grows in some of the mountainous evergreen-oak woods and is perhaps just a sub-species of *C. repandum*. Endemics crop up in almost every family. There are indigenous species of anemone, vetch, scabious and crocus. There are species which have no obvious close relatives on the mainland. *Petromarula pinnata*, an extraordinary member of the campanula family which resembles nothing so much as a giant, herbaceous, blue-flowered daphne, grows in rocky sites, especially near to the sea. The strange umbellifer *Lecokia cretica* has an outlier population here, but otherwise is a strictly Asian plant. And down in the south of the island the stumpy Cretan palm, *Phoenix theophrastii*, hangs on in a few sandy valleys near the sea. This is a very scarce tree, with a strange, melancholy beauty that comes I suspect, from its air of being a mis-placed and endangered waif.

The endemics that seem to thrive on the island's parched and now largely deforested landscape are those I found the most fascinating. Little annual *Anthemis* species creep about the beach, and over the wasteland near villa building sites. In the *garigue* there are intriguing endemic galiums, with whippy, goosegrass stems on wooden trunks, like cats-o'-nine-tails. (A climber and a shrub in one plant: how William Robinson would have admired them!)

The island's most famous native is Cretan dittany, *Ebenus cretica*, a dramatically beautiful shrub with silver-haired leaves and deep pink pea-flowers. For a highly restricted species its adaptability is awe-some. We saw it in glowing shoals on stony foothills, on roadside verges, and already starting to colonise the bare rock terraces which have been blasted out of the southern mountains for banana forcing-houses. It seemed positively to *like* the country, rather than to be confined to it, and put me in mind of the Oxford English Dictionary's expansive definition of endemics as 'having their ordinary habitat in a certain country'.

A few weeks after returning from Crete I was driving along the M25 and glimpsed an almost pure Cretan landscape: drifts of pink and purple sainfoin (ebenus's nearest relative) spreading down a sandy embankment. It is one of the new 'ordinary habitats' of the species, and I was srruck with the thought that endemicness is a quality that goes beyond the purely biological. Almost all plants have particular associations with 'a certain country', which are part of their attractiveness and meaning, and which one ought to try to conserve in gardens. They can be ecological, historical, literary, entirely private, a matter of habit as much as habitat. In the Chilterns I know two good landscape endemics – wood anemones growing on the tops of tree stumps and, after the hurricane, cherries which blossom at knee height.

Of course, it's usually impossible to transplant such associations and contexts into a garden. The point is that they very often create themselves, *in situ*. One of my personal endemics is a double-flowered variety of the greater celandine, which I grew rather proudly from seed from Kew, believing it to be such an ancient and highly bred cultivar that it probably teetered on the sterile. Now it ramps about as the most aggressive naturaliser in the whole garden. The other is more restrained, but even more loyal and laden with associations. It is a self-set specimen of the bramble, *Rubus laciniatus*, which grew on a heath next to my cottage in Suffolk, and whose seed stowed away to the Chilterns (and stayed viable) in a discarded jar of blackberry jam. More deliberate – but no less intimate – transplantings can produce neighbourhood endemics. I once found a village in the backwaters of central Norfolk where almost every tiny garden was stuffed with Crown Imperials. Another, in Hertfordshire, has montbretia as its botanical mascot, its dialect plant.

These intensely local constellations, generated by serendipity, gardeners' natural sociability and the quirky, cussed preferences of plants themselves, seem to me to be at the heart of the 'mystery and indefiniteness' of the best gardens, both wild and cultivated. And, respecting both the independent life of plants and the imagination of the grower, they define exactly what kind of art gardening is.

Tulipa

'A strang and forraine flower'

AUDREY LE LIÈVRE

Such was the verdict of John Gerard (*Herball*, 1597), who went on to comment that 'there hath not been anything set down of the ancient or later writers as touching the nature or vertues of the Tulipaes, but are esteemed especially for the beautie of their flowers'. He was right in so far as there is no tulip native to Britain (though the little yellow *Tulipa sylvestris* has in course of time become naturalised here): but there is that in the words he chose to hint of something aloof in this brilliant creature which, as he says, has left its nature and 'vertues' inviolate, not to be picked over by mere writers. To this day a faint aura of the exotic remains with the tulip, despite the cottage garden image with which it has come to be invested.

Gerard also tells us that his 'loving freind Master James Garret, a curious searcher of Simples, and learned Apothecarie of London' has been working on them for twenty years, and this marries up with the statement of Richard Hakluyt (a relation of the traveller) writing in 1582 to 'Master S' *A briefe remembrance of things to be indevoured at Constantinople* – 'And now within these foure yeares there have been brought into England from Vienna in Austria divers kinds of . . . flowers called Tulipas, and those and other procured thither a little before from Constantinople by an excellent man called M. Carolus Clusius'. Though it is possible that a few tulip bulbs may have reached Europe with the returning Crusaders, and though some writers mention Portugal as a possible channel, usually the credit goes to Ogier de Busbecq, sent in 1554 as envoy by Ferdinand I of the Holy Roman Empire on a delicate mission to the court of the Ottoman Emperor Suleiman the Magnificent. Making his way from Adrianople to Constantinople, de Busbecq passed drifts of flowers and paused to admire the splendour of their colours. He thought that the Turks called them *Tulipan* (deriving from *Tul(i)bend* and thence Persian *Dulbend*, Turban), a strange misunderstanding because the Turkish name, which was used also in Persia, Afghanistan and throughout Central Asia, had always been *Lalé* (which later became a favourite girl's name).

However, *Lalé* had no European connotations, whereas a word meaning 'Turban' better conveys a sense of brilliant colour. The ambassador on his travels collected plants, seeds and medicinal substances and sent some of these to friends in the Netherlands. In Vienna he came to know Charles de l'Écluse (Carolus Clusius), born in Flanders but at that time Praefectus of the Imperial Medicinal Garden, and on leaving the city in 1574 he left with Clusius a large consignment of bulbous plants just received from Turkey. About 1575 Clusius sowed their rather dried-up seeds: they germinated well and in due course he obtained a group of plants with yellow, white, red, purple and some variegated flowers. Meanwhile the Swiss botanist, Conrad Gesner, recorded in his *De Hortis Germaniae* (1561) that, some two years previously, he had noticed a flower like a red lily growing in the Augsburg garden of Councillor John Henry Herwart, who told him it had sprung from seed 'procured from Byzantia'. This also proved to be a tulip, and though it can take up to seven years for a seedling to reach flowering age, de Busbecq's original consignment could just have been involved.

The origin of the garden tulip may never be completely clarified, but the Royal Horticultural Society's *Dictionary of Gardening* (1951) expresses the view that it probably derives from a yellow-based species no longer traceable and perhaps no longer in existence, which gave white-based mutants under cultivation: and that inter-crossing of these variants gave rise to the garden tulips of Turkey [which, presumably, constituted most of the early arrivals in western Europe] and from which, through long process of selection and improvement, our garden tulips have been developed.

But merchants as well as diplomats were at work on imports, and Venice was probably involved as well as the Low Countries. The traffic in bulbs reflects the popularity of the tulip in Turkey itself, where legend had it that the flower arose from the blood of the Persian youth Ferhad, who threw himself from the cliffs on hearing of the supposed death of his much-loved Shirin. Presented by a young man to a girl, a red tulip with a black base betokened a heart on fire with her beauty, burned to a coal with love. From the Middle Ages tulips carried for the House of Osman a symbolism equal to that of the fleur-de-lis for the French royal family. Mehmed II, conqueror of Constantinople in 1453, was also a highly cultured man who set great importance on gardening and tulip-growing. Rows of tulips were embroidered on a brocade tunic belonging to Suleiman the Magnificent in the mid-sixteenth century: and from the mosques and tombs of Istanbul and Bursa come silk tunics with crimson tulips woven on a silver ground, and wall tiles from the fifteenth and sixteenth centuries embellished with tulips, hyacinths, narcissi and dianthus.

The Turkish idea of beauty in a tulip differed from later western European ideas: to them the flower should be almond-shaped with dagger-like petals, a little like *Tulipa acuminata* as available today. On the white earthenware made in the sixteenth century in Nicea (Iznik), the tulip is shown sometimes in its natural state, striped or with wavy-edged leaves, occasionally with a broken stem or drooping flower: and sometimes stylised – and there are said to be nearly 1000 versions of stylised tulips – with petals blue, white or red straying upwards like a strange six-fingered hand, and turquoise leaves. A frieze of tulips decorated the elegant 'tulip kiosk' built overhanging the waters of the Bosphorus by the Grand Vizier to ingratiate himself with his imperial master, Selim II, in the middle of the sixteenth century. We know that Selim commanded the Sheriff of Aziz to provide 50,000 tulip bulbs for the imperial gardens, and this was the first of the great periods of interest in the tulip. As time went on, however, the tulip slowly gave place to the ranunculus – and then, oddly, to melons and cucumbers, as noted by the botanist Tournefort on a visit to Turkey – to re-emerge at the beginning of the eighteenth century in the reign of Ahmed III. This was known as the *Devri Lalé* – the Tulip Epoch.

But we must return to western Europe, and to Clusius. In 1593 he too left Vienna, having been appointed Professor of Botany at the University of Leiden, and he took his tulips with him: but he was greedy and his prices so prohibitive that the people found it cheaper to steal them, and in this fashion the whole of the country was quickly stocked. He was not the only supplier, however. In 1562 a merchant in Antwerp received a cargo of bulbs from Constantinople, some of which were eaten with oil and vinegar, some planted and neglected, and a few rescued by George Rye (or van Rye), a merchant of Mechlin and an amateur botanist, who cosseted them and got good results. And in Leiden itself John Hogeland was growing them in 1590. Later, about 1610, tulips apparently obtained from Tournai were flowered for the first time in France by Fabri de Peires in his Aix-en-Provence garden, and by the time of Louis XIV (1643–

1715) no lady of fashion would have wished to be seen without a corsage of rare tulips (and very uncomfortable they must have been, too).

In England the tulip quickly became popular: Gerard's *Herball* in 1597 lists 14 varieties, and Parkinson has well over 100 in his *Paradisi in Sole Paradisus Terrestris* (1629). He described the phenomenon of 'breaking' (later called 'rectifying') by which a self-coloured tulip (known as a 'breeder') would suddenly produce a flower striped or splashed, often with very attractive markings and in colours much more brilliant than those of the breeder itself. The reason for this behaviour puzzled Parkinson and others, and indeed it took a further 300 years to identify the culprit as a virus transmitted by aphids. In the interval, the mystery of breaking served to make the beautiful

Drawing of wood-cut from *Stirpium Historiae Pemptades Sex* (1583) by Rembert Dodoens (1516–1585)

and variable results much more interesting and better appreciated than the more boring breeder.

John Tradescant, gardener to Charles I, grew tulips and is known to have bought 800 bulbs in Haarlem, which must have increased the flower's fashionable appeal in Court circles. And John Rea's *Flora*, which appeared in 1676, shows the growing interest in the tulip by including over 300 cultivars. The names betray the sources: some are English – 'Pretty Betty', 'Religious', 'The Rich Parot – this groweth tall and strong' – and some French or Flemish – 'Morillon Cramosine', 'Agot Robine Paragon', 'Admiral Vander Pool – of a dark red, inclining to liver-colour'. Rea here uses the French terms for certain kinds of striped tulips: and de la Chesnée Monstereul's work *Le Floriste François* (1658), which has been regarded as the first horticultural monograph, shows some of the differences as being very slight, even ridiculous: why 'Marquetine' for four or five colours merged, and 'Marquetrine' for those same colours when better demarcated? Similarly there was Morillon and Morillony, Agate and Agatine. Fortunately, the use of such terms was gradually reduced and became more sensible, but for 200 years they must have complicated the ordinary gardener's dealings with tulips quite unnecessarily.

The tulip had arrived, but it was still inescapably 'forraine'. The only legend which accompanied it into western European life was that of Fahrad and Shirin: no medical lore was known except the suggestion of Dioscorides that it might be helpful against a crick in the neck (though even then, the red wine in which it was to be mixed might have been more efficacious!). As for recipes, apart from preserving the bulbs in sugar, which Parkinson and others recommended, there seems to be only one, and that rather dull: 'Pease of the Seedy Bulbs of Tulips' it is called, and comes from *The Closet of the Eminently Learned Sir Kenelme Digby Kt Opened* (1669). A satirical piece of about the same period (Thomas Fuller's *Speech of Flowers* (1660)) runs down the nature of the tulip by making a disaffected rose remark '. . . and what is this Toolip? A well-complexioned stink, an ill favour wrapped up in pleasant colours'.

The double tulip was recorded in 1665 (though Clusius apparently found a rather miserable specimen in 1581, describing it as 'a poor tulip as tulips go now, its colour a bad green'), and by the end of the century parrot tulips were 'in' – though not approved by all ('monsters, frightful to look upon', commented Henry van Oosten in *The*

Dutch Gardener (1703)). During the seventeenth century several works on the culture of the tulip were published in France and the Low Countries, in which much good and some rather questionable advice was given: 'The Tulip', wrote van Oosten, 'is justly called the Queen of Flowers, and the chief Jewel of Flora: This Noble Flower must be sowed in the Month of September from ripe seed, in well-dunged Ground, according to Art . . .'. Monstereul, in *Le Floriste François*, recommended that tulips should be sown when a north wind was blowing.

In the midst of these developments the strange phenomenon of tulipomania broke on the world of the Dutch bulb breeder. This had little to do with the tulip as such: the flower was simply a focus, and as Messrs Step and Watson remark in *Favourite Flowers* (1897), 'Griffins and Unicorns of the heraldic type might just as well have been the subjects of the speculation'. It should, however, have been possible to see the mania coming. It originated in France, where in the 1620s huge prices were given for beautiful tulips in flower. The example is often quoted of a favourite red and white flamed tulip, 'Semper Augustus', the total stock of which was said to number 12 bulbs in 1624, for which 1200 florins had been paid. In 1625 3000 florins were offered for two of these bulbs, but refused. 'Semper Augustus' was perhaps unusual in holding its value for 13 years (no doubt because its stock increased slowly), for in 1636 one bulb was sold for 5500 florins, and another for 4600 florins with a new carriage and two horses. Such prices point to the profits which might be made. At the start (1634) sales took place during the period June to September, when bulbs were out of the ground: but presently even this hold on reality was lost, and they were sold and re-sold without even being seen by any of the parties concerned. Selling was itself a complicated business. The contemporary *T'Samenspraeken tusschen Waermondt ende Gaergoedt* – a discussion between two weavers – gives an account of the clubs for tulip trading which were based at various taverns. It was illegal actually to offer a bulb for sale, but it could be made known that bulbs were available, and two arbitrators were chosen to close the deal. Alternatively, bulbs could be sold by public auction. Rich and poor, all took to tulip-growing, so long as they had a small patch of ground and a few breeder bulbs: and at first everyone made profits. But soon the whole enterprise rode out of control. Houses and estates, horses and carriages, the very tools by which

Drawing of blue 'Dutch tile' tulip motif in Library fireplace, The Neuadd

workmen gained their living, all went to finance the so-called 'wind
trade'. Fraud was easy, for it was impossible to tell until flowering
time whether the bulb sold was of the promised cultivar. And then,
as swiftly as it had started, early in 1637 the tulip market collapsed.
Suddenly everyone wanted to sell, and there were no purchasers.
After some inadequate sparring the Court of Holland declared that
every vendor who could not make his purchaser pay could dispose
of his bulbs in any way possible, claiming the difference from the
purchaser. Contracts could remain in force till enquiries were made,
but many sellers preferred to cut their losses. Thus the trade sub-
sided to a normal level, and the only kind of fortune which lasted
was made by the tavern-keepers on the amount of food and beer
consumed during negotiations! Later, when it seemed that the advent
of the double hyacinth might provoke a similar flurry, a hasty
re-printing of *T'Samenspraeken* served to stifle it.

In England there was a time when it seemed that prices might be getting a little out of hand, but in *The Tatler* (31 August, 1710) Richard Steele's gentle satire helped to ward off an attack of tulipomania. Sheltering from a shower of rain, he explained, he overheard an earnest conversation on the merits of various crowned and coroneted heads: 'one said he valued the Black Prince more than the Duke of Vendosme, another that if the Emperor of Germany were not going off he would like him better than either the Prince of Hesse or the King of Sweden' – and so on until, stepping out of the porch in which he was sitting, he discovered that the conversation concerned only a bed of tulips – a bed which its owner solemnly declared that, though it was no more than 20 yards long and two broad, he valued more than he would the best hundred acres in England. The piece ended, 'I have often looked upon it as a Piece of Happiness that I have never fallen into any of these fantastical Tastes, nor esteemed any Thing the more for its being uncommon and hard to be met with ... For this Reason I ... make as many Visits to a Spot of Daizies, or a Bank of Violets, as a Florist does to his Borders and Parterres'. Common sense prevailed, fortunately.

But while Steele was calming the English enthusiasm, in distant Turkey the Tulip Epoch had begun. Ahmed III (1703–30) restored the gardens of his palace so that half a million tulips flourished there, and he also ordered the Mayor of Istanbul to regulate excessive tulip prices and to expel from the city anyone who broke the rules. In Turkey experts gathered to discuss and judge the finer points of the blooms before them, and a contemporary painting by Ahmet Yakuboglu shows a group sitting cross-legged on rugs under blossoming trees in a garden, drinking coffee and admiring tulips set around them in vases: behind them lies a flowery mead, and beyond that a bare, hilly countryside with cypress trees. Perfect tulips had to conform to the rules, as strict as any later applied in England, and verses were written in praise of new tulips. In a list of 1323 tulips compiled by Sheikh Mohammed Lalézaré ('Tulip Chief') wonderfully poetic names were given – 'Pink of Dawn', 'Spring of Life', 'Lightning Flash': Wilfrid Blunt compares them favourably with certain cultivar names of 40 years ago, but I think they sound even better alongside 'Milestone', 'Mickey Mouse' and 'Red Baby', taken from today's *Classified List*.

Magnificent festivities were held at tulip time, and the French

ambassador, writing to Louis XV in April 1726, describes one such
fête given by the Grand Vizier, Ibrahim Pacha. In the tulip beds every
plant which had come up blind was replaced by a flowering tulip,
and a candle was then set beside every fourth flower, level with the
bloom: along the alleys were hung cages filled with all kinds of birds.
The trellises were filled with a great quantity of flowers, set in carafes
and lit by a multitude of glass lamps of every colour, which were also
hung on bushes transplanted in from neighbouring woods. The colours,
the lights reflected in mirrors and the sounds of music *à la Turque*
enchanted the beholder, and continued every night while the tulips
were in flower, while the Sultan and his whole suite were lodged and
fed by his Grand Vizier. *La Corbeille de Fleurs* (1819) describes another
such occasion attended by the wives of the Sultan: 'Les femmes du
Sultan, aussi brillantes que les Tulipes, se répandent parmi ces fleurs'.

In Europe, flowers were now losing the symbolic meaning which
they had held in religious painting and were no longer used to decor-
ate the borders of illuminated texts. The date of the first tulip
engravings has recently been advanced by Ruth Duthie's charming
book *Florists' Flowers and Societies* (1988), which shows a coloured
illustration of tulips from the manuscript of P. A. Michiel of Venice
in the mid-sixteenth century. Others followed rapidly, and perhaps
some of the most beautiful are those which appeared in the *Hortus
Floridus* of Crispin de Passe the Younger, which first appeared in 1614,
and included the earliest representation of a 'broken' tulip: it quickly
went into six editions, including one in English and one in French.

The succession of William and Mary to the English throne in 1688
undoubtedly strengthened the links between the two flower-loving
countries, and as the century progressed fashionable artists from the
Netherlands – Jan ('Velvet') Breughel, Jacob Walscapelle, Ambrosius
Bosschaert, and others – began to produce brilliant flower studies
which added warmth and luxuriant colour to the drawing-rooms of
the wealthy, and are of special interest today because they show the
tulip as it then was, a decorative but rather outlandish flower, with
large, loose petals and splendid markings – half way in the development from the almond shapes of Turkey to the goblet-like flowers
which, as an eighteenth-century writer says, 'when they are in Perfection of Bloom . . . will contain an English Pint of Wine within their
Petals or Flower-leaves'.

The florilegia (albums of paintings for those who appreciated the beauty of flowers but lacked any great horticultural interest in them) included ravishing watercolours by Alexander Marshall, who recorded striped and flamed tulips in an album now in the Royal Library at Windsor Castle, and who spent his last years sharing Fulham Palace with the botanical Bishop of London, Henry Compton. Nicolas Robert was another prolific artist, adding 727 paintings to the royal collection in France and producing many of the life-size flower drawings engraved in the *Recueil des Plantes* (1701).

The tulip was not known in western Europe early enough to appear in the *milles fleurs* of medieval tapestries, but it is to be seen in other decorative arts. There is a charming example in furnishings in the Victoria and Albert Museum, where on a seventeenth-century bed-valance are embroidered tulips, with other flowers, rising from the earth, while on the bed curtain itself single tulip flowers are appliquéd at all sorts of strange angles, as though tossed about in a breeze. The tulip also appears among the enamelled flowers so beloved in jewellery and on watch cases, and sometimes a watch itself was made in the shape of a tulip. As one might expect, Dutch floral marquetry also gave it prominence. Wonderful Delft ware – blue and white tulip vases, made like pagodas – was also popular. Even playing cards took a role: in a pack produced in Switzerland in the mid-eighteenth century the Queen of Spades is shown sniffing a tulip rather disdainfully (perhaps it was one of those Parkinson accuses of having 'a strong ill sent'). Later William Morris used its strong, curving shape for wallpaper designs, and much later the postage stamps of many countries – among them the USSR, Turkey, Israel, and Iran – have carried their native tulips.

The eighteenth century showed a greatly increasing interest in gardens and flowers, hustled onwards by the quantities of flowers introduced from abroad. Ray Desmond in *The British Museum Book of Flowers* (1989) calls the whole century 'a glorious celebration of flowers' and describes beautiful hangings in Montacute House which are embroidered with a whole eighteenth-century garden, with trees in tubs and great numbers of tulips lining the grass plots. The still-life mode ended in the Netherlands, after about 100 years, with the death of Jan van Huysum in 1749, but a whole new school of late-eighteenth/early-nineteenth century flower painters and botanical artists – Georg Ehret, Ferdinand and Francis Bauer – were soon drawing rapt attention, followed by the tulips of Redouté in *Les*

Liliacées. At the end of the century the Impressionists rivalled the seventeenth-century painters in the warmth and colour of their flowers.

All this time, while the decorative arts were benefiting from the design possibilities of the tulip's attractively sinuous shape, the improvement of the flower itself was quietly going on, especially in the Netherlands. Classification of tulips was still very elementary: no more than early-flowering and late-flowering, with a few 'meane-flowering', as Parkinson had rather ambiguously termed it. The descriptive colour categories used by the French and Flemish writers and referred to earlier were gradually refined to three: roses (pink and red markings on a white ground): bybloemens (a word apparently meaning 'next in importance' – mauve or purple, also on a white ground): and bizarres (reds and browns on a yellow ground). Towards the end of the eighteenth century, English 'florists' began to interest themselves in the breeding of superior forms of a limited number of 'florists' flowers' – the auricula, polyanthus, anemone, ranunculus, carnation, hyacinth, tulip, and pink. Florists were usually working people – weavers, railwaymen, miners – living in tiny houses with back gardens, mostly in the Midlands and the North of England. The tulip fanciers among them spent their spare time most agreeably in raising their tulips, giving them good solid names, attending florists' feasts at local taverns, and winning copper kettles at florists' shows. *The Midland Florist* gives an account of the Great Northern Tulip Show held at the Corn Exchange, Manchester, on 28 May 1850, when the best exhibit was a break of a famous tulip called 'Lancashire Hero', with clear black feathering on a pure white ground. The convivial (sometimes too convivial) atmosphere is evoked by the comment that 'The meeting of florists, in the evening, at the Swan with Two Necks, was well attended. The Flagstaff Inn was also crowded: in fact we never before saw so many florists together'. Ruth Duthie shows an engraving made for *The Florist*, 1851 of just such a gathering, with portly bewigged florists at ease in the tavern, smoking their long pipes while the punch bowl is carried round and the finer points of a vase of flowers on the table are discussed. A whippet stands patiently by.

There was plenty of literature on the subject of the florists' activities. Robert Sweet's *Florists' Guide* was first published in 1827: Volume II shows many gaudy and multicoloured tulips, mostly variants of *Tulipa gesneriana*, the name which Linnaeus in due course bestowed on the earliest arrivals from Turkey. The great era of tulip shows was 1840–1860. Philip Miller in his *Gardener's Dictionary* listed the properties of a good florists' tulip: it should have the usual three inner and three outer 'leaves' (petals), a tall strong stem, a middling flower and 'leaves' which when open should stand erect. The bottom should be proportioned to the top, the upper part rounded and not pointed: and the stripes should be small and regular, arising quite from the bottom: if there are any remains of a self-coloured base the flower would be in danger of losing its stripes again (this phrase obviously had no other connotation!). The hives (anthers) should be brown, not yellow. Sheikh Lalézaré would have recognised, but not entirely approved them.

The nineteenth-century florists were developing these points: but in mid-century a 'tulip war' raged between northern and southern fanciers, the southerners declaring that a good cup and a clear base alone would make a good tulip, the northerners considering that fine and regular feathering and flaming was also needed to make a tulip perfect. ('Feathering' was delicate marking round the petal's edge, 'flaming' indicated markings down the centre of the petal.) Despite the in-fighting, however, it is nice to think of men like Tom Storer, a railwayman who raised many fine tulips in his garden by the railway track at Derby, including the bizarres 'Sam Barlow', named after one of the most stalwart florists of his day, and 'Dr Hardy', both of which broke to give many fine forms. 'Miss Fanny Kemble', severe but beautiful in her dark purple and white, was held to be the loveliest of all tulips: her whole stock cost Mr Davy of Chelsea 100 sovereigns in 1832, which some would consider to be tulipomania come again. The tulip names of the time were stuffy, to say the least of it – 'The Rev. H. Ewbank', 'Mabel', 'Universe' do not inspire interest. *The (Royal) National Tulip Society* was founded in 1849 and in the 1930s subsumed by the Wakefield and North of England Tulip Society: but in the interval it carried out some useful work, including the organisation of the Great Tulip Conference in 1897. The Wakefield and North of England Tulip Society was formed in 1836, and continues to hold a tulip show in Wakefield each May.

Late in the century the tulip grew ever more popular in England. It still retained an exotic feel, and it was still classified very loosely into early-, mid-, or late-flowering. But we are now within waving

i. *Tulipa biflora*; ii. 'West Point' (Lily-flowered); iii. *T. turkestanica*;
iv. 'Mr van der Hoef' (Early-double); v. 'Fantasy' (Parrot)

distance of modern times, and suddenly things were beginning to look different, for the world was on the threshold of exploration in Central Asia. Much of this was organised, or encouraged, by Dr Eduard Regel who had moved from Zürich in 1855 to become Director of the Imperial Botanic Garden, St Petersburg. His son Albert, a doctor, plant-hunted on the various missions to which he was attached in Dzungaria and the Tien Shan regions, where other Russian botanists also worked. Gradually, from these remote regions, a fine harvest of species tulips was gathered in. Eduard Regel, who was aware as no one else of the uncounted riches of Central Asia, wrote up the tulips in *Gartenflora*, the journal which he had founded in 1852. Some of them also were figured in the *Botanical Magazine*, but Regel considered that the material was not always accurately handled there. Not only in Central Asia, however, but also in Asia Minor (where the indefatigable plantsman and traveller H. J. Elwes was at work), Persia, Turkey and the south-west of Russia, new species were being sought by the professional collectors employed by the firm of C. G. van Tubergen of Haarlem and by Max Leichtlin, an amateur who ran his own private botanical garden and nursery in Baden for the supply of exotic plants to Europe [see HORTUS 5]. John Hoog of van Tubergen's planned that his collector, Kronenburg, balked by the plague from searching Bokhara and Afghanistan, should instead work along the northern slopes of the Tien Shan to Wernoje and then south along the Tien Shan proper, a route which Albert Regel had followed and found fruitful. Many of Regel's introductions, including *Tulipa altaica*, *T. iliensis*, *albertii* and *ostrowskiana*, had vanished from trade catalogues and were all worth re-introducing. In May 1900 Ellen Willmott, who had helped to finance the van Tubergen collectors, had the satisfaction of exhibiting at a Royal Horticultural Society show masses of Turkestan tulips brought in by Kronenburg and Sintenis, to the evident astonishment of the nurserymen Peter Barr, Wallace and others. Being aware that not a single one of these tulips had reached Europe since old Dr Regel's death in 1892, they could not understand where and how she had obtained them. But Ellen Willmott could keep very quiet when it suited her, and liked nothing better than springing surprises.

The received wisdom on species tulips had always been that they originated in Turkey, Asia Minor and Persia. The Regels had now proved that Central Asia was also an important source, but it has

i. 'Van der Neer' (Single Early); ii. 'Marechal Neil' (Double Early);
iii. *T. confusa*; iv. *T. kaufmanniana*; v. 'Keizerskroon' (Single Early)

taken a further two generations to arrive at a precise statement of the facts. Michael Hoog, writing in *Lilies and other Liliaceae* (Royal Horticultural Society, 1973) tells how, intrigued by the great range of colour and form, and the untold diversity, he felt that the tulips of Turkey might form only an element in the overall development of the genus. Careful examination of the distribution of species then revealed that the greatest concentration (40 per cent) of all known species lay within 1000 km of the Tien Shan in Central Asia, and more than 60 per cent within 3000 km. Michael Hoog concluded that the origin of *Tulipa* was located in Central Asia whence migration took place in all directions, until halted by cold conditions in Siberia and Central Russia, and by deserts in North Africa, Iraq and Israel. China had not been adequately searched for species. Turkey, with the Caucasus and Iran, should thus be regarded as a secondary gene centre rather than the main source: apart from *Tulipa sylvestris* and *T. sprengeri* no new species had been recorded there other than those which could have arisen from mutation, interspecific and remote hybridising and successive stabilisation. It is fascinating to speculate whether there are undiscovered species still in the heart of Asia.

Does this add anything to the known history of the garden tulip? Probably not. The original species could still have been one of the mutants mentioned by Michael Hoog, or it could have come with travellers along the Silk Road. But a number of changes were taking place among the garden tulips. It is surprising to find that, as late as 1887, 'broken' tulips were still regarded as far more interesting than breeders. It was not until the important Dutch nurserymen E. H. Krelage & Son began to distribute the new Darwin tulips (named after the scientist and naturalist), bred from the stock of M. Jules Lenglart of Lille where many generations of selection had already taken place before purchase by Krelage, that growers began to realise that the breeder could be an interesting and worthwhile tulip in its own right. Darwins, with their strong stems and squarish cups, were used in the crosses which formed both Mendel and Triumph tulips, as well as the Darwin hybrids. At the same time the nurserymen Peter Barr in England and W. B. Hartland in Ireland began to search out, from gardens and old collections, single, late-flowering tulips which they designated Cottage tulips. W. B. Hartland's selection was (in 1901–2) headed 'Late Border Cottage Garden Single Tulips – Bright Parisian Boulevard Colors' – conjuring up a Matisse-like palotte, though Matisse was scarcely heard of before 1905, and may not have penetrated to County Cork till long after.

With all this activity, it was rapidly becoming evident that some sort of classification was needed which went beyond the rough and ready divisions on which nurserymen worked, and which might include both cultivars and species, while retaining for the latter the old distinction between those with hairs on the filaments and those without. The Daffodil Committee of the Royal Horticultural Society in 1902 became the Daffodil and Tulip Committee: in 1913 the Society appointed a Tulip Nomenclature Committee composed of British and Dutch specialists, which reported in 1917. After a series of reports and trials a tentative list of tulip names was drawn up and in 1935 accepted at the Rome International Horticultural Conference. Twenty years later the International Horticultural Conference at Scheveningen appointed the Royal General Bulbgrowers' Association as the International Registration Authority, and finally in 1987 a classified list was issued – the *Classified List and International Register of Tulip Names*.

At last, here is something comprehensive, including both species and cultivars, and easy to grasp. I cannot resist quoting at random one of the entries from this fascinating list:

> *Juliette: Exterior:* outer petals flamed chrome-yellow, edged aureolin somewhat scarlet to the edges, inner petals aureolin with scarlet midrib and flames; inside lemon-yellow, base indian-yellow with signal-red flames, anthers plum-purple. Sport. 1985.

There is a tri-language glossary at the back, but no detailed colour code explanation. But it makes it clear at once how much more observant one ought to be. It should not be necessary to be losing one's sight in order to seek, as did E. A. Bowles, the compensation of looking closely into a flower to see its miraculous colours and patterns. And not only is the range of petal colour greater and more subtle than that of any other genus – though the lily, of the same *Liliaceae* family, is a close rival – but there are shadings and variations about every other part of the inflorescence. The colour, size and shape of the flower's base, about which the old florists used to argue: the ovaries, the style, stigma, the anthers and filaments which compose the stamens, the very pollen itself (can it really be *purple*?) are amazing in their colours – black, mauve, olive, orange, purple, red, yellow, chocolate, blue, white: *any* combination can be present in one flower.

Are all these variations for the purpose of guiding pollinators? No one seems to know. It would be nice to think that they are for the delight of any human being who cares to look.

Which brings me to the final question – what is the tulip like in itself, how is it perceived as a flower with a character, as a person, almost? When I was beginning to write this piece the editor of HORTUS sympathised with me because I was writing out of the tulip season, and had no bloom beside me to watch the colour seeping slowly up through the waxy bud. He was right, and I wish I had in my hand a brilliant May tulip; but that is partly because it is a dull January day, and it is natural to want to get on with the season. In fact I have come to feel that the written word can just as well evoke the presence, not only of the individual flower, but of great hosts of tulips stretching back into the distant past, and all along the Asian 40th parallel on which tulip species seem to have concentrated their origin.

From Sheikh Lalézaré's 'Pink of Dawn' by way of Parkinson's 'Gingeline' to Rea's 'Orenge, Brimstone, Hair and Dove' and the Juliettes and Olenkas of the *Classified List*, there seems to be no colour lacking. But this was not always seen as an advantage.

'Vainly in gaudy colours drest, 'tis rather gazed on than caressed' is how the tulip is seen in a Victorian *Language of Flowers*, and this unsympathetic but quite penetrating observation makes the tulip sound rather a sad flower. Others saw it differently: Vita Sackville-West in *Passenger to Teheran* (1926) talked of 'This roof of the world, blowing with yellow tulips', and I often think it a pity that we have lost this use of the word 'blow', for there is something of a trumpet call about the sight of a great multitude of brilliantly coloured flowers.

This was not the way in which Sylvia Plath saw the twelve red tulips which were brought to her in hospital: the poem ends with a metaphor of heartbeats, but gets there only via a series of protests – 'The tulips are too excitable, it is winter here': she saw them as taking her oxygen, as disturbing the quiet of her white hospital room with their loud insistent colour, as red lead sinkers round her neck . . . And yet the poet Vahid can say, 'Fireside is the tulip garden of the winter'.

The military tulip, the municipal tulip, even the nine formal, normal, cheerful cottage tulips of the lovely HORTUS logo, all take such very different views to make this a puzzling and intriguing flower.

For myself, I think that Gerard was right: the tulip *is* 'lorraine', and aloof: it is a proud flower, bolt upright. There is just one possibility which would make it seem, to me, a little more relaxed, a little more homely. I wish that the 'broken' tulip, with all the subtleties of its featherings and flamings, its rich variety of colours, could be given its place. And although Parkinson was wrong in thinking that breaking necessarily spelled the end of the bulb's life, it produced one of the best pieces he ever wrote: 'this extraordinary beauty in the flower, is but as the brightnesse of a light, upon the very extinguishing thereof [;] and doth plainly declare, that it can do his Master no more service, and therefore with this iollity doth bid him goodnight.'

ACKNOWLEDGEMENTS

My thanks are due to John Berkeley, Esq., of Spetchley Park, Worcester, who has kindly allowed me to use material from letters written by John Hoog to Miss Ellen Willmott. I am also grateful to the following for help and information: Dr Michael Avishai, Director of the Jerusalem and University Botanical Gardens; Victoria Matthews of the Royal Botanic Gardens, Kew; and the Staff of the Lindley Library.

BIBLIOGRAPHY

Most of the sources which I have consulted are named in the text, but I must add the following, which have given me material which is basic to the study but has not been specifically acknowledged:

Bazin, G., *A Gallery of Flowers*, 1960
Blunt, W., *Tulipomania*, 1950
Coats, A. M., *Flowers and their Histories*, 1968 (revised edn)
Hall, Sir Daniel, *The Book of the Tulip*, 1929
Solms-Laubach, H., Graf zu, *Weizen und Tulpe*, 1899
Stork, A., *Tulipes sauvages et cultivées*, 1984

Drawings by Simon Dorrell

Paradise in the Parks

JOHN FRANCIS

JOHN FRANCIS walks through Southampton's parks most mornings, after his night's work at the hospital. He lives in a flat; the parks are his garden . . .

Richard Andrews (1798–1850), son of a wheelwright, himself a coachbuilder of renown, friend of the deserving poor (how nice to be sure), prosperous and generous, owner of a manufactory in Above Bar, Southampton and five times – eat your heart out, Dick Whittington – Mayor of that county, now city, enjoys an enviable position in death, as he seems to have done in life. There he stands, a bit nibbled

There he stands, a bit nibbled by Time & car fumes.

by time and car fumes. Surely it is the pierced state of the ozone layer, old coal fires and acid rain that have rendered so lacey those parts of his mayoral gown that were not intended to be lacey? As I say, his position is enviable. To his left and to the right stretch avenues of fine horse chestnuts. Behind him, over his right shoulder, stands the poignant monument to the crew of the *Titanic*, realised in slippery-looking granite. Just to the right of the nape of his neck there live the sardonic-eyed, mocking élite of the aviary, much given to derisive bouts of laughter, struttings, twitterings, wolf-whistles; every last one of them glad to have won a place in the Royal Box, from which to observe the 'fairly' throbbing heart of Southampton, safe from cats and totally confident about the timing and the quality of the next meal.

But Richard Andrews' most desirable prospect is directly in front of those sightless eyes: the great Lime Walk stretching, if not as far as the eye can see, at least as far as a twenty-minute stroll takes. I see Mayor Andrews' statue every morning when I pass him on my way home. Home, or kipperwards, or boiled eggwards, even, in Babylonic mood, tomato and baconwards, after a night's work. Praising God and eyeing the hostas, you may say. That is, if I go by way of Brunswick Place.

Brunswick Place is the edging for the northern end of the parks. I say parks, for though they form a whole, it is to be hoped that tiresome roads will not punctuate them. I see Mayor Andrews; perhaps he sees me. It is more likely, for the little I know of him inclines me to suppose that he was a discriminating man, that he is regarding the vista of the Lime Walk. The late hurricane saw off several limes. I have noticed one adolescent replacement, planted to commemorate the life of Norman Dalrymple, cabinetmaker, born 29 November 1938, killed Clapham rail crash, 12 December 1988. How much better in this tragic circumstance to plant a tree than a stone. And a cabinetmaker surely would be pleased to know that more wood, so to speak, was on the way. I digress.

Parks are conducive to digressing.

The statue of Lord Palmerston, Prime Minister, Foreign Secretary, keen dispatcher of gun-boats, has a charming spot all its own, which he keeps an eye on. Such a mild eye, such a milky, innocent look! Clad in a dressing-gown with toga-ish overtones he seems to be in charge of a rockery, winding paths and pretty flowering shrubs. If all

Clad in a dressing-gown he seems to be in charge of a rockery, winding paths and pretty flowering shrubs.

one has heard is half true, he would be indulgent towards any lascivious goings-on in this section.

I admit that as I walk home at about six in the morning five days a week I am sometimes seized with a mild and harmless sense of megalomania. 'All mine!' The Siren voices of the kipper and the boiled egg are silenced. I feel at one with Louis XIV, whom one can imagine, roused by his faithful body-servant Bontemps, looking out after the curtains had been thrown back and seeing vistas. And not just vistas. With his inward eye he would also have seen another lovely day of sheer Kingship: snubbing a pushy courtier here, graciously receiving a humble petition there, having a spousy chit-chat with his sanctimonious old humbug of a second wife before invading somewhere; but before doing any of these mundane things, seeing the amazing park that he had created with the help of his wily old le Nôtre. The advantages of being Louis XIV seem very real when, sharing it with the dead eyes of Richard Andrews, you see the Lime Walk. Sets you up for a good day's sleep. And, of course, you got up twice: once for yourself, then officially, as King. 'Dawn broke in the Royal Bedchamber at . . . fill in the space yourself, your Majesty.' Then at a signal (this must have been a bit trying) a Royal flourish of fifes and drums alerted the waiting world – well, Versailles any-way – to the tell-tale tremor of the Royal eyelids. 'Yes, Sire, ghastly din but just swallow this aspirin, and the roses are looking lovely.'

At sixish the parks are all but deserted. All but. Once from out of a thicket of rhododendrons I was surprised by a vivid-voiced, red-faced old party bidding me 'Good morning' and asking me what the time

He was still cheerful and the source
of his cheerfulness, bottled Somerset
orchards, lay strewn about him.

was. He was still cheerful and the source of his cheerfulness, bottled Somerset orchards, lay strewn about him.

Of course, the fancy that you are the Emperor of China, le Roi Soleil or Lord Tom Noddy is forever being ambushed. For you are not really alone. Tulips like hock glasses filled with the wrong wine peer tremulously at you, borne on a tray of freakish mist which would be dispersed by the errant flight of a butterfly. You know the sort of local mist I mean; it clings over streams, it heralds pop groups on television; and it is regularly waded through by Vincent Price in a battery of old horror movies. Stand still, heedless of tomatoes and bacon: this is not a repeatable experience. It is not for storing on even the most sophisticated video machine, and banality lies in wait. Plump, plump, plump. Two stout ladies in track suits, keenly anxious to shed those ugly pounds, thud past the aviary. The peacocks, the cockateils, and me, distinctly hear one say (for even exercise must not dethrone gossip, thank goodness) 'I don't see how she can be a bridesmaid, not with those tattoo'd arms.'

" I don't see how she can be a bridesmaid, not with those Tattoo'd arms... "

Having no garden of my own, unless you count my window boxes, I number the parks of Southampton, whatever the Parks Department fondly imagine, among *my* most cherished possessions. They are a noted glory, conceded by even the most biliously hostile dweller in neighbouring Portsmouth to be not half bad. Not that they are perfect. I appreciate that parks, being large-scale, necessarily paint in bold colours. Even so, I question faintly the wisdom of egg-yolk yellow wallflowers topped off with puce tulips. Again, fiendish experiments by mad horticulturists who produce regrettable pelargoniums should be resisted, not encouraged. It's odd the way Parks people seem to long for a vivid tropical look to northern European gardens. I've noticed bits of Cheltenham, of all places, attempting to pass themselves off as Brazil. Better to have a space of uncut grass and a few primroses; and what I often ask is wrong with foxgloves?

I like rhododendrons, but I'm against those blue azaleas that seem to be plugged into the national grid.

> If thou wouldst view fair Melrose aright,
> Go visit it by the pale moonlight.

If thou wouldst view Southampton's parks, moonlight might reveal some growths of a monstrous aspect which are best avoided. No. The best time to view parks is a little after six in the morning in early summer, more particularly if you work at night and have no garden of your own. Then it's paradise.

Drawings by John Verney

The Art of Gardens

ANDREW LAWSON

I have been looking at paintings all my life, but I only started to look seriously at gardens quite recently when well into my middle-age. With some surprise I find that familiarity with the language of painting is a useful background from which to view gardens. Curiously it does not seem to require a great quantum leap for the eye to adjust from a familiarity with pigments and forms arranged within a frame to coloured flowers and leaf shapes distributed upon the broader canvas of the garden.

I find I now get the same thrill of pleasure from a good garden as I have always got from paintings that I admire. This pleasure is a cocktail of sensory delights, spiced with admiration for the skills of the artist. I confess I have been moved to tears in admiration for gardens, just as I have so many times in front of paintings. And I am pleased to say that while I have often wanted to 'take my hat off' figuratively to my favourite artists, I have sometimes been able to do so literally in the garden.

Two casual remarks made to me, separated by twenty years, brought home the close parallels between the arts of gardens and paintings. Freddie Gore, my painting tutor at St Martins, told me that 'Every artist has a limited range of colours to which he returns again and again'. More recently, Rosemary Verey made more or less the same remark with reference to her planting: 'I know what colours work best for me', she said, 'and I try to stick with them.'

Of all the gardeners I know, Rosemary Verey is the closest to a painter in her attitude to colour. She will pick a flower to hold against a prospective partner – like a draughtsman squinting to measure a model against the line of an outstretched pencil – and if she likes the association she will lift the plants and put them together without further ado. Once, when moving plants was impractical, she picked whole swathes of flowers from one patch of plants and threaded them among a complementary group, so that for a few hours one complete border was a glorified flower-arrangement, undetected by her visitors.

One colour association that works especially well for Rosemary Verey is lilac-purple with pale yellow. She often wears these colours herself and so looks particularly harmonious in her own garden at

Barnsley House. Her most triumphant celebration of purple and yellow is the famous laburnum walk. Here the tall lilac-coloured globes of *Allium aflatunense* rise to meet the hanging yellow racemes of *Laburnum × wateri* 'Vossii', through which also hang the occasional flowers of *Wisteria sinensis*, its lilac colour picking up an echo in the hue of the alliums. It is a colour combination that finds further echoes in the adjacent border, where yellow-leafed trees, gleditsia and ulmus, are underplanted with lilac-flowered *Campanula lactiflora* and *Thalictrum aquilegifolium* among many others. Nearby, the purple flowers of *Clematis macropetala* clamber through a golden privet, pruned to give a compact and tight-leafed shape. The whole effect is a concerto on two colour-instruments. These borders are a masterly statement of colour, of the kind that one might encounter in a Bonnard painting – but of course Bonnard never had to wrestle with the gardener's additional problem of orchestrating his colours to perform together at the same time.

As far as I can tell, Rosemary Verey's use of colour is intuitive, as it is with many artists, but her choice of colour combinations would have found favour with the Post-Impressionist painter Georges Seurat. Seurat was one of the great theorists of recent art, working as he did at a time when chemists and philosophers such as Chevreuil and Goethe had just revealed the physical basis for colour perception. They showed that certain colours could be regarded as diametrically opposite to other colours, which are called 'complementaries'. Red and green, for instance, are complementary, as are purple and yellow, blue and orange. Complementary colours provide the maximum available contrast. Nothing could be less purple than yellow. Green is the furthest one can go from red.

The effect of putting complementary colours side by side is the enhancement of each colour. A red looks all the redder for being put beside a green. Perception of purple is increased by an adjacent yellow. To see this effect, go from the laburnum walk at Barnsley House to the National Gallery in London and look at Seurat's painting 'Une Baignard' made in 1884 when the artist was twenty-five. ('Hats off, gentlemen, a masterpiece'.) You will see that Seurat intensified a dominant colour by putting a touch of its complementary beside it. Wherever the blue of the water meets the flesh colour of the bathers, Seurat puts a few dots of orange pigment along the edge of the flesh. This intensifies the blue. Elsewhere in the painting, areas of yellow are set off by adjacent purple, and red by green. The painting is all the more subtle because Seurat also uses enhancement of tone (lightness and darkness). Each tone is lightened at the edge of its meeting with a dark one.

Colour in painting was liberated in the late nineteenth century in the hands of Seurat and other artists, who were also labelled 'Post-Impressionists', such as Van Gogh and Gauguin. Just after the turn of the century a group of artists that included Matisse, Derain and Braque were called 'Fauves' (wild beasts) by virtue of the intense colours they used. Since then, the story of art has been a gradual unfolding of any remaining constraints of colour, form, or materials. Strangely, I would say that the reverse holds true in garden art, certainly in the field of colour. For sheer exuberance of pure colour in the garden we need to turn to the Victorian gardeners, or to their successors in our municipal parks and suburban gardens who maintain the Victorian tradition of annual bedding schemes. This uninhibited use of pure colour for its own sake is sometimes derided by garden writers. Yet the brilliant bedding schemes of the best municipal parks are seen and enjoyed by more people than any other kind of garden, and without a doubt they lift the spirit of all who see them. Judging by the great art of our time, pleasure in pure colour can hardly be dismissed as unsophisticated. Rather, pure colour seems to satisfy a fundamental sensory urge.

Another curious feature of modern gardening is that while the breeders of new strains of plants are producing bigger and brighter ranges of the familiar garden plants, there is a tendency for the *cognoscenti* to reject these 'improvements' and to turn back to the more modest wild originals. I think this is a missed opportunity – you would not hear of Matisse rejecting a new pigment if it was offered to him.

In appreciation of art, the true art-lover ignores fashion, for there is pleasure to be had from every smallest corner of the world of art. So it is with gardens. Fortunately my advocacy of courageous colour partnerships does not prevent me from promoting the more subdued garden schemes that we English seem to do so well. In painting, Gwen John and Ben Nicolson are, for me, quintessentially English artists – 'laid-back', quiet and refined, and Gertrude Jekyll is their gardening equivalent. Remember that she was trained as a painter and turned to garden design when her eyes became too poor for her to paint. The Jekyll influence is still enormously strong today, and when it has been well absorbed it has contributed to some of our most spectacular contemporary gardens. Peter Healing's garden at The Priory, Kemerton is the best example I know, with its long border in which the plants are graded horizontally by colour, vertically by height, and in time according to their flowering period. It is a sensational achievement, with plants of any one colour coming into their best at one time.

Monochrome plantings, like the red borders at Kemerton and Hidcote, or the white gardens at Sissinghurst, Crathes Castle and Brook Cottage, Alkerton, are the ultimate refinement of the Jekyll influence working on the fundamental bedrock of English 'good taste'. They correspond, if you like, to the drawings of the masters of art, limited in means perhaps, but all the more revealing of the character and style of their creators. When you look at a border made up of plants of a single colour, your attention becomes all the more focused upon the little distinctions of texture and shape.

Texture and shape take us into the realms of sculpture, and there are English gardens whose makers appear to have the sensibilities of sculptors of the landscape. I am thinking of David Hicks, a brilliant architect and designer in other fields, whose garden in Oxfordshire has hardly a flower in sight. Instead he weighs one texture against another by interplantings of foliage plants, and one volume against another by carefully pruning his trees and hedges into solid-seeming structures. Rectangles of grass are allowed to grow long, framed by fillets of tightly mown grass for contrast. The trunks of a hornbeam hedge-on-stilts stand out against a background hedge of the same species. The artist is in command of his elements: the cubist sculptor.

Can there really be such a thing as a cubist garden? Cubism, you remember, was one of the most revolutionary movements in twentieth-century painting, initiated by Picasso and Braque around 1907, and subsequently insinuating an influence in much painting up to the present day. Expressed simply, cubism represented a new way of seeing the world – fragmented and viewed from several angles at the same time; a world split up into its elemental cubes and cones; a world divided into interconnecting compartments. And what does that remind you of? Why, Hidcote, of course, the most revolutionary and influential English garden of this century. It seems to me more than a coincidence that Hidcote was also born in 1907, the year that

Lawrence Johnston first moved into the Manor and began to make his garden. I am not suggesting that Johnston knowingly created a cubist garden, or even that he was aware of what Picasso and Braque were up to in Paris. It may just be another instance of an idea, when its time is ripe, appearing in several places at the same time, as so often happens with discoveries in science.

Having given you a cubist garden, my next trick is simple – a surrealist one. The surrealists, like Dali and Magritte, enjoyed delivering a shock to the spectator by putting together familiar things in an unfamiliar way. My favourite surrealist garden was, I suspect, knowingly surreal. It was created by Lord Berners at Faringdon House. In a pool in front of the orangery reposes a solemn bust of the Victorian dignitary Sir Henry Havelock. The water laps around his shoulders. He looks like a seal coming up for air. In the dovecote nearby the living birds have been dyed brilliant magenta, lemon and blue like so many eggs on Easter morning. Likewise, a blue dog lurches around the garden. It is all a great joke. And why should a garden not be funny?

The English are inveterate collectors of things, and many a garden is a depository of some arcane collection or other. When you visit Stowe you get the impression that the Temple family collected temples as you or I might collect paperweights or first editions. I know a garden in Cornwall which contains a collection of cast iron Victorian kitchen ranges, all proudly polished and burnished. In Bournemouth there is a garden constructed entirely from shells collected around the world and cemented into surfaces together with broken fragments of china. Garden gnomes are another example of this collecting phenomenon – The Gnome Reserve in Devon occupies over an acre of woodland in which hundreds of gnomes gambol and frolic in every imaginable activity.

The French painter Claude Lorraine remarked that there are only two branches of the fine arts – painting and pastry-cooking. That may be the case for the French. For the English, I like to think that there are two fine arts too – painting and the creation of gardens. Of the two, I would say that we are lucky enough, through climate and inclination, to excel at the second.

Colour from Plants

DAWN MacLEOD

In the spacious Surrey of my childhood, residents cultivated such a wealth of flowering plants to provide garden colour in summer and to brighten conservatories in winter that it looked like a perpetual flower-show to me. By the time I was four, seeking to rival in my own little plot those opulent displays put on by parents and neighbours, I had discovered how to wheedle such favourites as pansies, double daisies, marigolds and forget-me-nots from the gaunt old Scotsman who kept a plant nursery next door to our home.

Clutching a new Saturday penny with the polished face of King George V on it, I would creep among earthy-smelling sheds and stacked clay pots, hoping to find Mr Crawford disengaged. Seen like this, peeping round a bank of cold frames, I must have resembled Peter Rabbit with his wary eye on Mr MacGregor. Luckily for my future as a plantswoman, I wasn't shouted at or chased off with a threatening rake, but kindly allowed to choose the best specimens at knock-down prices. Where else, even in those non-inflationary times, could such gorgeous plants have been had at four for one penny?

Recalling the upright nature of both my parents, it seems odd that they should have permitted their small daughter to exploit the old man to such a shameless extent. Although nothing was ever said to me about it, I now suspect that a few coins must have been added to their own purchases, in order to balance the books while preserving an artless friendship between the solitary gardener and his youngest customer. So long as he wasn't engaged in the fiddly job of 'pricking out', I felt that Mr Crawford was quite glad to see me, even though his smile had a long journey and was very slow to arrive at his face.

The crimson lips of plump double daisies; pansies of bronze and purple velvet like Grandmother's sofa cushions; marigolds as bright as the August holiday sun on Weymouth sands, and smelling equally hot; and forget-me-nots growing bluer by the minute: were all these really so much brighter then than they look now, or was a purer glow distilled from their petals by some lost alchemy of my youthful eyes?

Many years (and much reading) later, I discovered that an entirely different range of hues lay hidden in plants – pigments which could be unlocked from flower, foliage, twig and root and then transferred to wool and other fibres used for the adornment of homes and persons.

My earliest practical initiation into the age-old craft of dyeing with plants came from a Hebridean crofter-wife. Who could have guessed that the water-lily whose white cups shawled the inland loch near her cottage held in its roots the finest black dye-stuff? Although her need to be customarily clothed in black from fingers to feet for Sabbath kirk attendance put her to immense trouble, it seemed certain that Mrs Macalister obtained what is now called 'job satisfaction' from her messy task.

First of all she had to wade in the mud at a season when the loch water was at its lowest level, around July. Having detected with her bare toes the thickened rhizomes which store up the dye, she must then detach these from a tangle of anchoring roots, while preserving the skins undamaged. Like beetroots, the rhizomes of water-lily will bleed if they are scarred, wasting valuable pigment.

An iron pot filled with rain water was used to extract the dye, suspended over a fire of peats built outside her cottage door for this purpose. I was delicately informed that, to clear and fix the colour on fleece, use would be made of stale urine collected over a week or two from 'the goesunders' (chamber-pots) and stored in pails in an outhouse. Her eyes on the seething cauldron, Mary Macalister described this as a natural process. Wool culled from her sheep, dyed by roots from the loch and fixed with urine supplied by people who would wear the finished article, seemed to her a ritual possessed of an almost mystical quality, and in no way offensive.

As for those unfortunate residents on the mainland whose lochs failed to provide water-lilies, they were obliged to wear inferior Sunday blacks dyed with roots of dock (*Rumex crispus*), iris (*Iris pseudacorus*), or meadowsweet (*Filipendula ulmaria*), known in the Gaelic respectively as *Bun na Copaig*, *Bun Sealasdair*, and *Lus Cuchulainn*. To these names she gave utterance with a shamefaced air, while the splendid *Bun an Lilidh* (*Nymphaea alba*) merited ringing tones and a gratified smile to match. The old Queen Victoria herself couldn't have been more complacent about the fine quality of her Sunday church-going attire.

Few urbanised visitors from the south seemed capable of understanding how this humble woman, poor in money and possessions, living in a remote, sparsely-furnished cottage, managed to feel so rich within herself. She was proud of her Gaelic-speaking race, of its traditional life-style, and of her own store of wisdom and local anecdote. Nor was she the only example I came across. In the 1950s, while working at Inverewe with Mairi Sawyer, I observed an even more memorable picture of Highland pride.

A short distance further north on the coast of Wester Ross, an elderly widow kept house for an unmarried son in his fifties, who combined part-time crofting with a job driving a local bus. One day Mrs Maclennan disclosed to us, in a reverential tone, that her son Murdo was 'too grand' to wear any garment not made from the wool of his own sheep. Each shearing time a portion of fleece was set aside for him and despatched to a mill in Inverness. There suitable yarns for weaving and knitting were spun, dyed with the rock-grown lichen known as 'crottle' or 'crotal' (*Parmelia saxatilis*), which yields a range of pale, medium and dark browns. Tweed was handloomed and then tailored to Murdo's measurements by a local firm, while Mrs Maclennan's needles busily clicked in the fashioning of pullovers and socks. This was grandeur indeed. Can any peer of the realm boast of being clad in such attractive and hard-wearing material, made of wool shorn from his own flock?

As for the thrifty use of natural waste products, long before people in the 1980s began to embrace 'green' ideas, we inhabitants of the Scottish Border country had as neighbour a retired naval commander, an early member of The Soil Association, so committed to its tenets that he was known locally as 'The Compost King'. Lady Eve Balfour (of the family of Whittingehame in East Lothian) had produced organically-grown crops at her Suffolk farm since 1939, seven years before founding The Soil Association. This great pioneer, fourth daughter of the second Earl Balfour, died in Dunbar in January 1990 at the age of ninety-one.

Her ardent disciple, the late Commander Stuart, ran a private hotel in Berwickshire (known familiarly as 'The Compost Heap'), where guests feasted on the very finest whole-wheat home-baked bread, made by the skilful Mrs Robertson, who also cooked organically-grown fruit and vegetables from the large walled garden, all of superb flavour. Proof of the pudding is in the eating, and our Commander had of course chosen the best possible way of advertising his then novel creed, by putting it into practice.

He had other promotional gimmicks, one favoured ploy being to take from a pocket a handful of dry brown granules, which he fingered without uttering a word. Some luckless guest, new to the game, would voice the magic word *compost*. After a slight but telling pause, Commander Stuart replied smoothly 'Yes, this is composted sewage from Scandinavia.' The compost heap, which Lady Eve and he did so much to publicise in the face of many a snide remark and snigger, became accepted as an essential adjunct to every garden, while the words 'muck and mystery' died unmourned. But the Commander failed to persuade local authorities to process human excrement for use on the land in place of chemical fertilisers. Maybe that will take another fifty years.

Our friend, who was interested in many uses of plants, heard of my experiments with vegetable dyes and urged me to make a trial ground for growing dye-plants in two kinds of soil, one patch organic, the other chemically fertilised. I am sorry now that in a busy life I couldn't find time for this investigation. It would have been fascinating to discover if the 'organic' plants gave superior colours to those obtained from chemically-fed ones – or perhaps the reverse. We were both well aware that it takes a long time to set up such a comparison, for you have first to ensure that one patch is completely free from chemicals.

If Mary Macalister voiced a dim view of black dyes produced by dock, iris and meadowsweet, I wonder what her reaction would have been to a macabre pigment brought from Egypt by tourists four hundred years ago. The dyes manufactured by chemists which we now take for granted weren't known until the nineteenth century, and so our forebears tried any and every substance from which colour could be extracted.

The Travels of John Sanderson in the Levant, issued in 1586, contains an account of how some English visitors were lowered into a cave somewhere near the Great Pyramid, there to pick over in the flickering light of candles a large heap of mummified corpses. 'They gave no noyesome smell . . . but were like pitch, being broken. I broke all parts of their bodies to see how fleshe was turned to drugge, and brought home divers heads, hands, arms and feete.' As the writer's reference to 'drugge' indicates, this material was in fact prescribed for medicinal purposes, though for what supposed benefit isn't stated.

Then there was an artist's colour known as 'mummy', in use over a long period and well referenced. The painter Alexander Brown, who gave lessons in water-colour to Samuel Pepys, wrote of it: 'Mummy is in every way ill-conditioned and hard. It will not flow unless you burn it in a crucible. So prepared, it may make a good black.' At a later date *The Compendium of Colours* is more enthusiastic: 'The finest brown used by Mr West [probably Benjamin West, P.R.A.] in glazing is the flesh of mummy. The most fleshy are the best parts. It must be ground up with nut oil very fine.' So even this gruesome pigment depended on a plant extract for its usefulness as an artist's material.

Until the discovery of aniline dyes, colouring matter used on textiles came most commonly from plants – although the Phoenicians of Tyre derived their gorgeous 'Tyrian purple' from molluscs. In Mediterranean lands the Kermes oak (*Quercus coccifera*) and Holm oak (*Quercus ilex*) are hosts to the scale insect, which yields an excellent red dye described by William Morris as '*The* scarlet of the Middle Ages'. He despised as an inferior hue the red introduced by a Dutch chemist in 1656, produced from the cochineal insect with a tin mordant.

The Greek physician Dioscorides, whose *Materia Medica* has kept his memory alive, wrote also on the subject of dye-plants in the ancient world. His list includes madder (*Rubia tinctorum*) for red; saffron (*Crocus sativus*) and weld (*Reseda luteola*) for yellows; and woad (*Isatis tinctoria*) for blue. Much information has been handed down over the centuries about this biennial member of the brassica tribe.

In Britain its history usually begins with the story of Julius Caesar's invasion and his discovery of natives who stained and patterned their bodies with blue pigment obtained from the woad plant. Some historians prefer to think that the Romans introduced woad to England. At all events, it is known to have been cultivated in Egypt very early in the Christian era and was widely distributed in the wild throughout Europe, Asia, and North Africa, so was almost certainly used by the Romans.

There are accounts of woad cultivation in Britain in Saxon times, and the term 'saxe blue', familiar in my youth, may well have been a corruption of 'Saxon blue', originally denoting material dyed blue with woad. In addition to the home-grown plant, there are records as far back as the twelfth century of woad imports from France, chiefly 'Picardy woad' from the country near Amiens. During the Middle Ages English woad-growing was largely centred around the towns of Tewkesbury, Wisbech and Glastonbury. It is thought that the syllable '*glas*' in the last name derives from a Celtic word meaning blue-grey, and was chosen to depict the glaucous foliage of *Isatis tinctoria* colouring acres of farmland on the outskirts of that little town. Woad is a hungry plant. For good crops it had to be rotated every second year, so it became customary for bands of woad-growers to travel the country hiring fields for its culture.

In medieval England the best rich blue cloth, known as 'perse', was properly dyed with woad alone on white wool, mordanted with ashes. Some tradesmen tried to achieve perse by putting woad-dyed material which hadn't coloured well into secondary baths of madder. If detected, this malpractice got them into serious trouble, for it was an offence to describe such adulterated colour as perse. The genuine blue cloth was highly prized, fetching as much as six shillings a yard in the thirteenth century.

Some time during the fifteenth century our cultivation of woad unaccountably dwindled and began to fail, although the demand for this dyestuff continued. To fill the gap, shippers – and in particular the Merchant Venturers of Bristol – began importing quantities of French woad, mainly from Bayonne and Bordeaux. The value of that trade may be judged by the frequent mention of woad in local wills and bequests. One rich merchant of Bristol left stocks of woad to pay for his burial in the splendid church of St Mary Redcliffe, while another bequeathed 'eight measures of woad towards a new pair of organs in St Werburgh's Church'.

In France, it so happened that the cloth-weaving industry of Languedoc declined at a time when British cloth manufacture was on the increase, so the scarcity of home-grown woad made England a good customer for the surplus stocks of French growers. This was a small, early instance of ever-changing trade patterns, which in our time so exercise the minds of EEC statesmen – although European farmers no longer cultivate woad.

Because the dyeing process was inordinately tedious and smelly, it seems unlikely that the woad-men were able to take a pleasure in their work to equal that of Mrs Macalister in Uist with her water-lily rhizomes. The first crop of *Isatis tinctoria* would usually be reaped when the stalks began to turn yellow, before the flowers opened. About six weeks later a second cutting would be made, and in a good year this might be followed by a third. After being washed in the nearest stream, and sun-dried – which must be done quickly to ensure the best dye – the woad was sent to a mill and ground to a smooth paste.

After that, the woad-men made the stuff into heaps, pressed down and shaped smooth like overgrown blancmanges. Carefully sheltered from rain, they formed a black crust, which must not be broken for fourteen days. Then the crust was beaten into the soft centre, and the paste shaped into spherical moulds, emerging to be dried upon hurdles. The woad now resembled a batch of shabby cricket balls; some specimens, of a dull purplish colour, are stored in the Museum of Economic Plants at Kew.

In this form the woad arrived at the dye-works, where the balls were beaten to powder with mallets on a stone floor. Again it was piled into heaps, three to four feet high, well moistened and left to ferment. For twelve days the stinking mass was stirred about by men with shovels, after which they left it alone until by some sixth sense they judged it to be fit for use.

At last it was ready to be dissolved in a dye-bath of boiling water, where it stood for some hours in a closed vessel with one-twentieth its weight of newly-slaked lime. Given gentle heat, this liquor when stirred produced a blue froth, first sign of the desired end-product. But the mixture beneath the scum had a reddish hue, and cloth entered into the bath came out a bright green. Only on exposure to the atmosphere could oxidation take place, producing the true woad blue, a permanent dye. The smell of this process was so disagreeable that Queen Elizabeth I refused to visit any place where woad dyeing was carried on. How glad everyone must have been when, with the opening up of sea routes to the Indies in the sixteenth century, indigo was imported to supersede woad. The plant *Indigofera tinctoria*, a member of the pea family, yields an equally fast blue with considerably less trouble.

To those who are interested in flower-arranging, woad may be worth growing in some out-of-the-way spot – perhaps *en famille* with edible brassicas in the kitchen garden. After the commonplace yellow flowers are done, if a warm autumn facilitates a good supply of ripened seed, the plant has decorative value. During a stint at the American Museum in Britain (at Claverton Manor near Bath) I experimented with some fifteen-inch dried stems hung with purple-black pods which dangled like earrings, in an arrangement where they stimulated a great deal of curiosity. Combined with silver moons of honesty (*Lunaria annua*) and handsome 'clocks' of goat's-beard (*Tragopogon pratensis*), which are bigger than seedheads of dandelion and may be preserved with a light hairspray, this group looked attractive for many weeks.

In one article it is possible to cover only a small fraction of the dye-plants and lichens – about a hundred and twenty – which I have so far investigated. Periodicals designed for gardeners are strangely reluctant to admit this aspect of horticulture. I recall some years ago spending a whole day in the Vincent Square library of the Royal Horticultural Society. Having searched more than sixty annual indices for mention of dye-plants, I was about to pack up and go home when I found an entry: 'British Dye-plants' by Dr Plowright. That volume of *The R.H.S. Journal* had been issued as far back as 1901. Such neglect of this subject seems strange, for the long saga of colour painstakingly extracted from plants forms an important facet of social history.

Drawing by Simon Dorrell

The Artist as God

Louis Comfort Tiffany and the gardens of Laurelton Hall

MITCHELL OWENS

When Louis Comfort Tiffany sat for his official portrait at the age of 63, the man who reinvented the stained-glass window chose to be recorded in a situation far removed from his professional endeavours. Executed in 1911 by the Spanish impressionist Joaquín Sorolla y Bastida, and hanging today in the galleries of the Hispanic Society of America in New York City, the painting shows a bearded, surprisingly youthful dandy in a suit of white linen. He is seated before an easel; a brush is grasped lightly in his hand; his mouth has the set of self-satisfaction. Most significant, however, is the setting: the father of American Art Nouveau is posed for posterity against an absurdly luxurious bank of white and blue hydrangeas in the gardens of his country house, Laurelton Hall.

All that Louis Comfort Tiffany ever wanted out of life could be found behind the gates of his private estate. A friend once wrote that to Tiffany, 'The garden [was] his school, the flower his companion, his friend, and his inspirer.' Excepting rogue daylilies and unkempt box hedges, however, there is practically nothing left to see of the extraordinary gardens of Laurelton Hall, on which Tiffany lavished so much attention. The house, itself an amazing creation, disappeared long ago, the victim of fire, vandals, and the demolition contractor's wrecking ball; the exotic grounds fell prey soon after to neglect and developers. But enough faded photographs and crumbling newspaper clippings remain to piece together a portrait of a feverishly creative man determined to turn his world into a picture.

The son of the founder of the eponymous silver-and-jewellery emporium, Louis Comfort Tiffany (1848–1933) bore all the hallmarks of genius from earliest youth – precociousness, acute sensitivity to criticism, and an implacable belief in his own brilliance. 'The more I teach him, the less he knows,' said one exasperated tutor, but even he grudgingly admitted that the boy had talent to spare.

Tiffany's sensitivity to colour and shading was astounding, a gift he would use to tremendous effect when planning his gardens. It wasn't enough simply to make a brooch in the form of Queen Anne's lace; the enamel, garnets and silver used in its creation had to recreate as accurately as possible the subtle shading of the original blossom. And though he initially won international acclaim as an interior decorator and a designer of memorial windows, by the turn of the century his focus had shifted almost entirely to naturalistic subjects: fish, birds, insects and, above all, flowers.

Perhaps this sudden preoccupation with floral imagery, with living, growing things, had something to do with Tiffany finally becoming a man of property. Despite two marriages and a growing family, he had continued to live at his parents' Romanesque mansion on 72nd Street and Madison Avenue in New York City, and spend summers at their Hudson River compound. It was a convenient arrangement but no doubt confining. (It was no secret that Papa Tiffany preferred to keep a close eye on his wilful, spendthrift heir, whose high-society friends he considered 'fast company'.) It is conceivable that Tiffany *fils* turned a spade or two here, but it wasn't until 1889, when he became master of his own estate, that gardening became an essential part of his life.

The land Tiffany found for his first real home lay on the north shore of Long Island, a densely wooded bluff overlooking Cold Spring

Harbor. Here he built a house christened The Briars. Unfortunately, Tiffany the acclaimed artist and designer wasn't much of an architect. The Briars was an ungainly neo-Georgian building, comfortable but clumsy, its unfortunate proportions effectively obscured by a romantic accumulation of Virginia creeper.

The arrangement and contents of the gardens were decidedly conventional for so Bohemian an occupant; perhaps Tiffany was just testing the horticultural waters, enthusiastic but conscious of his limitations. He was, however, quite certain about the type of flowers he liked. Unlike the fashionable gardeners of the day, who cultivated showy, multi-petalled hybrids, Tiffany was happiest in the company of charming, unsophisticated flowers, and he favoured naturalised varieties above anything bred in a greenhouse. Paths led to a pretty dry-wall garden of Cherokee, briar, and dog roses and to a shady wilderness area planted with bird's-foot violets. Cut into a grassy slope on the harbour side of the house were a pair of broad terraces foaming with alyssum, arabis, cerastium, stonecrop and saxifrage. Elsewhere were carpets of ground myrtle (vinca) and beds of ferns and cacti. Friends offered cuttings and seeds from their own gardens, notably Caroline Starr Balestier, the American wife of Rudyard Kipling, who sent Tiffany a rare sweet pea from her East Sussex home.

Tiffany lived in apparent contentment at The Briars, dogs scampering behind as he walked the dew-soaked gardens at dawn. 'To watch the flowers grow from bud to full bloom was his greatest pleasure,' recalled his youngest daughter, Dorothy. Family life became an apparently unceasing round of outdoor activities: picnics, charades, impromptu pageants, and buggy rides. Only one condition marred the bucolic splendour – the master's decree that flowers were to be admired, not picked. Dorothy Tiffany recalled that her father considered the destruction of a flower, even accidentally, a crime worthy of the strictest punishment. Flowers, it seemed to her, were more important to Tiffany than his children. Her poetically-inclined sister Comfort lamented: 'Blooms, blooms, everywhere;/was one single flower loved?'

The serenity of the country was too good to last. In 1902 Tiffany's father suddenly died, and it was as if the weight of the world had been taken from Atlas's shoulders. At the age of 54, Louis Comfort Tiffany found himself free of his father's stern gaze and meddlesome ways. It was a situation ripe with possibilities, and he took full advantage of it:

le roi est mort, vive le roi. To his family's dismay, he quickly bought 580 acres of land adjacent to The Briars and broke ground for a new country house. What followed was surely one of the most amazing achievements in the history of American architecture and gardening. Once again the egotistical Tiffany acted as his own architect, and came up with a house that managed to be both graceless and beguiling. Laurelton Hall was a million-dollar folly in the Persian mode, a sprawling stucco palace built for a New World Nebuchadnezzar. The buff-coloured structure was the size of an ocean liner: 280 feet long, 84 rooms, 25 bathrooms. Guests marvelled at the stained-glass galleries, the grand loggia with its column capitals shaped like poppies and lotus blossoms, the booming pipe organ, the stencils copied from originals at the Topkapi Palace, the museum-quality collections of Native American and Oriental art. It was a modern Xanadu unlike anything seen before in the United States, but the massive house and the treasures it contained were as nothing when compared to the gardens.

When first encountered, the gardens of Laurelton Hall must have seemed as unassuming as those of The Briars. Visitors approached the house via a serpentine drive of blue gravel that wound through a tantalising series of painterly scenes built up as carefully as any Impressionist landscape. First came field upon field of lemon-yellow daffodils, then flowering banks of *Phlox subulata*; the latter's pink and white blossoms gave the wooded landscape a snowy frosting that was much commented on in magazine articles of the day. The road rolled onward, through shady groves of red cedar, chestnut, mountain laurel, and salmon rhododendrons; beneath a pink-blossomed tunnel of espaliered apple trees; down to the rocky beach; and as it curved back to meet the house, the road followed a stream planted with day-lilies, Joe-Pye weed [*Eupatorium purpureum*], wild rice, Japanese iris, and golden-rod. To the eye of the unsuspecting visitor, so far, so good.

Behind the house, however, awaited a melodrama of breathtaking proportions, 'the dream, in both theme and execution', a critic reported, 'of an intensely original mind.' Actually, the mind responsible for Laurelton Hall was less original than eccentric. Relying upon such disparate inspirations as the Grand Canyon, ancient Babylon, and the Islamic world's reverence for water, Tiffany conceived a majestic scheme of fountains and hanging gardens for the east or harbour side of the house. Water from a 40,000-gallon tank was pumped into a fountain inside the entrance hall, then channelled outside to a high terrace where it burst into a gentle geyser. Plumes of water splashed over a boulder of jagged rose-quartz crystals and flowed into an octagonal pool. As if by magic, the water disappeared underground, only to be reborn at another octagonal fountain on an adjacent terrace, and so on down the steep hillside, until the water ultimately gurgled into Cold Spring Harbor. It was an amazing marriage of nineteenth-century romanticism and twentieth-century engineering that never failed to impress even the most jaded guest. This Ziegfeld Follies calvacade was rendered even more stupendous after dark, when rotating coloured lights turned Tiffany's elaborate waterworks into iridescent rainbows.

On each terrace, shallow flights of steps led past tiers of octagonal flower beds, each thick with heavily-scented petunias or old-fashioned roses and surmounted by a dwarf cypress. A snarling bronze-and-mosaic Chinese dragon presided over the bottom-most fountain, backed by a wall of potted New Zealand cabbage trees [*Cordyline australis*].

Another of Tiffany's flights of fancy was his method of displaying wisteria. Steel wires and cables were attached to the upper walls of the house, stretched straight across the lawn, and fastened into the surrounding trees. This airborne trellis was quickly smothered, the pendulous purple flowers hanging into the air as if from one of Tiffany's celebrated stained-glass windows.

'Art is man's nature,' Tiffany once proclaimed; 'nature is God's art.' In his mind, there could be no higher calling than to meld the two into a gratifying whole. He felt that he had achieved this mission in Laurelton Hall. Here he spent his declining years with his mistress Sarah Hanley, who retreated into fervent Catholicism after his death, doing penance for her days as an artist's paramour by painting portraits of God floating above fields of flowers. One supposes that Tiffany would have been pleased with her efforts: the Almighty always had *his* face.

Portrait of Louis Comfort Tiffany by Joaquín Sorolla y Bastida.
Oil on canvas. © The Hispanic Society of New York

The Gardener's Diamond Year

ELIZABETH SEAGER

'Odd as it may appear, a gardener does not grow from seed, shoot, bulb, rhizome, or cutting, but from experience, surroundings, and natural conditions' wrote Karel Čapek in *The Gardener's Year* – and it was my childhood experience of reading his book, first published in Britain sixty years ago, that opened my eyes to plants and gardens.

In its diamond anniversary year, I would pay tribute to this little gem, recommend it to others, and urge its reissue for the delight of future generations. The book is vividly descriptive of buds, seeds and seasons; sharply observant of gardeners and their quirks; and whimsical in the best sense of the word – inventive, full of humour and self-mockery.

Karel Čapek is best known as playwright and author of *R U R* (Rossum's Universal Robots) – a vision of the future in which robots take over from their creators. He was born on 9 January 1890 in north-west Bohemia, the son of a doctor. In 1907 the family moved to Prague – but he did not wish to follow his father's profession, and ten years later he was working as a journalist. A keen interest in drama led to his appointment as Director of Prague City Theatre in the early twenties.

In 1925 he and his brother Josef, a leading Czech artist, decided to make a home together, and had a house built on Úzká Street – subsequently renamed Street of the Brothers Čapek. It was here that they both indulged their love of gardening, pottering in the 'ample yard', where they grew rare plants and alpines, and had a greenhouse packed with orchids and cacti. Photography was another passion, and soon Karel was contributing photographs of his flowers to several magazines, and reviewing gardening books for the *Prager Presse*. The brothers worked in old clothes, and 'Karel was never so pleased as when a deliveryman would approach and ask him rudely if Dr Čapek were at home.' In 1935 he married the actress Olga Scheinpflugova, after a long attachment to her, but he died only three years later, on Christmas Day 1938.

The Gardener's Year was one of several books inspired by Čapek's varied leisure activities. It was illustrated by his brother and published in Prague in 1929. The first British edition appeared in 1931, published by George Allen and Unwin, and translated by M. and R. Weatherall. I was nine when I discovered it in the mid 1940s, in the revolving bookcase of a rented house that was then our home. The

bookcase itself was fascinating to a child, whirling round smoothly at a touch – and so was the chair beside it, with elegant wooden arms and back, and an intriguing tapestry-covered triangular seat. An omnivorous reader then, as now, I worked my way through the books, devouring long-forgotten thirties novels, together with *Masterman Ready*, *Rodney Stone*, and much narrative poetry, before reaching *The Gardener's Year*.

A child looks first at illustrations, and they enchanted me. Line drawings, cartoon-like in their simplicity, showed the gardener (always male, for gardening was still a predominantly masculine hobby) contented and happy, despondent or perplexed; crouched confidingly over the earth; bent beneath the sun, bottom up, head down; or floating fantastically over his plants on butterfly wings.

The pictures of compost heaps delighted me, and I am convinced that they inspired my later passion for making them. Čapek's enthusiastic gardener 'hunts about at home for eggshells, burns bones after lunch, collects his nail-cuttings, sweeps soot from the chimney, takes sand from the sink, scrapes up in the street beautiful horse-droppings, and all these he carefully digs into the soil; for all these are lightening, warm and nutritious substances.'

One picture depicts steam rising from a manure heap to form a fat cloud full of flowers. In 'the reeking and strawy heap of manure' the gardener can imagine the perfume of the flowers which will eventually benefit from it – 'he sniffs approvingly, and he carefully spreads this gift of God over the whole garden as if he were spreading marmalade on his child's bread'.

Having sampled the pictures I began to read, starting with the chapter on buds. 'There are buds deep scarlet and rosy with cold . . . brown and sticky like resin . . . whitish like the felt on the belly of a rabbit . . . violet, or blond, or dark like old leather. Out of some pointed lace protrudes; others are like fingers or tongues, and others again like warts. Some swell like flesh, overgrown with down, and plump like puppies; others are laced into a tough and lean prong; others open with puffed and fragile little plumes. I tell you, buds are as strange . . . as leaves and flowers. There will be no end to your discoveries.' I went out and looked around our garden. It was March and the buds were there, just as Čapek said – and I have been looking and marvelling ever since at the small miracles of the garden.

I rediscovered *The Gardener's Year* in 1972 in a second-hand bookshop in Oxford, and carried it home with great delight. It is one of my treasures – I see myself in every chapter, I have shared all the author's

discoveries, enthusiasms and mistakes. So apt are his comments that I think of him every time I step into the garden, and hardly a summer passes but I murmur his garden prayer. 'O Lord, grant that in some way it may rain every day, say from about midnight until three o'clock in the morning . . . gentle and warm that it can soak in . . . and grant that the sun may shine the whole day long, but not everywhere . . . and not too much; that there may be plenty of dew and little wind, enough worms, no plant-lice and snails, no mildew, and that once a week thin liquid manure and guano may fall from heaven. Amen.'

I remember Čapek when I sow seeds 'winged, prickly, downy, naked, and hairy; big like cockroaches, and tiny like specks of dust.' I recall his words when I dig the soil in November – 'to lift it with a full spade gives you a feeling as appetizing and gratifying as if you lifted food with a full ladle, with a full spoon . . . it ought to be like bread, like gingerbread . . . like leavened dough . . . when you turn it over with a full spade, it ought to breathe with pleasure and fall into a fine and puffy tilth.'

In autumn I savour his description of a bulb, 'a bomb out of which a spring flower will burst'. In spring I identify with Čapek's gardener who 'with a fading plant in his hand, runs round his little garden twenty times looking for an inch of soil where nothing is growing. ... but in two days ... will discover that he has planted it right on top of the scarlet shoots of the evening primrose.' I think of him ruefully when I am ensnared by the hose: 'with a hydrant hose ... one can water faster and, so to speak, wholesale; in a relatively short time we have watered not only the beds, but the lawn as well, the neighbour's family at their tea, the passers-by, the inside of the house, all the members of the family, and ourselves most of all.'

The Gardener's Year was reissued in paperback in 1966, but it is now out of print, though it can still be found in second-hand bookshops, a slim green volume, often tattered and well-thumbed. It is high time for a reprint of this minor gardening classic, to delight and inspire a new generation.

Author's note:

In compiling this article I have consulted Karel Čapek *by William Harkins, Columbia University Press, 1962 – a study of his life and literary works; and my own copy of* The Gardener's Year *by Karel Čapek (fifth impression, 1931)*

Illustrations by Josef Čapek from The Gardener's Year

The Annapurna Sanctuary

A Close Brush with Death

TONY SCHILLING

The great massif of Annapurna sprawls for almost fifty miles along the northern edge of the central region of Nepal and acts as a 26,500 ft (8077 m.) high Himalayan buffer against the Indian monsoon. Annapurna, which means 'the giver of life', is a revered mountain, for its melting snows help feed the sacred waters of the river Ganges. Beyond its icy ramparts lie vast windswept steppe-deserts which lead northwards to merge into the high arid plateau of Chinese Tibet, while immediately to the south are lush forests and deep valleys fed by thundering rivers.

The largest of these rivers is the Modi Khola which forms a wild and savage cleft nursing leech-infested bamboo forest. At the head of the Modi Valley lies an incredible glacier-riven amphitheatre ringed by many giant peaks including Annapurna I, Fang, Glacier Dome, Gangapurna and Annapurna III. Its gateway is guarded on either side by the towering peaks of Hianchuli (21,132 ft / 6441 m.) and the twin summits of 'The Fishtail', Machapuchare (22,943 ft / 6993 m.). From the ice-fluted crests of these two great sentinels, complex shattered cliffs fall a vertical distance of $1\frac{1}{2}$ miles (2.41 kms) to end abruptly at the edge of the pounding river. Even on a sunny day it's a grim and oppressive chasm and fills the minds of those who enter with a great sense of awe.

Less than twenty-five years ago it was a semi-forbidden area held sacred by the local Gurung people, who discouraged outside intrusions into the Sanctuary. Particularly resented were non-believers in their faith, all women, and sheep, but with the passing of time these attitudes have significantly mellowed and in order to gain entry now the only qualifications required are a stout heart and a strong pair of boots. In the spring of 1977 I led a trekking party of friends along this wild path; we were in search of plants, beauty and adventure, and we found all three in plenty.

By the time we reached the Gurung village of Chomro we had already experienced the botanical highlights of the journey. On our approach we had camped at Gorapani amid great forests of *Rhododen-dron arboreum*, one of the monarchs of the genus. The hillsides were alight with their blossoms, in shades ranging from scarlet through rose and pale pink to the occasional pure white form. This variable species, which attains a height of 75 ft (22.5 m.) or more, is the national flower of Nepal and occurs right across the central Himalaya from Kashmir to North Burma.

Among this dominating species also occurred the holly-leaved oak, *Quercus semecarpifolia*, a wide variety of plants representative of the laurel family and, best of all, *Magnolia campbellii*. The typical form of this great tree magnolia blooms pure ivory-white in Nepal, which comes as a surprise to those who have been brought up to enjoy the pink form so common in cultivation. In ideal natural conditions this noble species grows to over 100 ft (30 m.) in height, and makes many of the so-called giants in gardens look like mere saplings in comparison.

The spring season also rewards the explorer with the fragrant white flowers of *Osmanthus suavis*, and drifts of *Daphne bholua* var. *glacialis* bearing abundant mauve-lilac flowers with a perfume strongly reminiscent of clove carnations. The variety *glacialis* is a deciduous plant and far hardier than the evergreen type species which comes from lower altitudes and is horticulturally inferior. In 1962 Major Tom Spring-Smyth collected a particularly good form of the decidu-ous variety in eastern Nepal and this has since become commercially available under the well-chosen clonal name of 'Gurkha'. There may be even better hardy clones awaiting introduction to our gardens, as the plant ranges in colour from pure white to deep maroon.

Berberis concinna is a neat and dwarf sub-evergreen species also com-mon to these hillsides, but seldom seen in gardens. Its small spiny-toothed leaves are a shiny green above, glaucous-grey beneath and slowly turn purple, orange and scarlet in a beautifully erratic manner from autumn through to spring. This character, coupled with the brilliance of the disproportionately large scarlet, pear-shaped fruit, makes it a doubly desirable barberry.

We moved on through this colourful tapestry of plants towards the 10,500 ft (3230.8 m.) Deorali Pass. This lovely grassy ridge-top is encircled with rhododendron forest out of which jut black-green, sentinel-like trees of a silver fir, *Abies spectabilis*, while at the forest edge grow shrubs of the pink-flowered *Viburnum grandiflorum*. In

spring the whole world seems to pulse with the song of birds. Beyond the col our trail pitched steeply downwards through broken ground which required measured caution and a steady head. Thin wayside waterfalls tumbled clear of saturated mossy bluffs upon which were massed an autumn-flowering form of *Primula boothii*, a joy to find at the end of a long and tiring descent. Hard by, on the domes of mossy rocks, we found two or three plants of *Primula drummondiana*, a rare and tender plant in cultivation and probably only to be found in the most specialised of private collections.

Next day our way was one of descent, ascent and then more descent, mostly though a wild tangle of forest and broken mountainside. There were many epiphytes on the trees, especially orchids and various ericaceous genera, including *Agapetes*, *Vaccinium* and *Gaultheria*. Other interesting 'hangers-on' were *Euonymus echinatus*, *Rhododendron dalhousiae* and the club-moss *Lycopodium herteranum*. Climbers included *Clematis montana* and 'claspers' were represented by *Hydrangea anomala*, the Himalayan counterpart of the more familiar east Asian *H. petiolaris*. We were indeed beginning to experience the real wealth of flora which abounds in the lush monsoon-influenced forests of Annapurna's southern flanks. Later in the day we dropped out of the darkness of the forest onto more open hillsides, and then continued very steeply down between cultivated terraces of rice, millet and buckwheat to camp at the attractive village of Khimnu.

The following day, beyond the village on the cliffs above the river, we located several clumps of *Bergenia ciliata* var. *ligulata* clinging to rock ledges, their white, pink and rose-coloured flowers lighting up the sombre hues of the grey rocks. Every *Bergenia* species I have ever seen in the wild has been in a rocky home, either clasping the cliff side, or growing in broken ground among boulders on stabilised screes. In cultivation, although a perfect subject for the larger rock garden, it is more generally used as a ground-cover plant, or perhaps as a random subject in the front part of a mixed border. Either way, it is a useful and reliable flowering plant and a cottage-garden favourite. Eventually, late in the day, we pitched our tents beyond the larger Gurung settlement of Chomro high on the western flank of the deep and narrow Modi Khola gorge. We were now poised for the final leg of our adventure – into the fabled Annapurna Sanctuary.

The dawn of 13 April broke clear and bright. After a hasty breakfast of chapatis, we struck camp and in high spirits headed on into deep forest, pushing ourselves hard in the hope of reaching the Sanctuary that evening. The four previous days had been cool and stormy with heavy snowfalls in the high mountains, and we were therefore glad of the improved, warm weather and clear views.

The giants of the forest here were the oaks, and the best of all was *Quercus lamellosa*, the species which Sir Joseph Hooker described in his *Himalayan Journals* as 'the noblest of oaks'. It attains a height of well over 125 ft (37.5 m.) in this sheltered valley, thriving in the high rainfall of the area. Leaves from the species have been recorded as much as 15 inches long and 9 inches wide (38 × 23 cm.), bearing up to thirty-five pairs of veins. Our enjoyment of the forest was blunted by the tedium of the rocky trail which bucked, lurched and wound its wild way above the western bank of the river. The narrow and deep valley in itself created a threatening feeling of confinement and this was further amplified by the density of the vegetation, now altering to accommodate great brakes of bamboo, *Himalaycalamnus falconeri* var. *cupreiciliatus*. In summer monsoon periods this dank trail is a leeches' paradise; even in spring and early autumn their numbers are remarkable.

Above us, a green swathe of mixed forest led obliquely upwards across the mountainside and merged gradually into the more subtle purple-brown tones of a blanket of leafless forest. This 'blanket' was composed of the Himalayan birch *Betula utilis* which, as its specific name implies, is used by the local people for a variety of domestic purposes. In ancient times its attractively peeling bark was used as paper, and many holy Sanskrit manuscripts were written upon it. The bark is also believed to have magical powers: spells written upon it are placed in an amulet and tied around the neck in the belief that this will ward off demons and evil spirits.

All that morning we pushed our way along the narrow trail. The strangely spectacular aroid *Arisaema griffithii* thrust mottled shoots out of the leaf mould, some already unfurling their purple-green leaves and producing large cobra-like hooded flowers, adding a bizarre touch to the already eerie atmosphere. The glossy green leaf-rosettes of the giant lily *Cardiocrinum giganteum* glistened in the sunlight which filtered down through the delicate filigree of bamboo foliage, and *Meconopsis napaulensis* was a common sight, its hairy leaves sparkling with silver beads of moisture and smothered by ladybirds.

Soon after midday one of our lead Sherpas, Mingma, suddenly pointed ahead and said 'After big black rock maybe we have trouble!' The trouble proved to be of the technical kind, for the trail suddenly became slippery and exposed. After another half-hour we found ourselves flanking around a great bluff of rock which fell at an awkward angle from the eastern wall of Hianchuli, the peak of which was now immediately above us on the left. As we turned the shoulder I suddenly became aware of the great mass of snow-ice which dominated the way before us. It was avalanche debris, some old, hard-packed and a dirty-grey, some quite recent, soft and white. Several of our porters had already crossed the huge convex, fan-shaped chaos and others, plus the lead Sherpas, were close behind, but unwisely high on the central section of hard snow-ice. Immediately above us hung a high, evil-looking black cliff down which wept a thin, ice-encrusted waterfall descending from heaven knows where. It was an uncanny place and one could clearly sense danger.

After due consideration, two of us cautiously started kicking steps obliquely outwards and upwards across the slope in the wake of our Sherpas, aware of the difficulties of the situation. I remember reassuring my companion that 'real avalanches only happen in books', and that 'all should be well if we hurry'. My comments, which appeared to cheer him, left me secretly unconvinced of the wisdom of our actions; but, given the circumstances, we had little alternative.

Just as we were approaching the point of no return, the taut silence was shattered by a terrible roaring sound and all order was suddenly turned to noise, fear and confusion. Blind instinct coupled with terror gave wings to our hurried retreat as we slipped, stumbled and ran back to the safety and shelter of the cliffs we had so recently left. A second or two later I saw Sherpas, grey-faced with shock, running back to join us; two porters were falling, running and stumbling down the very centre of the slope in a ferment of head baskets, rucksacks and scattered equipment, all of which seemed to be driven along by a wild sea of snow, ice and flying rocks until wind-blasted spindrift completely enveloped the scene. I was convinced that both the porters had been engulfed, but for the moment we were helpless to move as the terrifying avalanche continued to thunder past our refuge point. For at least three minutes the deafening 'trundle' continued; they were undoubtedly the longest minutes of my life. When at long last all was quiet and still, a sense of momentary relief was immediately replaced by renewed panic as we hurried towards the nose of the avalanche-cone. For ten dreadful minutes, I feared the worst. Mixed waves of anger, shock, guilt and grief, washed over our frantic movements and discussions; discussions made difficult because of tensions and language problems. Eventually horror and tears were replaced by great relief and nervous laughter as a careful count of heads revealed that all, miraculously, were unscathed. One badly shaken porter had lost all his personal belongings, and some of our kitchen equipment was missing, but otherwise all was well.

It's strange how very close actual disaster and unharmful excitement can be to one another, the former leaving a scar on the memory for life, the latter actually adding a zest to life and causing merriment in the story-telling which follows. Nature is always neutral, but thankfully fate sometimes takes sides.

We retreated to a glade in the bamboo forest where we pitched camp, and then, frightfully British – we all had tea!

In addition to the refreshing effects of that incomparable beverage, an overdose of adrenalin sharpened my reactions and apparently brought about an acute stimulation of my senses. The nearby plants of *Rhododendron arboreum*, *Piptanthus nepalensis* and *Viburnum grandiflorum* which I had noted some time earlier were now doubly attractive, and the mighty sweep of the beetling cliffs and sheer ice turrets of Machapuchare almost overwhelmed me with their aweful majesty. I remember making a deliberate note of these exaggerated feelings, and mentally asking myself why it was that one had to be almost exterminated before it was possible to obtain such a clear and intense perception of beauty. The sensation was only momentary, but I have never forgotten its powerful impact.

Russian roulette is definitely not my favourite game of chance, so the next morning we wisely but tediously detoured down by a longer route which took us safely around the base of the now much enlarged avalanche slope.

Mingma took the lead cutting steps for the party with his ice-axe, pausing now and then in the intense cold to cast his sharp Sherpa eyes across the tilting sea of avalanche debris, hoping for signs of our lost kit. It must have been very deeply buried: the massive proportions of the debris were quite incredible to observe, and Mountain Travel Kathmandu (our trekking company) would never see its table-cloth and kitchen cutlery again!

We cut our losses, as well as our steps across the slope, and three hours later safely attained the target of our venture: the lonely Annapurna Sanctuary. This immense mountain fastness is one of the greatest of Nature's amphitheatres. Within its icy bowl plant life gives up the battle to survive and surrenders to the stern, sterile world which stretches up towards the five-mile-high mountain crest.

We had risked a lot to realise our objective: the irony was that the only plant we saw beyond the 'firing range' which we hadn't already seen lower down was that very well-known and common garden plant, *Primula denticulata*. If anyone had foretold that I would chance my life in order to see the drumstick primula in the wild, I'd have called them crazy; yet, unintentionally, that's precisely what I'd done. Strangely enough, in spite of everything, it all felt worth it.

Two days later, when we had safely returned to Chomro, we learned from the villagers that there is a wayside holy shrine near the entrance to the Modi Khola gorge. Apparently it is considered wise and polite to pause there in order to make some small, reverent gesture of appeasement before venturing on. If I ever go back, I'll follow convention.

Decoration by Simon Dorrell

Gardening Myths and Commandments

JOHN KELLY

The latter part of a wise man's life is taken up in curing the follies,
prejudices and false opinions he has contracted in the former.

Jonathan Swift

Gardening is troubled by two distinct schools of thought. The first
consists of the accumulated attempts of would-be academics to turn
it into a learned discipline, and the second is the result of that other
quasi-priestly ambition – to control the mysteries.

In the first instance the symptoms are well known. Prolonged pon-
dering over irrelevant minutiae is one. It usually culminates in
pronouncements about truth that would have frightened Socrates to
an even more premature death. 'No, it can't be the true *despicabilis*,
you see. It lacks the forked cilia on the sterile pollen grains which are
– and I'm sorry about this, old chap – positively diagnostic.' Another
is the self-conscious language used in planty articles in amateur
specialist publications: 'Upon attaining the sub-summit ridge, it was
instructive to observe the eco-geological inter-relationships which
existed among the saxatile leguminids . . .'.

Guardians of the mysteries more often than not develop, if they
were not endowed with them in the first place, regional accents of
orotund ripeness. 'Do 'ee be sure to set they 'taters on Good Friday
now, my sunner.' Or, 'Raht, lad! Sithee, soar tha seed in roars of five.
Set 'um in roars of fower / and they'll noar coom oop 'til June be
ower'. Alternatively, they produce the sort of vocal delivery designed to prove that their rooms at home are so vast that they have
to project in order to be heard. 'Of course, Wessex always puts his in
the bed by the stables. I told him in The House – deep litter 'em
with marigolds. Works every time. Been known in the family since
Bannockburn'.

The fruits of these intellectual flights are the myths that weave
themselves like hyphae throughout the collective gardening consciousness. They often take the form of commandments, such as the
one that was current as the 1960s turned into the 1970s: 'Thou shalt
not use plastic pots.' Dire consequences were foretold for those who
were considering the move. Devotees of terracotta could be seen

crossing the street rather than walk on the same side as a shop selling red plastic pots. Plastic pots could not possibly drain. Plants incarcerated therein were doomed to creeping rot and the sinister attentions of slime moulds. Oxygen would not be able to reach the roots through the non-porous corsetry that would inevitably bring on attacks of the botanical vapours. They are still largely unacceptable on the show bench. Any geriatric clay container is preferable, so much the better when encrusted with lime, tidemarked with algae, and bearing the name of a pottery long since buried beneath a polystyrene New Town.

The plastic revolution redounded greatly to the benefit of those who had the foresight to anticipate that terracotta would, after a few years, become fashionable and therefore capable of being priced far beyond the reach of the many. However, it did not succeed in laying to rest a commandment connected with clay pots that is still alive today. This states: 'Thou shalt fill the lower part of thy clay pots with crocks; yea, unto one quarter of the volume thereof.' It is still meticulously obeyed and is repeated in guardian-of-the-mysteries style in contemporary books, especially those on alpines. Indeed, in the more thoughtful volumes it is further suggested that 'inverted turves' be placed over the crocks, so that the compost shall not seep downward and block the 'drainage'.

Inverted turves! Well, to be fair, some books, with a nod to modernity, recommend that 'coarse peat' be used instead. Of course, that advice has now run into shoal waters – another story. Meanwhile, the terracotta industry feeds on the myth to the extent that it is its own product that comprises the crocks. What do you do when you take delivery of your first batch of pristine clay pots? You have to break one or two to make crocks with!

Nobody uses crocks with plastic pots. They just fill them up with compost and get on with making the plants feel at home. So why crock clays? The answer lies back in the dream time, when it was wisely predicted that you would need a much more gritty compost in plastic pots. Nurserymen, turning for economic and storage reasons to folding-bag pots, discovered from the start that it was physically impossible to deploy crocks in them, so they simply shovelled in the gritty compost and hoped for the best. The best was beyond their wildest dreams, and that should have been the end of crocking. Unfortunately, the drainage holes are rather larger in a clay pot than in a plastic one, and it is necessary to prevent the compost pouring out through them like sand in an hour-glass. An inverted clay shard – a crock – does the job perfectly, but 'crock the pots' is shorter to write than the necessarily specific instructions. Hence the continued practice of robbing the plants of about one third of the space available for nutritious compost.

Plant names offer wonderfully fertile ground for the pseudo-academic. The pronunciation alone is alive with opportunities for the kind of avant-gardism that is such a British social accomplishment. In Britain, élites create and sustain themselves by inventing manners. They are not necessarily *good* manners – just ways of doing things that are acceptable within a limited circle. The British way of pronouncing Latin botanical names is a similar trap for the unwary. Woe betide anyone who pronounces *caespitosa* as keye-spit-oh-sa! The British pronunciation is cesspit-oh-sa. Beware, too, the 'ah' sound that is so necessary in Received English. In the traditional English pronunciation of plant names, it is said as in 'plane' or 'lay'. Thus to pronounce *nana* as nahna is to court social oblivion; neighna is OCD (our class, dear). And heaven help the person employing the short *i*. To render *minus* as meenus is fatally to label oneself a foreigner, while lack of care with the pine genus is a short cut to social death. None of this is all that surprising in a nation that can perpetrate 'Veye-vat Redge-eye-na' at its coronations.

There is no myth here, merely an indication of the unthinking way in which tradition overrides thought. When it comes to the application of names, however, pseudo-academicism rides triumphantly over botanical science. Reputations are made or broken upon the rocks of rightness and wrongness in plant names, and yet such things do not exist. No plant has a 'right' name. What it is known as at the moment is the result of consensus among botanists. It is instructive to note (as the saying goes) the career of the name *Lithodora diffusa*. In Gertrude Jekyll's time it was applied to the plant that was later renamed *Lithospermum diffusum*, and kept its new designation until very recently. Now it is *Lithodora diffusa* again. Sceptics with durable labels from the 1920s will have saved themselves a few bob over the years. Is there really anyone who can put hand on heart and say that it will never change again?

The perennial dismissive pronouncement by show judges, 'Disqualified, I'm afraid: wrongly named', should be enough to disbar the judge. It won't happen, of course; such things never do. If you actually know that *Gladiolus callianthus* is now generally accepted as more appropriate than *Acidanthera murielae* and you are a big, gruff guru with a seat on a committee, who is to balk your didacticism?

At the other end of the horticultural social scale is the large body of opinion in favour of 'common' or 'English' names. It is against the use of 'long' Latin names and sees them as élitist and difficult. People who think like this are not wrong; in fact, their protestations at the constant changes in botanical names elicit real sympathy even from the botanists who offer them. Complaints about Latin names are often based on the misconception that all plants have common names, but this in its turn derives to some extent from the keepers of the wildflower mysteries.

These are enthusiasts who never use anything other than English names. For example, they would perish rather than utter the Latin name of the bloody cranesbill. Fair enough, up to a point; *Geranium sanguineum* has half as many syllables again. But what happens when they wish to refer to *G.s.* var. *lancastriense*? Do their principles force them to call it 'the light pink form of bloody cranesbill that grows on Walney Island, off Barrow-in-Furness'? The Latin name is in fact a shorthand that cuts out circumlocution. Mind you, they are strangely selective, and much more likely to say 'sempervivum' than 'Welcome-home-husband-though-never-so-drunk', which is fun and therefore to be avoided at all costs.

Myths and the commandments that are based on them almost all derive from make-work. Genuine academics love to introduce complications – they would not be human otherwise. One has only to think of the activities of 'lumpers' and 'splitters' among botanists. The former tend to be monographers (fatter monographs), while the latter are mostly taxonomists (more taxa). How much more likely is it, then, that the pseudo-academics will strive to complicate things? The mystery-controllers are, of course, bound by their priestly role to introduce ritual.

If you want to get on in the upper reaches of the gardening world – well, perhaps not quite upper; just . . . not quite – you simply must not try to question the faith. An example of this is the story of the painting of tree wounds. For some time it was thought that the stumps of severed branches should have their surfaces painted with a fungicidal paint. The arguments for it were convincing enough for professionals to recommend and carry out the practice. Later the same professionals, who, after all, do the job every day, noted that as time passed the painted stumps decayed more rapidly and dangerously than those left unpainted. By now, however, the guardians of the arboricultural mysteries had taken stump painting to their collective bosom. It had become as indispensable to the perceived health of trees as purging had once been to the treatment of malaria. To this day, it is demanded of tree surgeons that they paint the stumps of branches they have removed; and they do so, otherwise they would lose business. However, they now use cheap household emulsion from the Penny Bazaar, in the hope that it will wash off only after their bill has been paid.

Most myths, though, are the result of poor observation or the drawing of conclusions from insufficient evidence. Among the former is the assertion that you should never water the garden in sunlight. This is perhaps the most oft-repeated of all gardening canards. It is based on the idea that droplets of water act as magnifiers and concentrate the rays of the sun onto the areas of leaf beneath them. The trouble with this one is that it is so plausible.

However, were it really true, nowhere would you see a single leaf in all nature that was not covered in burn marks – even to the extent that the leaf surfaces would have became inadequate, the plants would have died, and we would not have evolved to be here to see them in the first place. In tropical regions, the sun's rays are vertical and can burn human skin through cloud. Rain usually comes in short, heavy bursts, after which the sun beats down from a clear, blue sky. Its intense rays fall on leaves covered with glistening water droplets, and yet – do you see a mark on them? In Florida, where they insist on having gardens where it is 70° F in January and almost rainless, they start watering before sun-up, but are still doing so at nine a.m. as the sunbathers crank up the sunbeds for another day's basting. You do not see the philodendrons and hibiscus suffering from scorch. Surely the sun of the British Isles, operating at the latitude of Labrador, is unlikely to be all that fierce, despite its never having set on the Empire. And yet the myth lives on.

Another myth concerns what happens to plant roots in a drought. It states that inadequate watering or spells of rain that are too short cause the roots to turn upwards in search of water. The end result is supposed to be that the plants develop shallow root balls and become unstable. What wonderful piffle! Roots are positively geotropic; they have to go downwards, even if forced to make a detour on the way. Plants that are adapted to dry places, such as grape vines and olives, keep going until they find a constant source of moisture; the more constant, the better the wine and the olive oil. However, those that are used to moister climates are not equipped to go mining for water. What happens in a prolonged drought is that the roots begin to die. Light watering, whether natural or artificial, prevents death among the roots nearer the surface and, moreover, stimulates them to proliferate at a great rate to compensate for the failing roots below. The result can well be a shallow root ball and instability, but not for the reasons given by the myth. So what? Well, anyone with any sense hearing the myth might well fail to see a credible reason for administering a copious, drought-breaking soaking. A reason that appealed to his logic could well be the saving of the plants.

Observation and evidence are anathema to the myth makers because they threaten the foundations of their authority. They counter contradiction by labelling it the product of false logic, such as arguing from the particular to the general. Proper evidence is usually particular; to use it to propound a general rule is as logically viable as Newton's derivation from experiment of the laws of motion. In special circumstances they may not work, but in general, in the practical world in which we daily live, they do.

To be particular, I offer as an example twelve years of constant observation of the non-existence of a universally accepted horticultural phenomenon: that lime-hating plants will die if watered for any length of time with limy water.

Over that length of time my staff and I propagated, either from seed or cuttings, many thousands of calcifuge plants each year. Camellias alone accounted for a thousand cuttings, evergreen azaleas another thousand, rhododendrons the same, and pieris, andromedas and other lime haters at least another two thousand. Some plants highly sensitive to calcareous environments, such as Asiatic gentians, were propagated from time to time. The strike rate of cuttings was 100 per cent – almost unheard of – and attained annually. With other plants it was commensurately high.

The plants were mainly grown for sale and had to be of high quality. In many cases they remained on the propagating bench, which consisted of a mist system, from midsummer until the following spring, after which they were potted and repotted three times, coming to point of sale after two, three or four years – sometimes more. The water supply was from the same line that fed my house. Our kettle had to be de-scaled once a month and the vertical pipes feeding the mist nozzles developed into stalagmites. The water came, unsoftened, from aquifers in the chalk downs of Dorset. It was probably the most 'limy' water it was possible to use for watering plants, and yet not one plant – ever – showed signs of chlorosis or did anything but grow away lustily, unless attacked by pests or diseases in much the same small proportion that you would expect from any well-run production unit.

How many of you with hard water supplies but lime-free soil have gone to great trouble and expense to arrange rain water collection for your lime haters? Why did you do so? Was it because of observation, or was it because:

> The great enemy of the truth is very often not the lie – deliberate, contrived and dishonest – but the myth – persistent, persuasive and unrealistic.
>
> (John F. Kennedy)

The Laskett

The Story of a Garden

ROY STRONG

I always wish creators of gardens had written more. Few do, and we are the poorer for it, as nothing is more fascinating than learning from the pen of the only begetter. Nor do many gardeners have any archival sense. One is horrified by the paucity, in the era of the camera, of visual evidence, for example, for those two horticultural war-horses of our age, Hidcote Manor and Sissinghurst Castle. Well, no one need fear that in the case of our own garden, should it join the ranks of the survivors. From the moment of its inception every bill has been kept, every design and thousands of photographs too, besides, in recent years, the advent of our garden diaries. In addition, through over fifty volumes of scrapbooks we can trace the story of The Laskett garden from field to folly. But even that is not enough; fascinating though visual and archival evidence may be, it only tells When and How, evading that most compelling question of them all, Why.

But let me begin at the beginning, with the house itself. The Laskett, a word in Herefordshire dialect meaning a strip of land without the parish, lies on the fringes of the village of Much Birch midway between Ross-on-Wye and Hereford. As my wife, Julia Trevelyan Oman, always says, it is building rather than architecture, a pink sandstone box from the 1820s evoking the modesty of a rectory in a novel by Jane Austen. That a huge garden might be made was certainly never part of our plans at the outset, as is reflected in the fact that no one who was going to make a large formal garden would ever have chosen a house sited, as ours is, in the corner of a three-and-a-half-acre triangle of land, thus eliminating any possibility of the classic progression through parterres, bosquets and walks radiating from and related to the house. But in the long run that deficiency has been found to have its advantages. The first is the one of surprise: nobody visiting the garden for the first time can ever guess at the spectacle that suddenly unfolds as they cross the drive past a fountain and through a slip in a beech hedge. Turning sharply left there is a great vista falling away into the distance, through three gardens, towards glimpses of a pleached lime avenue. That is where the garden proper begins. To a sense of surprise I would add the ability to indulge in certain grand effects which, if sited in proximity to the house, would have appeared too pretentious and out of place. The ten-foot-high column topped by a golden ball, the nine-foot-high Shakespeare Urn (commemorating the award to me in 1980 of the FVS Foundation of Hamburg's Shakespeare Prize), and the small classical Victoria & Albert Museum temple (built in memory of the years 1974 to 1987), which make up the eye-catchers at the ends of the grandest vistas, are so far from the house that they have taken on the character of total fantasies in an imaginary landscape.

Both house and garden are south-facing and the land gently slopes away, presenting us at the outset with few level surfaces except that of the site of an Edwardian lawn-tennis court. And that was where we started, for it was in the field attached to the house let to a farmer as pasture for his cows. His decision in 1974 not to want it any longer set us on our way. Together we stood and looked at the three-foot-high grass and realised that something had to be done; and it was on the flat surface of the court, when mowing had revealed the fine turf beneath the grass, that we began, in the December of that year, to plant one of our first yew hedges, around what was to be the Pierpont Morgan Rose Garden. At the time I felt the lack of flat terrain a tremendous disavantage, but now I realise our good fortune, as changes in level, as every true gardener knows, form some of the most thrilling experiences. That only dawned much later, when we learnt that built structure could be added as and when it could be afforded. So, piecemeal over the years the flights of steps and paving came, necessitating only a realignment of hedges, letting one side grow up to re-establish levels within the composition.

But what about the soil? It is light and sandy, reddish in colour, too quick-draining and calling for constant compost and mulch to keep the moisture in. It tolerates rhododendrons and azaleas but they cannot be said exactly to thrive. Willows won't grow, and all except the most common of prunus are fated. Putting those black marks aside, practically everything else does pretty well and some things spectacularly so. Yew hedging, one of my great loves, shoots up at the rate of a foot to eighteen inches a year and, as most of the garden's most important rooms are formed of it, this has proved a great blessing. Sprigs two feet high become eight-foot walls in a decade. And, of course, Herefordshire being the cider county, malus flourish, and my wife's passion has become old apple trees and the decorative crabs, of which altogether she now has some hundred or so. This soil is also an ideal one in which to grow grey foliage plants but, as they are tender, one has to protect them from the wind. Wind, in fact, even more than rabbits and moles, was to be and still is our greatest enemy, horrendous gales blowing from the Black Mountains felling branches, even whole trees. The garden's climatic history has included the great drought of 1976 and the bitter winters of the early 1980s; in one of those we suffered from 24 degrees of frost which wiped out much, including a fifteen-foot-high avenue of *Nothofagus procera*. To these minuses we can add that on arrival we had to take down seven elm trees, that the chestnut avenue up the drive promptly died, followed a few years after by a superb beech and a turkey oak. None the less, an ever-open cheque-book and a succession of tree surgeons have ensured that the mighty Cedar of Lebanon which holds the whole house in its arms still presides over the front lawn.

But I have yet to explain what led us to do it, apart from the necessity of filling the field with something. Nineteen seventy-four was my first year as Director of the Victoria & Albert Museum. It was the period of the fall of the Heath Government, the oil crisis, and industrial and social unrest. The feeling of uncertainty about the future of things was encapsulated in the first exhibition I rushed into the museum, *The Destruction of the Country House*. This brought home

to the public, by using the museum as polemic, the full horror of
what we had lost in this century, in terms not only of houses but of
gardens, too, and went on to spell out the dangers ahead. It was a
time of deep gloom, and I clearly remember that the act of planting
that garden was a deliberate and defiant one. In spite of it all I believed with a great passion that that most English of all art forms, the
classic country house garden, would go on. With no money, little
labour, but much love and not a little vision, we would make one.
We would plant our yews in this dark hour and hold fast in the
knowledge that they would grow and we would live to clip them
into pinnacles and peacocks, and so it has proved. But that could not
be foreseen amid the turbulence of the second half of the 1970s.

By 1975 we had a plan; in fact, I still have what I drew in the summer of that year. Its design emerged out of what I loved and knew

best. There was never any question but that the garden was to be formal. Indeed, I was mesmerised by the country house views in Kip's *Nouveau Théâtre de la Grande Bretagne*, recording late Stuart gardens with their stately avenues, pattern planting and enclosures. It also struck me as being a not particularly labour-intensive form of gardening, for it gave architecture and articulation purely through the ordered siting of trees and shrubs, some of which would only call for an annual prune or clip. Next for inspiration came the photographs by Charles Latham in *Gardens Old and New* (of 1910), that set of volumes which records the country house gardens of Edwardian England on the eve of the deluge of 1914. Constantly I would go for walks in those photographs looking for ideas for The Laskett – ideas, that is, that we could afford. Then there were the real gardens. Hidcote Manor, of course, first visited by us on a chill winter's day with the late Lady Hartwell. Pamela's husband Michael has made a marvellous garden of this kind at Oving, which was another inspiration because it consisted purely of trees and shrubs held together by sculptural ornament. Two other friends provided further impulses, Sir Cecil Beaton and John Fowler. Cecil was actually the first person ever to walk me round a garden, which he regularly did at his house at Reddish. This seemingly simple act, like so many in one's life, was seminal in opening up to me the very idea that one could actually make a garden at all. Although Beaton's garden was beautiful, its design never affected me as much as John Fowler's miraculous creation at King John's Hunting Lodge at Odiham in Hampshire. This is the most perfectly articulated small garden I have ever seen. It excited me above all as to the effects which could be achieved by training. Features such as the stilt hedges and the use of clipped box for formal accents stayed imprinted on my mind.

The trouble is that, almost twenty years on, so many other influences have come tumbling in. Italy certainly, which I first fell in love with in 1955, but the gardens only came in the 1970s. The Villa Lante or the Villa Farnese haunted me; it was fifteen years before we could afford to grace the first grand vista with steps, balustrading and a distant temple, but such artefacts were always in my mind's eye from the very beginning. Het Loo, that supreme restoration of a late seventeenth-century garden in Holland, constantly seized my imagination during the 1980s, with the result that more box and ground pattern began to spring up everywhere. The Yew Garden near the house, where I planted my first minute box parterre, suddenly exploded in size. A box and gravel parterre with our initials entwined at its centre was laid out on the far side of the garden and, in front of the house, a design from John Marriott's *Knots for Gardens* (1615) was planted, adding a carpet at the feet of a statue of Flora.

The main layout of the garden has never really radically changed over two decades, but it has been developed and refined enormously. This is not only the result of having seen new things, but also of having made terrible mistakes, or of finding that a particular scheme was either unmaintainable or simply didn't work. Garden ornaments in particular have frequently migrated before finding their final resting-place. Over ornament I have no snobbery, and ours is a happy mishmash of old and new, in fact whatever I think I can get away with at a distance. I would like to have new things, and perhaps we shall achieve that one day. The Associates of the Victoria & Albert Museum presented me with our only new artefact as a farewell present, a plaque by Simon Verity which is like a medal, in which my profile is sandwiched between that of the Queen and the Prince Consort.

The achievement of any garden must be considered in relation to the commitment in terms of both time and labour. Contrary to general belief, formality and size are marvellous concealers of untidiness and lack of finish. Through the fourteen years that I directed the Museum, I was never able to give the garden the input it demanded. But it was during these very years that its vital infrastructure of shrubberies, hedges and screens grew, making the later elaboration possible. All of this has been achieved by just the two of us, plus the equivalent of an untrained gardener one day a week. We had to accept a relaxed philosophy over what got done and what had to be left. If the weeds sprang and the branches got entangled, we merely looked at those areas through romantic eyes. This year for the first time we have a gardener three days a week, and cannot contain our excitement as to what we hope to achieve in this new era.

Inevitably, until recently plants have had to take something of a back seat. One of the great joys of this present phase is to see that position being slowly reversed. Four years ago I planted a Flower Garden: it is rather Reptonesque in shape, but for the first time I have been able to indulge in and learn about herbaceous borders, and also to start thinking more intensively about the seasonal sequences.

The Silver Jubilee Garden, once only at its apogee in a froth of white and lilac in June, now has an autumn finale of Michaelmas daisies coinciding with the second flush of the 'Iceberg' roses. Julia has turned her hand to the spring planting, which now unfolds in a complex rhythm which begins in January and lasts until the close of May. Flora in her glade is never without a bloom at her feet from the earliest snowdrops, through scillas, chionodoxas, tiny daffodils, fritillaries and aconites. The formal beds are planted in succession to achieve a display of tulips and hyacinths over as long a period as possible. The stunning great *allée* of daffodils along the pleached lime avenue is succeeded by purple alliums amid cow parsley, like a Sisley painting. The winding walk, the Serpentine, is thick with ribbons of 'White Lion' daffodils, which fade as the Flower Garden springs to life. Recent new planting at the boundaries is aimed at giving glorious sunset-coloured foliage to enliven the autumn skyline.

The Laskett is an autobiographical garden, for our life together is etched into its many compartments. They have to be called something, and often they were constructed with money made through a book or a theatrical production. It must sound eccentric to visitors as they are guided through the Pierpont Morgan Rose Garden (I gave the Walls Lectures there in 1974), along the pleached lime avenue, Elizabeth Tudor (my wife and I did a little book on her in 1972), or sit in the Ashton Arbour of clipped yew (named to recall Sir Frederick, two of whose ballets Julia designed), looking towards a tableau of topiary peacocks set, as it were, on a stage which we call Covent Garden (where Julia also designed three operas). It is all a bit arbitrary and sometimes, in the case of the statuary, just plain dotty. A recumbent stag will be christened Franco because of a book I wrote for the brilliant Italian publisher Franco Maria Ricci, or a classical female bust Lucia because we were in an E. F. Benson phase.

But it does mean that every space in the garden is thick with association and memories of a life together and of our mutual creativity. Of course, it is rich beyond that with other memories, above all of people. A sundial from Cecil Beaton's garden stands at the centre of the garden we planted in honour of the Queen's Silver Jubilee in 1977. That to me symbolises a precious friendship, for I often stayed with him and the exhibition of his portrait photographs at the National Portrait Gallery in 1968 lit the blue touch-paper of my career. Julia's family, the Omans, is recalled by an urn at the centre of the Rose Garden which came from her aunt, the writer Carola Oman's house at Bride Hall in Hertfordshire. A pinnacle from All Souls and a lion from the Houses of Parliament are evidence of her distinguished grandfather, Sir Charles Oman, the historian and MP

for the University of Oxford. These came from Frewin Hall where he lived, as also did a descendant of a quince tree which now flourishes at The Laskett and the agapanthus which have been multiplied and passed down through the family for almost a century. Every year we look forward to that heavenly blue bursting upon us on the terrace.

I have not yet mentioned either the orchard or the vegetable garden, which are my wife's domain. Apple trees are her obsession and we have over sixty varieties, going back to the twelfth century, all of them on dwarf rooting stock. They look beautiful in spring with their explosion of bloom and equally ravishing in autumn laden with fruits. A Finnish apple steamer bubbles away during the fruiting season producing juice which we bottle and lay down. A second, smaller orchard contains peaches, and in a good year a tree can produce up to thirty. But it is the vegetable garden which is our real cornucopia. It makes no claim to be a decorative potager, although it has at its centre a small arched tunnel heavy with honeysuckle, 'Albertine' and what the friend who gave it to me calls the 'Gardener's Rose'. Spilling over amid the vegetables will be pot marigolds, nasturtiums and hardy geraniums and herbs of every kind. But it is the edible produce which is its heart. Joy Larkcom's oriental vegetables have given it a new dimension this year, but we also always purchase seeds in France and Italy and cast them upon the earth in hope. The fact that for ten months of the year we eat our own salad greens is some measure of

Plan of
The Laskett

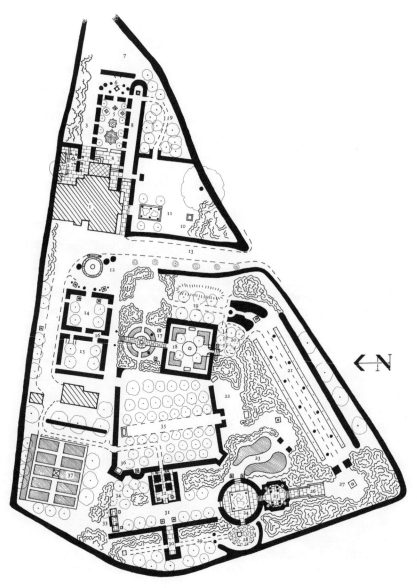

the success. There's asparagus, onions, potatoes, carrots, leeks, spinach, as well as gooseberries, Jerusalem artichokes and rhubarb.

Beyond this wired enclosure about a dozen compost heaps are dotted, many held down by black plastic sheeting with rubber car tyres, monuments to the impact of our visit to the compost queen of Dieppe, Princess Sturdza, who manages to transform beech leaves into black soot with the wave of her wand, in only six weeks.

Rosemary Verey, to whose encouragement one owes so much, once wrote that The Laskett is the largest formal garden in England to be planted from scratch since 1945. I wonder. If you asked me what The Laskett garden was about, I might reply that it is the portrait of a marriage, the family we never had or wanted, a unique mnemonic landscape peopled with the ghosts of nearly everyone we have loved, both living and dead. It has always been conceived as an enclosed, private world, and that indeed is the key. There is no borrowed landscape. It deliberately shuts out the glory of the rolling hills of Herefordshire and remains a sealed, hermetic, magical domain of its own. And yet there is never a sense of being shut in, of claustrophobia. Just one of serene tranquillity, or as much of it as can be granted in this transitory life. For me its making has been a more extraordinary achievement than any of the books I have written or museums I have directed. To take a basket with two glasses and a bottle of wine up to the Victoria & Albert Museum temple on a summer's evening and sit contemplating the vista together in silence is happiness quantified. What more can one ask?

KEY TO PLAN

1 House	14 Small Orchard	25 Roy's Birthday Garden
2 Glyndebourne	15 Schönbrunn Orchard	26 The Beaton Steps
3 The Canal	16 Tatiana's Walk	27 Shakespeare Urn
4 Terrace	17 Silver Jubilee Garden	28 Hearne's Oak
5 Yew Garden	18 Pierpont Morgan Rose	29 Winter Rose Walk
6 Torte's Garden	Garden	30 Ashton Arbour
7 Service Area	19 Sir Muff's Parade	31 Mary Queen of Scots Walk
8 Fledermaus Walk	20 Scandinavian Grove	32 Covent Garden
9 Spring Garden	21 Elizabeth Tudor	33 Victoria & Albert Temple
10 The Glade and Flora	(Pleached Lime Avenue)	34 Julia's Birthday Garden
11 Knot Garden	22 The Serpentine	35 Christmas Orchard
12 Fountain Court	23 Flower Garden	36 Gothick Arbour
13 The Drive	24 The Hilliard Garden	37 Kitchen Garden

Drawings and Plan by Simon Dorrell

Pugs, Peacocks and Pekingese

The Garden at Garsington Manor

DEBORAH KELLAWAY

There was something operatic about Lady Ottoline Morrell's appearance: larger than life. She was very tall, with an exaggerated nose and jaw and a thickly powdered face; her hair was mahogany-red under huge plumed hats or turbans, and she wore a sort of fancy-dress, sometimes silk Turkish trousers modelled on Russian ballet costumes, sometimes jewel-coloured dresses that trailed along the grass. Virginia Woolf described her as 'all velvet and pearls', and the pearls were a triple string of antique, irregular stones – like childish molars, one observer said. Even her voice was a recitative, full of emphasis and sing-song modulations.

You would expect her garden to be operatic too. And so it was, if that means a garden that a stage designer would like to copy, with statues standing against dark, clipped hedges, and well-placed openings for exits and entrances. But it was not flamboyant; it was controlled and calm. Juliette Baillot, the Belgian *mademoiselle* who came to Garsington to be governess to the Morrells' nine-year-old daughter, Julian, walked round the place with her young charge and found 'a sort of brooding austerity' there.

That was in early summer, 1915. The Morrells had moved in three weeks before. In the house, carpenters were still replacing rotten doors and window-frames. Lady Ottoline, in holland overall, was helping a 'nervous and artistic' workman to paint the oak-panelled drawing-rooms to match the colours of her vision, and her husband, Philip, was dredging the monastic fish pond at the bottom of the garden and replacing its old stone coping. The May weather was beautiful; in the evenings the Morrells sat outside and together planned what they should do with the garden: what to keep, what to change, what flowers to plant.

It was full of flowers already: blossoming fruit trees – apple, pear and quince – and Ottoline had a strong feeling that she belonged there and had known it always. But she thought the garden 'rough', in spite of its resident gardener. With her extraordinary mixture of taste and originality, she set out to clarify and enhance its latent beauty.

The ground behind the Elizabethan manor house sloped south-wards downhill past a spreading ilex tree (*Quercus ilex*, the holm oak) to the weed-choked pond. Far over to the east stood a square, seventeenth-century dovecote with hipped roof. To the west lay a string of other fish ponds in a half-wild setting of pollarded willows. And below all this, on the far side of a rough hedge, were an orchard, poplar trees, water meadows full of buttercups and cowslips and then a panoramic view past the 'Wittenham Clumps' to the Berkshire downs where, as L. A. G. Strong was later to observe, 'the distance distilled itself into the sky'. To most ambitious garden-makers at any time from the eighteenth century onwards, this place would have invited romantic landscaping. The big pond (fed by springs from the series of other ponds) could have been enlarged into an ornamental lake, with natural verges and groups of deciduous trees beyond, framing the view in the manner of Capability Brown. It would have been quintessentially English. D. H. Lawrence saw it thus, as autumn came at the end of that first year:

> . . . this house of the Ottolines' – it is England – my God, it breaks my soul – this England, these shafted windows . . . the elm trees, the blue distance – the past . . .

But to Ottoline, sitting under the ilex tree in May, it was Italian: 'more Italian than any other place in England that I have ever known'. It was something to do with the sloping site, the few dark evergreens that were already there, and the presence of water. Un-hesitatingly she planned to recreate the sort of garden she had known at the Villa Capponi outside Florence, where she used to stay, as a girl, with her Aunt Louise (Mrs Scott) and where the garden des-cended through three or four terraces to a swimming pool on the lowest level, screened by cypresses. The villa's saloon windows opened onto a broad terrace with a spell-binding view – not of blue, rural distances, but of the red roofs of Florence. This was the garden that gave Garsington its pattern.

'We hope in time to terrace the slope down from the house,' Otto-line wrote in her journal of 1st June, 1915. 'We have made one terrace and a walk round the pond, and in the autumn we are arranging to plant yew hedges that will grow like a tall, dark wall round the water . . .'

The 'one terrace' at Garsington ran along the south face of the house – a broad, unbroken sweep of lawn which was later edged, above its retaining wall, with yew. The other terraces were never built. Below that one retaining wall, the grassy slope fell naturally to the pond. Thus the translation of Garsington into the Villa Capponi was only partial, and all the better for it: one terrace was right, three terraces might have been too much.

But the pond at the bottom of the garden was thoroughly Italianate, converted with extraordinary determination and speed into a formal, stone-edged rectangle some thirty yards wide and sixty yards long, with an assembly of Italian statues standing around it. 'Rude figures', the Garsington locals called them. In later years it was said that if the Morrells had to choose between a second bathroom and a garden statue, they would always choose the statue. They started to buy them at once, shopping, not in Italy, but at Crowthers in London, and paying a maximum of £50 apiece. A strong Vulcan, legs crossed, hammer in hand, was placed on the far side of the pond facing back towards the house. Opposite him was a seated female figure. On an artificial island in the middle of the water Venus reclined, Cupid at her feet. Apollo and various nymphs completed the company. Goldsworthy Lowes-Dickinson admired them so much that he wrote an imaginary dialogue supposed to take place between them. They were spaced at seemly distances from each other round the pond, making a symmetrical composition. The horizontal rectangle of water outlined by the verticals of statues and yews was echoed, at the top of the slope, by the low, long, silver-grey stone house with its great chimney stacks and pointed gables. Lady Ottoline's instinct had been right: Garsington belonged to the English Renaissance (the house was built some time in the sixteenth century) and was far more in tune with an Italian Renaissance pool than it would have been with a romantic English lake.

The Garsington pond proved to be, from the first, the magnetic point of the garden: tragic, comic and beautiful beyond Ottoline's imaginings. In the first year the old cowman mysteriously drowned himself in it. Four years later, the painter Mark Gertler *nearly* drowned there. In between, a land girl called Lucy *pretended* to be drowning under the fascinated gaze of Asquith, the Prime Minister; and, finally, the big black boar fell into it.

A small weatherboard boat-house – a white-painted pavilion with classical pediment – was transported by the Morrells from Peppard (the Morrells' previous country house, near Henley) and re-erected at one end of the pond; from it, stone steps led down into the water. Bathing parties and boating parties were the order of the day. Summer visitors borrowed bathing costumes on arrival and ran down the grassy slope to the pond – a scene immortalised in one of the set-pieces of Lawrence's *Women in Love*. The water was terribly cold, and to Dora Carrington, the painter, unappetising. 'I lie exhausted in the sun', she wrote in the hot summer of 1916, 'after swimming in that cess-pool of slime.' Later, she took off her clothes and posed beside the pond for her photograph, along with Julian and Juliette and Ottoline herself – living statues among the stone.

But it was the beauty of the pond that mattered. The yew hedges duly went in at the end of 1915 (D. H. Lawrence helped Lady Ottoline plant some of them) and soon peacocks were trailing their tails along the grass walks beside the water. W. B. Yeats remembered them thus, strutting

> With delicate feet upon old terraces . . .
> Before the indifferent garden deities . . .
> (*Meditations in Time of Civil War*)

On the far side of the pond a second yew hedge was planted behind the first, making a dark *allée* down which both birds and people could process, past *claire-voies* or peep-holes cut in the outer hedge to give framed views of the wide landscape beyond. They walked there in moonlight, reciting Verlaine, or in the afternoons, locked in *tête-à-tête*. Mark Gertler tried persistently to paint it all: the pattern of right-angles, the verticals of statues, the shining light of the water barred by the deep reflections of trees. But when he set up his easel on a sunny weekend, perambulating guests continually bore down on him. It was like painting in the middle of a market place or pleasure ground, he said.

From the very first year, a legendary company of people descended on Garsington. They lay on rugs on the grass, or reclined in a motley assortment of chairs, some with ramshackle canvas canopies over them, while Ottoline prowled with her camera, taking their photographs. She was clearly not a snob about garden furniture; in her snapshots, Lytton Strachey perches, cross-legged, on a kitchen chair; T. S. Eliot leans back in a deck chair; E. M. Forster tilts a cane chair forward while he reads the paper; but Virginia Woolf, in wide-brimmed hat, puffs a cigarette on a heavy wooden seat with a decorative Chinese Chippendale back beneath the ilex tree.

After the pond, that venerable tree was the centrepiece of the whole garden. Aldous Huxley described it, in *Crome Yellow*: 'Like a great wooden octopus, it spread its long arms abroad.' From its shadow the peacocks would walk forth with prancing steps into the sunlight, 'trailing their shabby finery across the turf on the lower lawn'. (The tree still stands today; its scarred and corrugated trunk tells of its handsome past, but its long wooden arms are gone. When the greatest of them fell, a few weeks after the Morrells had sold Garsington and returned to London, the news seemed so portentously tragic to Ottoline that she lost her temper with Philip for continuing to eat his lunch.)

Ottoline's idea of beauty was governed by a desire for harmony. The sloping, south-facing garden at Garsington was a muted composition of greens and greys and silver, bright grass, dark yew, leaden ilex, stone, steel-grey water. She instinctively understood that the surest, strongest gardening effects come from repetition. Everything at Garsington came in pairs, if not in avenues Accordingly, the vast old ilex tree was reinforced by two new ilex walks, one on either side of the lawn sloping down to the pond. After the war, two lime walks were planted across the tract of wild garden to the west – one along the path that led from manor house to church, the other parallel with it but further down the slope, keeping it company. D. H. Lawrence had originally seen this part of the garden in a different, softer light; he thought it called for an 'arbour', and built one there himself in a matter of hours. 'Absurd and suburban', other Garsington inmates called it, but Ottoline loyally covered it with climbing roses and propped it up when it threatened to fall down. Her own view, even of the wild garden where she and Lawrence together planted purple irises beside a pond, was both simpler and grander, and if you stood on the terrace looking down towards the swimming pond, there was scarcely a flower to be seen.

The flowers were in the flower garden. When the Morrells arrived, a great square kitchen garden lay to the east of the house above the dovecot, walled with brick and stone and criss-crossed by paths. To Lady Ottoline, with her memory of the Villa Capponi where flowers grew in box-edged beds in a separate part of the garden from the lawn, the metamorphosis of kitchen garden into flower garden was an obvious step. First came the traditional things: madonna lilies, bearded irises, clumps of delphiniums, borders of pinks. Standard fruit trees were planted on either side of occasional seats where people could sit for tea, warming their backs against the old walls. But, as with everything that Lady Ottoline touched, traditionalism was transfigured by the strength of her taste.

She required three things of her flower garden: colour, scent and shape. Her colour sense was better, according to the painter Henry Lamb, than that of most painters. 'You beat us all at colour,' he wrote. She loved the hot colours that many a modern gardener shrinks from, the very colours that her new biographer, Miranda Seymour, found in the silks of her sewing box: 'orange, red, gold and lemon silk reels lying in carefully graded rows . . .' (*Ottoline Morrell: Life on the Grand Scale*, 1992). In the early August of 1917, two years after her arrival at Garsington, she reported herself as feeling

. . . so happy watching the flowers – the brown-ringed sunflowers, the red-hot pokers, the phlox and montbretia, the zinnias and the marigolds –

all crowded together with snapdragons and poppies in the square beds. But she also loved moonlit flowers of luminous white. When, through a window at night-time, she saw the garden lying 'blue-white, green-white, opalescent', she would come down and walk through the moonlight, swinging her Chinese lantern over tobacco flowers and night-scented stock.

Scented flowers were essential – to fill the bowls of pot-pourri that stood, along with pomanders, in every room of the manor house. She recorded picking 'Herbs, sweet geranium and lemon verbena, the rose leaves and rosemary'. Jasmine mingled with roses on the walls and there were 'continents' of lavender. 'The lavender was ripe for cutting', wrote Ottoline in her journal of 1917, 'and Katherine and I with knives and scissors cut and cut and made great piles of it, laying it out on a sheet to dry.'

'Katherine' was Katherine Mansfield, who seemed, of all the visitors, the most responsive to the flower garden. She remembered it as 'a bright dazzle, an exquisite haunting scent, a shape so formal and fine' that she almost doubted its reality and was 'tempted for one bewildered moment to stoop and touch and make *sure*'. Many people wrote about Garsington, its pond, its tree and its astonishing hostess; Vita Sackville-West summarised her visit there in 1924 as

'Pugs, peacocks and pekingese . . . photograph albums, talk . . .' But Katherine Mansfield cried: '*Who* is going to write about that flower garden?'

She roughed out a story herself in which pairs of people would walk up and down the paths, some in harmony with the flowers, others 'extraordinarily odd and separate from them' – but she never finished it. The best – if not the only – attempt at catching its enchantment comes in Huxley's *Antic Hay*, where he likens it to 'a great tank of warmth and perfume and colour . . . The place was shadeless and one breathed hot, dry perfume instead of air . . .'

That was before the ninety-six Irish yews had grown, one in each corner of the twenty-four box-edged beds. These yews were trained into points, to look like Italian cypresses. Down the middle of the garden on either side of the central grassy path ran low hedges of English yew, out of which the pointed Irish yews rose like candle-snuffer turrets above a roof-line. This was the shape 'so formal and fine', an eccentric and inspired geometry that Ottoline imposed on her bright garden.

But she herself, like most garden-makers, sometimes disparaged it. Returning after a time away, she found it 'terribly untidy and dishevelled' and at once set about weeding it herself. The Morrells were not as wealthy as their friends supposed. Ottoline is on record as painting a garden seat herself (she painted it blue-green). The gardener, Reuben Yates, doubled as coachman and pumped up the water for the weekly baths. In hot summers village children were paid to water the plants. Only when Philip Morrell's mother died in 1926, and some extra money came his way, were the Morrells able to commission the architect Philip Tilden to design the stone loggia with its three arches and Doric columns (modelled on the arcaded south loggia at Cranborne Manor) which now connects house and flower garden so gracefully that it might always have been there. In the event, its cost was one of the reasons why they decided to sell Garsington.

Another reason seems to have been a growing unhappiness, a feeling that, beautiful as Garsington was, it could not last, and its visitors could not respond adequately to it. Some of them, like Bertrand Russell, scarcely seemed to notice the beauty that was there. At least three others mercilessly used it in their novels. 'I have made human beings, individuals, my work,' Ottoline had written as early as 1913, 'and it is hopelessly unsatisfactory.' Her enduring creative work was to be her garden, but few people thought to tell her so. 'And here we all sit,' she wrote, 'and we all remain outside each other and never really blend and live together as the flowers do.'

The Morrells moved back to London in 1928, twenty-four years after the moonlit night when Ottoline first drove past the manor house with her sister-in-law and saw its gabled stone façade looking deceptively small and modest on the far side of a forecourt, buttressed by towering yew hedges and lying a little lower than the road. She did not know then that she would ever live there, but she did not forget its 'romantic, haunted grange appearance'.

No one ever forgets their first sight of Garsington. It comes upon you unexpectedly as you reach the top of the hill; there is no oblique view – the high hedges prevent it. Then suddenly there are tall stone gateposts, ornamental wrought iron gates, and you are looking through them straight at the stone façade. 'My only words were the obvious ones,' wrote Siegfried Sassoon of his first arrival there from an army hospital in 1917, 'an absolute dream of beauty.' Later he looked down from his bedroom window and saw the same scene from above: 'a green forecourt,' cut across by a paved path from front door to gates: 'and the little Morrell girl playing with the pug Socrates, and a peacock was parading with tail outspread.'

The forecourt he remembered as 'green' is gravel now, but the stone *putto* the Morrells placed in its centre is still there, and the 'enormous smooth dense green yew hedges' are just as Virginia Woolf described them in 1918. Garsington has been lucky. Nobody has ever spoilt it. There are no clamorous Victorian extensions, for during the nineteenth century the owners were absentees and it was let to tenant farmers. Since 1928 it has had only three owners. Dr and Mrs Heaton, the Oxford don and his wife who bought it from the Morrells, did nothing to change the Italianate garden, and buried their dogs beneath the lime trees leading to the church; but they levelled the slope outside the dovecot for a fine new tennis lawn, and made a pretty terraced walk to demarcate this part of the garden from the pond; it talks a different, small-scale garden language – English rather than Italian, with little level lawns between twin flower borders, stone retaining walls, pairs of slender junipers marking the changing levels, and the whole thing overhung by laburnum flowers in May. They also planted a mulberry outside the dovecote –

now in its shapely maturity; its succulent crop stains the stone paving
below it in October and it is unthinkable that anyone – least of all
Ottoline – would wish it wasn't there.

But the Heatons could not stay at Garsington during the Second
World War; petrol rationing made it impossible to drive regularly
into Oxford; the house was let to the painter Thomas Lowinsky, his
wife Ruth (the celebrated 'society' cook) and their family, and the
garden entered its austere wartime phase, with flowers giving way to
vegetables in the flower garden, and farm animals grazing on the
lawns. Lowinsky looked down from his bedroom window at the
pond, the statues, the hedges, two tall poplars rising high from
the yew *allée*, and wide fields beyond, and spent a year painting the
ordered sequence of spaces in a beautiful green composition of
horizontals dissected by slender verticals.

After the war, Mrs Heaton's brother (the Oxford historian Sir
John Wheeler-Bennett) and his American wife, Ruth, bought Garsington and began to put the place back into shape. The lawns were
mowed, the hedges cut; the walled garden furnished with bedding
plants beneath standard roses; the Queen Mother planted a magnolia
near the dovecot, and an ornamental wooden bridge was built to link
a tiny island in one of the fish ponds to the shore. But they were
historians rather than gardeners; they respected the recent past and
did not seek to change it. Perhaps the most important thing they did
was, in 1949, to engage a fifteen-year-old garden boy called John Prior.

John Prior is still at Garsington today. It is he, largely, who has
saved the garden from the threatening forces of decay. For forty years,
now, he has been keeping the whole place in order. Armed with
electric hedge-clippers and the tallest ladders on the market, he and
his young off-sider, Craig Pym, cut the towering walls of yew that
enclose the forecourt. He came to it gradually. 'I wasn't allowed up
there at first,' he says, shaking his head. Now he climbs 'up there'
each summer, and though the ancient hedges inevitably have a gentle
sea-swell along the tops, they still flourish: the tallest yew hedges, it
is said, in England. It takes six weeks each summer to cut all the
Garsington hedges. The sentinel Irish yews in the flower garden
wear wire corsets to prevent any unseemly spread, and every three
years the corsets are loosened and the trees pruned to shape. The
result is a faithful realisation of Lady Ottoline's idea.

Nothing at Garsington is lovelier than the view of the flower gar-

den from the stone terrace of the loggia. You see it between the two very tall, pineapple-topped gateposts which completed the Morrells' design. It lies at your feet, five steps lower than the loggia, not quite level, but tipped towards the sun. The pointed Irish yews, stretching away from the gateposts in a straight double row, are not evenly spaced, but seem to come in pairs, because the paths between the square beds are narrower than the beds themselves. So there is complexity as well as symmetry in the pattern and, above all, there is abundance. Step down into the flower garden and walk along any of the grassy paths, and you are half-lost among the beds; you cannot see it all at once, and you are wrapped in a sense of mystery and bounty.

But ground elder has entered this enchanted place, and encroaches upon the neat box edgings of the beds. John Prior fights it, but when someone says to him (pointing to a particularly infested bed), 'Shouldn't you dig everything out and treat the soil with chemicals for a year?' he smiles indulgently and replies: 'We don't like empty beds.'

He could not have kept Garsington going as he has done without this tough determination to resist voices of doom, this refusal to let difficulties get him down. But to keep twenty-four large beds full is not an easy matter, and he admits to the familiar gardener's predicament of not *quite* keeping up to schedule: he says he often gets his sweet peas in late. He raises scores of half-hardy plants for bedding out in summer: there are still snapdragons and nicotiana at Garsington; there are also whole beds of dahlias and of fuchsias, and in spring the classic recipe of tulips rising amid wallflowers and forget-me-nots.

Spring, it is said, is now the loveliest time at Garsington. The wild

garden round the lime trees is full of snowdrops, daffodils. An ancient sickle-pear tree still survives to blossom against the house, perfectly ladder-trained. Wisteria climbs along one end of the south front, and at the other there is still a handsome *Magnolia grandiflora*, as there was when Dorothy Brett, the painter, posed there for her photograph. But there is a new climber on the dovecot – 'Cooper's Burmese' rose; it looks an established part of the Garsington scene, beautifully pruned and covered in large, single, creamy-white roses from top to bottom in the summer. But it is the choice of Garsington's present owners, and so is the sturdy shrub rose 'Scharlachglut' with huge, single, red-velvet flowers and bright orange heps, which grows in their newly created kitchen garden on the west side of the house.

Since 1982, Mr and Mrs Leonard Ingrams have owned Garsington. If you ring the doorbell now, a little dog comes barking, just as Ottoline's pugs used to do. Rosalind Ingrams follows – small and slim, with the merest suggestion of red in her hair. She has written an illuminating leaflet on the history of Garsington Manor which is available to visitors (the manor garden is open to the public twice yearly under the National Gardens Scheme). She is sensitively aware of the problems that confront new owners of famous places; she is wary of turning the place into a museum and has planted a young magnolia at the top of the sloping lawn; but she has that 'instinctive tact' which Siegfried Sassoon detected behind all Lady Ottoline's arrangements. She has done one bold thing – she has made a wide gap in the yew that edges the top terrace: now you can see the pond from there, as well as the distant view. She is sure that Ottoline would have done the same if she had known how high her hedges were to grow. The new gap is formalised with a young Irish yew at either end, and is infilled with a low hedge of lavender, just as if Ottoline herself had supervised the plantings. 'If I leave here,' she had written in her diary in 1925, 'I wonder what will happen to my lavender hedges and the Irish yew . . .'

When the Morrells left, they took three of their favourite statues with them, and erected them in the communal garden behind their Gower Street house. The Ingrams have bought them back; they are reinstated in their old places. Another of the statues has been expertly repaired. It is a draped female figure with a sunflower at its feet; it stands alone in a glade, perfectly positioned, as always at Garsington, lyrical, covered with lichen, almost as green as the pale lime trees behind it, and if you stand on the grass terrace and look westward, it completes the view. Rosalind Ingrams loves this statue, as no doubt Ottoline once did.

Love of the place is the driving force that keeps it going. Every year, in early spring, the big pond is drained, cleaned and refilled. New plantings are in sympathy with the old. Clipped box has been introduced along a new side entrance, young standard fruit trees are growing below a barn. The diseased standard roses in the flower garden have been replaced by shrub roses or ramblers, trained on stout tripods, one in the centre of each bed. Mrs Ingrams has her own vision of those flower beds; she sees them filled with tall, mixed flowers rising high above the neat squares of box-edging: lupins, delphiniums, peonies, Japanese anemones. She does not make pot-pourri but she dries flowers and arranges them on the drawing-room hearth; here the dried delphinium spikes retain their living blues.

She has a special reason for wanting the flower garden to be at its best in June: opera has returned to Garsington. It was there first in the person of Ottoline herself, as well as in her imaginings, where she saw Garsington as 'a ravishing decor recalling . . . a Mozart opera.' But she also saw it as a theatre, '. . . where week after week a travelling company would arrive and play their parts . . . a queer, strange, rather ragged company.'

Now, in summer, it is a company of young professional musicians who arrive at the high iron gates. They rehearse on the stone terrace; producers make full use of Philip Morrell's double flight of steps leading down from it, and of the pillared entrance to the flower garden; the three-arched loggia is the backdrop – Don Giovanni disappears sensationally through the central arch to an inferno of flame and smoke.

In late June, the season starts. The audience parks its cars in a field, and enters the garden at the point where the new clipped boxes grow, walking past the young fruit trees below the old barn where refreshments will be served. This barn has just been lined with the 1930s limed-oak panelling from the old auditorium at Glyndebourne. There are tiers of seats on the lawn facing the stone stage. If summer rain pours down, a huge blue canopy keeps people dry. If the evening is benign, the critics give the garden setting rave reviews. For a few summer weeks, Garsington is home to the arts again. Strains of Haydn, Mozart, Benjamin Britten float down towards the pond, as once the strains of Hungarian dances from Philip Morrell's second-hand pianola pulsed out through the ground-floor windows, and young painters and poets danced on the lawn.

Drawings by Simon Dorrell

William Robinson and the Art of the Book

JUDITH B. TANKARD

In his book *Gravetye Manor or Twenty Years' Work round an Old Manor House*, Robinson noted that during the summer and autumn of 1895 four landscape painters had painted the water-lily pond, and had found that the garden was indeed 'full of pictures'. Mark Fisher, H. G. Moon, H. A. Olivier and Alfred Parsons were those mentioned, but many other artists also painted Gravetye. Both Beatrice Parsons (1870–1955) and Margaret Waterfield (1860–1950) painted the paved garden, showing the famous self-coloured pansies and carnations, along with Robinson's collection of Tea roses all planted in simple masses. Miss Parsons' brilliant watercolours, which captured the essence of floriferous Edwardian garden borders, and Miss Waterfield's more impressionistic, less detailed style, portraying somewhat idealised 'garden snapshots', were reproduced in a number of popular gardening books with colour plates. But William Robinson sought neither of these stylistic qualities from the artists he chose to illustrate his own books and periodicals: landscape painters working in a no-nonsense style, making a 'faithful record of beauty', were what he required.

For his two most popular publications, *The Garden* magazine and *The English Flower Garden*, Robinson used many artists, including Edward William Cooke (1811–1880), George Francis Miles and Alfred Dawson, and numerous photographers, such as Gertrude Jekyll, Ellen Willmott and Frank Mason Good. But Robinson was erratic in acknowledging the sources of his illustrations, and often his engravers, H. Hyde, Armand Kohl and C. Pochon, received the only credit. Artists whose work he used in some of his early books, such as W. H. Hooper and J. W. Whymper who illustrated the first edition of *Alpine Flowers* (1870), were later replaced, although Robinson continued to use their illustrations. For several of his books Robinson was fortunate in having the services of two extraordinary artists, Henry Moon and Alfred Parsons, whose work he made a point of acknowledging.

While he was working in a London solicitor's office and joining evening expeditions with the Gilbert Garret Sketch Club, Henry George

Moon (1857–1905) answered Robinson's advertisement for an artist who could draw flowers from nature. The drawing 'the tall, rather dark youth' produced on the spot, of a spray of white azalea, was in the naturalistic style that Robinson sought, and soon after giving up his job in 1880 Moon began work at *The Garden*. Robinson abhorred the highly stylised renderings of flowers in popular gardening books and manuals, and it fell to Moon to create a new style of floral illustration for reproduction.

Although Moon's drawings were simply executed, they are full of life rather than rigidly diagrammatic. Robinson felt that they were well suited to his particular printing methods, being neither 'overcrowded nor overcoloured'. One observer reported that Moon arranged the flowers simply and naturally, then sketched a faint outline which was infilled with full brush strokes of the predominant colour; he then employed a damp brush here and a touch of colour there, 'until the form and curl of the petals, with their gloss and sheen, grew up before one's eyes'.

Throughout his association with Robinson, which lasted until his death, Moon produced hundreds of drawings for *The Garden*, most of which were featured in 'An Artist's Note-Book'. Some of his illustrations were included in *The English Flower Garden*, in later editions of *Alpine Flowers*, and in Gertrude Jekyll's *Roses for English Gardens* (1902). Moon is better known for the supplemental full-colour plates that he prepared for *The Garden*, which were lithographed and printed by J. L. Goffart, and later for *Flora and Sylva*.

Another of his botanical triumphs was not prepared for Robinson, but for Moon's father-in-law, Frederick Sander (1847–1920), the famous orchid-grower of St Albans. *Reichenbachia*, a four-volume monograph with Moon's colour plates, was produced between 1886 and 1894. It is considered one of the most lavish gardening books ever published, and the chromolithograph plates of Moon's paintings required numerous colour printings.

In 1891 Moon and William E. Norton, an American artist whose painting of Moat Mead, Gravetye appears in *The English Flower Garden*, spent the year painting the garden at Gravetye, and the following year they exhibited their work in London. A number of Moon's paintings of Gravetye embellished the walls of the Manor, in company with Robinson's collection of Corots and Fantin-Latours.

Moon's brooding landscape paintings and sketches, inspired by

Corot, are not so well known. In addition to Gravetye and the surrounding Sussex woodlands, he painted scenes in the Norfolk Broads,
Suffolk, and Essex. These paintings and oil sketches reveal a completely different side of Moon, who, as Robinson said, 'like a poet . . .
had what he called his landscape days and his flower days'. Three
examples of his landscapes appear in *Flora and Sylva*. During his lifetime he infrequently exhibited his paintings at the Royal Academy
and the Royal Society of British Artists; his largest exhibition was a
memorial one organised by the Fine Art Society in 1912. Robinson
lamented that, had Moon been less occupied with plant-drawing for
reproduction, his work as a landscape painter might have taken a
different turn.

The best-known artist associated with Robinson was Alfred Parsons (1847–1920), whose illustrations enhance *The Wild Garden*, *The
English Flower Garden*, *Flora and Sylva*, and *The Garden*. His most famous,
however, were his illustrations for Ellen Willmott's *The Genus Rosa*,
which like Robinson's books was published by John Murray. Miss
Willmott commissioned Parsons, who had painted her garden at Warley Place, Essex, but when she ran into scheduling and financial difficulties, both artist and publisher suffered. When the book finally
appeared, Parsons was particularly displeased with the quality of the
reproductions. While Miss Willmott ignored Parsons' recommenda-
tions regarding papers and printers, Robinson probably admired him
for this very knowledge.

As a young man Parsons gave up a career in the civil service to
paint, and became a well-known and regular exhibitor at the Royal
Academy. He was also president of the Royal Society of Painters in
Water Colours. His output as an illustrator, in particular for the
American publication *Harper's Magazine*, was enormous. He lived in
Broadway, Worcestershire where there was a group of American
artists which included Edwin Austin Abbey, with whom he shared
his home. Another American, Henry James, was particularly enchanted by Parsons' work. In 1889 he commented that his work
'forms the richest illustration of the English landscape that is offered
us to-day. . . . One would like to retire to another planet with a
box of Mr Parsons' drawings and be homesick there for the pleasant
places they commemorate.' James was also enchanted by Robinson's
gardens at Gravetye Manor: 'Few things in England can show a
greater wealth of bloom than the wide flowery terrace immediately

beneath the grey gabled house, where tens of thousands of tea-roses
. . . divide their province with the carnations and pansies . . . [and]
the medley of tall yuccas and saxifrage.'

Parsons was also a garden designer; most of his work was carried
out in the Broadway area, and included his own garden at Luggers-
hill. He designed a garden with topiary peacocks at Court Farm for
Mary Anderson de Navarro, and gardens at Hartpury House which
were later remodelled by Thomas Mawson. Mawson also followed
him at Wightwick Manor, in Wolverhampton, where Parsons laid out
a rose garden surrounded by clipped hedges and topiaried yews.
Robinson, whose dislike of topiary and 'vegetable sculpture' is well
documented, must have turned his eyes from these gardens. It is unlikely that Robinson sought Parsons' advice at Gravetye, but he did
seek it on the remodelling of the porch at Moat Cottage, in 1883.

Their friendship lasted until Parsons died in 1920, and it is thought
that their initial contact, in the late 1870s, may have been through
his father, who was an expert on rock garden plants. Parsons' illustrations appear in the second edition of *The Wild Garden* (1881), which
had originally been published in a more modest form in 1870. Robinson himself thought this book one of his best, perhaps due in part to
his pleasure with Parsons' illustrations and the quality of their reproduction. The numerous editions of *The English Flower Garden* were
beset with all sorts of technical problems which proved exasperating
to Robinson (see HORTUS 17), and one of Parsons' illustrations for
The Wild Garden, 'White Willow in Hampshire', was engraved three
times before Robinson was satisfied.

In some ways *The Wild Garden* was more revolutionary than *The
English Flower Garden*, as it treated a completely new type of gardening, rather than cataloguing existing ideas. Gertrude Jekyll referred
to the importance of the book, not only in her writing but in her own
woodland garden at Munstead Wood, a living example of Robinson's
principles. Here she had shrubbery-edge plantings of lilies and ferns;
naturalised stands of foxglove in the woodland; and grass paths lined
with trillium, bracken, and dog's-tooth violets. In *Wood and Garden*
she wrote that she 'always devoted the most careful consideration to
any bit of wild gardening', and cautioned 'unthinking people [who]
rush to the conclusion that they can put any garden plants into any
wild places, and that that is wild gardening'.

The Wild Garden was in print for nearly seventy years, in seven different editions. Part of the popularity of this title, aside from the timelessness of its subject, was due to its attractive design, featuring illustrations primarily by one artist – unlike most of Robinson's other publications, with their multiple sources. In 1894 Robinson, thinking the book had stood the test of time, had copies of the ordinary fourth edition bound in soft vellum, with silk ties, possibly for private distribution. The next year he brought out a de luxe edition, with Parsons' illustrations engraved in Paris and printed on handmade paper from a French mill; this edition is the basis of a new facsimile edition to be published next year by Sagapress, New York in the hope that it may captivate another generation of garden lovers.

After many years of concentrating on plants for English flower gardens, Robinson began to shift his attention to trees and the surrounding landscape. With the publication of *Flora and Sylva* ('I married Flora to Sylva, a pair not far apart in Nature, only in books'), Robinson's interest in the art of book-making accelerated. 'Witness of the hot chase after process illustrations, small type, tin-shine paper, smudge lithographs, tomb-stone weights, and the less delightful features of modern books', he sought a typesetter who knew traditional fonts, colour printers who could do justice to his drawings, paper mills that could still 'make real paper', and engravers who understood his artists' drawings. Such pursuits continued to consume him for many years.

Flora and Sylva (1903–5) may have been short-lived, but this exemplary, quality monthly periodical was handsomely designed and illustrated, obviously aimed at a more élite market than *The Garden*. The handmade paper did justice at last to the engravings of photographs and drawings, and the splendid colour plates were extravagant additions. Who has not seen skeletons of this three-volume publication, with the plates excised for individual framing? For the most part those colour plates are of Moon's work, although the last volume contains fewer of his drawings. Several weeks before he died, Moon was working on drawings of "*Lilium myriophyllum*" and "*Lilium sutchuenense*", which appeared in the final issue of *Flora and Sylva* in December 1905.

With the first issue of *Flora and Sylva* Robinson began a feature entitled 'The Garden Beautiful: Home Landscapes and Home Woods', and this became the title of his twelfth book, published in 1907. Its purpose was to turn his readers' attention to an appreciation of native trees, and away from a preoccupation with 'the exotic, the curious and the tender'. He also took the opportunity to slip in his current thesis on 'Garden Design and Recent Writings Upon It'. Although the engravers' names appear on the plates, no acknowledgement of the photographer appears.

Robinson ran into some unusual problems with *Garden Beautiful*, originally scheduled for publication on October 30th, 1906. Not only did negotiations for an American co-publisher fall through, as Robinson's minimum price could not be met; more serious were one reviewer's pre-publication comments about the book. Edmund Gosse, literary editor for the *Daily Mail*, challenged Robinson that most of the book had already been published elsewhere, especially in *The English Flower Garden*. 'Will you kindly tell me what to say to the editor?' Murray asked Robinson. Robinson called in the book and made 'haste to rectify my mistake', preparing an entirely new text. A. C. Curtis was annoyed by the title, so similar to that of his own book, *The Small Garden Beautiful* (1906). Robinson's original book was pulped (but not before a few copies escaped), and the new (and only) edition of 1000 appeared in December 1907.

In August 1914 Robinson wrote to Murray that he had 500 copies of a new book ready; Murray found both text and illustrations charming, but suggested that it was an exceedingly bad time to publish anything. Robinson wished to offer *Home Landscapes* in half-bound vellum only, at a cost of 50 shillings. Murray cautioned him that booksellers disliked such a delicate binding as it was apt to be spoilt, but Robinson pointed out that this de luxe book was meant for country homes, not for display on booksellers' shelves among the Christmas offerings! Robinson often received scant encouragement from his publisher when he enquired about possible American sales for his books. This time, Murray reported that on a recent visit to London Mr Doubleday had said that the subject of *Home Landscapes* was 'rather too limited' and that he 'couldn't do much with it'. It was duly published late in 1914, and sold for £2 12s 6d.

No sooner did Robinson finish one project than he began to plan the next. August 1915 found him contemplating the addition of several more plates to *Home Landscapes*, plus a second volume with fifty new plates to show the best old country houses in relation to the landscape. The idea of a two-volume set was abandoned when Robinson ran into difficulties with the plates, and in 1920 he settled for reissuing *Home Landscapes* in a cloth binding, with a small supplement. The full title of the new edition reads: '*Home Landscapes:* With Views taken in the Farms, Woods, and Pleasure Grounds of Gravetye Manor. Second Edition, with pictures of old English Houses showing the value of natural form in relation to good building; to compare with the disfigurement of the Dutch and Continental Gardens.' The coherence of the book is spoiled by the inclusion of chapters on some of Robinson's pet peeves, such as Italian Gardens, the distortion of trees, and the art of landscape architecture – all subjects which had occupied him for decades.

The attractive folio-sized book is illustrated with full-plate 'sun pictures' by George A. Champion, a photographer whose work Robinson admired, and had used in *Flora and Sylva*. Champion recorded the seasons at Gravetye with extraordinary views of the surrounding woodlands and farms, supplementing areas featured in a previous book, *Gravetye Manor*. Less successful are the eleven plates of English houses that indirectly illustrate the extraneous chapters. Unquestionably Champion's photographs outshine Robinson's text, and one tends to agree with Doubleday's comment.

The book that combines the best of all Robinson's publishing ideals is *Gravetye Manor*. Published in 1911, it was based on a two-volume tree and garden book which Robinson kept from 1885, when he bought the manor house, until 1911. Beautifully presented on handmade paper, in a folio format similar to *Home Landscapes*, this book is particularly appealing for the same reason as that for which he chose his landscape artists: it is a faithful record. The dogma pervading most of his other writings is toned down in a highly personal and straightforward account of his own gardening work. As he wrote to Mr Murray, 'I do not like blowing my own trumpet much, but it might be stated that it is an account year by year of the forming of gardens and plantations in an estate of some beauty and extent.'

Although the illustrations are not as uniformly splendid as the ones in *Home Landscapes*, Robinson carefully selected only those which he felt necessary to illustrate his points. In addition to several photographs by Champion and sketches by Moon, the numerous vignettes throughout are new material; Murray recommended even more illustrations.

Robinson fussed over the details of the paper, over printing quality, and about quantities for the ordinary and the vellum-bound editions, but in the end must have been pleased with the book. The printer, Horace Hart of Oxford, thought it the best-printed book they had done. *Flora and Sylva*, *Gravetye Manor*, and *Home Landscapes* were printed on Unbleached Arnold paper, which the printer 'rolled and re-rolled' until the right surface was produced for the fine woodblocks. But Hart was exasperated by Robinson's method of sending in the book in bits and pieces, and by changing the title page at the last moment.

Murray suggested that a plan of the grounds would be an asset, in helping the reader sort out the various garden areas, but Robinson curtly replied: 'The aim of my work was to give pictures rather than plans, as I have never seen in any work on landscape or landscape gardening any plan that taught the general reader anything.' Murray's cautions were usually on the mark. Even with a modest print run of 750 copies priced at £3 each the book was slow to sell, and in 1929 several hundred were remaindered at £1 1s each. *Gravetye Manor* was reprinted in 1984 by Sagapress, New York.

The excerpts from Robinson's correspondence are quoted with permission from John Murray (Publishers) Ltd.

Blue Pleasure

JIM GOULD

As I entered my garden I removed the dark glasses I had been wearing, and halted in astonishment. There was a cascade of wonderfully clear, bright blue where a flax plant threw up a fountain of blossom. It was delightful. Why hadn't I fully appreciated it before? I placed one hand over my left eye: the blossom vanished, and only when I approached close to the plant could I discern the flowers, now a greenish-grey shading into the foliage; I covered my right eye, and the wonderful blue returned. I looked up at the tall hawthorn hedge now in full bloom, its branches covered in dazzling, snow-white flowers. I covered the other eye. This time the blossom did not disappear; instead, it went a dingy yellow. Bluebells growing under a lilac tree were in full flower, but their flowers were almost as invisible as those of the flax when I covered my left eye. They could just be seen, darker than their foliage. It was with great pleasure that I looked at them with my other eye. Though they were much darker than the flax, their colour was a revelation.

Of course, I had just returned from the Wolverhampton Eye Infirmary, after a stay of four days during which a cataract had been removed from my left eye. It must have been dirty yellow to so affect the blue flowers. The very dark glasses I had worn until entering the garden had concealed the pleasures in store. There were no more blue flowers to look at, in fact nothing else in the garden beds was in bloom. I then remembered the hugely colourful auriculas in the greenhouse. Their blooms were over, save for those of 'Apple Cross', a gold-centred alpine auricula with deep-crimson, shaded petals. This was the one disappointment. The golden centres were dazzling, far too gaudy for the velvety red of the rest of the petals. Their centres dominated the plants, as bright as the glowing golden buttercups in the adjacent field. Still, I consoled myself, come the spring there would be the blue show-selfs such as 'Blue Jean', 'Stant's Blue', and 'Foreign Affair', as well as the alpines 'C. W. Needham', 'Frank Crossland', 'Mrs Hearn' and 'Roxburgh'.

I looked down and saw my socks. Horror! One was royal blue and the other black – I had worn the dark glasses when putting them on

that morning. I went and looked at all the socks in the drawers upstairs. Grey, black, blue and brown were all mixed up together. Why
had no one told me? (I am a widower and live alone.)

My reaction to the flax blooms was of course emotional, yet I had
always considered myself to be unemotional. I recalled a discussion I
had had with a psychology student some years before. He contended
that reaction to all colours was emotional. If deep, bright colours (but
not pastel shades) could be isolated from everything else – shape, past
experience, associations, et cetera – all emotionally stable adults,
whether in England, Africa or elsewhere, would (he claimed) prefer
either blue or red, with green in third place. Children and the emotionally immature would prefer yellow or orange, while the emotionally disturbed would prefer purple, brown or black. Perhaps my
delight in the blue flowers reflected my maturity. I was vain enough
to hope so, though I have also found some purple auriculas, such as
'Lilac Domino', very pleasing. I have also been very glad to see
glossy-black cock blackbirds in the garden. Can I be both mature *and*
disturbed? That of course was a nonsense thought. The auriculas
have form and elegance as well as colour, and the blackbird's activities
and song are enough to override any colour reaction. Still, I have
always wondered about those who profess great admiration for all-
yellow or all-white herbaceous borders. I must banish such silly
thoughts, concentrate on enjoying the flax, and perhaps read again
what Gertrude Jekyll wrote about colour in the border.

For some months before my visit to the Eye Infirmary, I had been
a little alarmed by those who, taking my age into account (approaching 75), considered I ought to try to grow old gracefully. I reacted
strongly to this idea, for any such an attempt would surely lead to the
dreaded slippery slope that ends in vegetable senility. Surely it would
be better to aim deliberately at a little irascibility, even at the risk of
ending up a grumpy old curmudgeon? No sooner was this resolved
upon than to hand came an excavation report that I strongly objected
to. Carrying out my resolve, I sent the editor of an archaeological
journal a broadside on the matter. The paper has been accepted, and
though the editor insisted that some phrases be watered down, it is a
step on the path I intend to follow. Or at least, I *had* intended, until
I saw the flax and the bluebells. Perhaps after all it is too soon
to degenerate into contentious bad temper. The new appearance
of those blue flowers has made me feel years younger, and almost

cheerful. My priority now must be to search the catalogues for more blue-flowering plants to add to my garden.

I do not know what my socialist friends will think of my blue appreciation. I am told that Dennis Skinner, MP (the 'Beast of Bolsover' and star of *Westminster Live*) is often to be seen, in the appropriate season, strolling in Kew Gardens in the morning, before parliamentary business begins, enjoying the rhododendrons. I don't think there are any blue ones – if there were, would Dennis on those days be less bellicose (but also provide less enjoyable TV viewing)? Or does he have cataracts, too?

Companion Planting
or Gardening with Walter

CATHERINE UMPHREY

It may be impolitic to say so, but Margery Fish's first book on gardening reminds me of a children's story. The title, *We Made a Garden*, is simple and straightforward, and prepares us for nothing ambiguous or untoward. Its subject, the attempt by two laymen to put together a garden, suggests little in the way of either sophistication or expertise. And yet, *We Made a Garden* is a subtle garden primer. By recalling details of her own early experiences, Margery Fish provides us with an initiation into gardening fundamentals. That this initiation should include a tribute, a reckoning, even an odd sort of love story which appeals to both realist and romantic, is perhaps surprising. But it is all of a piece: as every child knows, it is not an easy or even a simple thing to do what one wants, and in order for Mrs Fish to make a garden and record its making in a way useful to others, she had to brave a host of complications.

First published in 1956, *We Made a Garden* is Margery Fish's account of how, in 1937, she and her husband Walter bought a run-down house in the Somerset village of East Lambrook and set about transforming their derelict grounds into a proper English garden. She

begins by recounting their search for a suitable house, then describes
the general condition of the land surrounding the house they decided
upon and proceeds to explain the work involved, not only in making
a lawn, laying paths and gravel drives and establishing hedges, but
also in planting, staking, watering – each task or subject assigned its
own chapter. As the garden took shape so, it seems, did the book –
except for the scattered but numerous hints that the garden's development describes an even more personal drama, of which modesty
and propriety prevent a fuller telling. But even so, Mrs Fish relates
some wonderfully revealing stories. These are enough to arouse our
curiosity, while giving shape to our surmises and quieting any mis-
givings that by collecting and rearranging her various clues (so as to
emphasise what she has not), we are invading a privacy meant to
remain inviolate.

Mrs Fish admits that in the earliest years of their garden-making
she was a complete novice. It was an easy mistake to assume that her
husband was as much so as she. But the mature Walter Fish (the
Fishes were evidently well into middle age when they purchased the
manor) had a secret history of gardening, or at least of directing a
gardening staff, at Sydenham, before their marriage. So Mrs Fish
ended by spending her first gardening years under the tutelage of her
husband. She also found herself doing much of the heavy lifting;
although Mr Fish made a commanding figure in the garden, doing
the summer watering outfitted in a panama hat and a light silk
waistcoat (worn to hide the braces needed to hold up his trousers), it
was his own assessment that he 'hadn't the figure for a belt', and
perhaps his weight precluded an enjoyment of the more strenuous
tasks of garden-making. Whatever the cause, Mr Fish took a great
delight in supervisory work, and it was established early on that his
role was that of master-mind, hers of helpmeet. Naturally, these roles
did not always suit. When Walter solved the problem of what to do
with the wealth of old oil stoves, broken farm equipment and discarded furniture found throughout the demesne, deciding the larger
debris should be piled in a heap, covered with soil and turned into a
handsome rock garden, it was left to Margery to wonder how it
ought to be done as well as to finish the deed. Occasionally, Walter
preferred to carry out one of his ideas himself. When the newly
planted climbers proved disappointingly slow in clothing the out-
building walls, he bought a large collection of mounted animal heads

at a London sale room, hung them all about for instant effect – putting the most splendid specimens on the three-storey-high malthouse walls – and took pleasure in his display of trophies until exposure to weather brought about their decay. We can well imagine that Mrs Fish, developing ideas of her own, may have anticipated some problems in gardening with Walter.

Of course, this is *Mrs* Fish's story, so we might expect a certain bias in reporting the contributions of *Mr* Fish. Indeed, according to the Introduction (provided by Henry Boyd-Carpenter) to the fourth Impression (1970), the first version of *We Made a Garden* was entitled *Gardening with Walter*, and rejected because there was 'too little gardening, and too much Walter'. But a good deal of Walter persists in the published version, and for good reason. When it came to the garden, the man simply could not be avoided. The chapters devoted to watering and staking might well have been called 'Watering according to Walter' and 'Walter's Staking Lessons'. It seems that Mr Fish was like the sun: his guiding light shone on every aspect of their garden enterprise, and his warmth and brilliance were not easily avoided. More importantly, once it becomes clear that his tastes and manner of gardening were in key respects the very opposite of his wife's, we begin to suspect that Mr Fish was not only Mrs Fish's gardening mentor, but her nemesis.

Walter, as it happened, loved really big flowers – those which in show and size gave ample return for their owner's investment. Dahlias the size of soup plates, in mixed colours, staked with good stout poles upon planting, were Walter's idea of exemplary garden plants. He taught Margery how to care for his fleshy beauties, making her lug great heaps of manure and buckets of water in their service. These tasks were to be performed regularly, with method and without fail. Margery, however, found herself captivated by tiny, unassuming, even difficult plants, and with plantings soft and subtle. She also loved to coddle her treasures, to tuck small bits of compost around their roots, or gravel about their necks, and to give little drinks to the young and tender. Often, as Margery went on her rounds, she would find that Walter had been before her, leaving a trail of withered green clumps upon the path. These were the hapless remains of those plants, usually hers, judged too weak and unpromising to keep company with the flourishing. To Walter's mind, such stragglers merely took up space which might be better used by something else – a dahlia, perhaps.

Walter was a man of principle. Fortunately, most of his principles were sound. He preached the value of basics – of well-maintained lawns and edges, of simplicity in overall design, of an unsentimental eye for the thrifty plant, of the efficient use of time and materials. With remarkable generosity, Mrs Fish expresses her appreciation for all the truly useful lessons Walter gave her on how to do what was worth doing, although one would guess she got carried away when she agreed that ruthlessness is the only way to get a job done. At any rate, she never flinched from giving credit where it was due, not even when by so doing she hints at the delinquency of her own debts of gratitude. While conceding much to opinions she apparently did not defer to, Mrs Fish is also honest enough to admit when she was wrong and Walter right. He was right to demand that weak-stemmed flowers be staked early, to debunk the myths about the benefits of supplemental watering, and to insist that a garden full of flowers is of no account if the surroundings are unkempt. Honesty, no doubt, also prompted her to record Walter's own violations of the very principles he espoused. For instance, his habit of leaving dead-heads and prunings where they fell (confident that someone else would pick them up) did not promote that well-kept look he favoured. And I fancy Mrs Fish cannot have helped but notice, silently of course, that dahlias are not the most thrifty of flowers, that a decorative scheme involving scores of decrepit animal heads is decidedly unusual, and that the time required to tidy up after them might be better spent.

Like many men of principle, Walter not only had strong opinions but was fond of impressing them upon others. In brief, he liked to have his way, to rule his roost, and to cut short outbreaks of opposition on the part of those under his authority. His handling of insubordination was memorable. When a gardener in his former employ – a man who above all else loved chrysanthemums – was found to be spending too much time doting on his favourites, Walter gave him a lesson in the folly of such fondness by slashing each and every 'mum to the ground. Margery became all too well-acquainted with the lesson. When she was still supposed to be learning to grow the simple and ordinary plants Walter recommended, she once had the good fortune to coax several flower buds from *Delphinium nudicale*, a de-cidedly difficult and therefore cherished specimen. She never saw it bloom, however. Whether Walter cut it off by mistake while dead-heading, as he maintained – or on purpose, as punishment for her defiance of the principle that a mastery of gardening basics should precede esoterica – she never really knew. That he was not at all apologetic argues against the innocence of this flower-slayer, in either case. Indeed, his love of the sword was such that, were it not for the fact of his alliance with the good-natured Margery, one might be tempted to think rather severely of Mr Fish. One might even think him a tyrant.

It is clear that her newly-awakened talent for gardening could not altogether flourish during the years that Margery Fish gardened with Walter, though it was not for lack of trying. She was blessed with backbone, energy and nerve, all of which she called upon to preserve her integrity, her composure and her sense of humour, in the face of endless Walterian assaults. But I think it not excessive to deduce that she also had passion. While devising strategies to distract her husband's attention from plans he was likely to overrule, plants he would wish to evict and projects he would want to supervise might have been amusing for a mind content with game-playing, Mrs Fish must (I think) have realised that she could never properly learn to grow and place the plants she admired while Walter was there. His death, less than fifteen years after the garden's conception, was therefore most opportune. It is a shocking statement to make, but it is possibly more shocking still to think that, had Mr Fish's indomitable spirit not departed, Mrs Fish might never have achieved her own potential, as the Margery Fish who at the time of her own death in 1969 was a gardener of world renown and the author of eight original and authoritative books on the subject.

We Made a Garden was published several years after Mr Fish's death, and it is apparent that sufficient time had passed for a number of changes to have been made. Walter's gravelled paths and drives had been paved, his ampelopsis removed from the walls, and all the borders reworked to include the early spring and late autumn flowers which he would never countenance. But, most importantly, Margery Fish's gardening genius had been liberated. We do not know how much it cost her; surely the pleasures of single-minded work and application are not as heady as those of well-matched monomachy. But it is to her credit that in the twenty or so years in which she subsequently gardened without Walter, she pursued an active routine of growing and sharing, writing and lecturing, and continued to perfect the garden the two had begun together. It is to the credit of both that she should have begun her career as a garden writer with so engaging a memorial to Walter Fish.

The interplay of the two Fishes makes *We Made a Garden* a favourite among gardeners. If it is also considered a classic, it is probably not for its descriptions of hedge-making or the need for deep watering, or for its tips on herb garden placement or how to make the most of floppy Sweet Williams – although the advice given on all such matters is useful and reliable. Those who enjoy artless and charming prose, which transforms the deeds of a man obviously difficult to live with into the diverting stuff of stories, will take these qualities as sufficient. But the book's most enduring virtue is its calm, untroubled revelation that the act of making a garden is, like writing, profoundly expressive, and that to make a garden with another is to risk unearthing considerable differences not easily concealed by the usual devices of evasion and duplicity. In Margery Fish's book, this lesson is not a sad or bitter one. She happily employs Walter's excesses for comic relief, slipping in less welcome truths while her readers are either laughing or gaping with horror. And it is unlikely that her impulse to garden was responsible for disabusing her of any fond illusions concerning her husband's tender-heartedness or democratic spirit. She was a sensible woman who found that in her desire to make a garden she was required to make new accommodations to her companion's tastes and temperament, then found that such attempts at accommodation were unsatisfactory. A room of her own, outside among the flower beds, was tempting. There is no need to heap blame upon Walter for a problem which, to be frank, was not as singular as he. Many of those who garden as well as live together find themselves in a role similar to that of either the hero or the heroine of *We Made a Garden*; as gardeners, most of us learn that our own garden creations, the ones we love, require us to exhibit our true selves by doing what pleases us, whereas the people we love require – and occasionally insist upon – no such thing. Elementary as it is, this problem is hardly simple, and it is rarely resolved as gracefully – or as successfully – as between the lines of *We Made a Garden*.

(Page 165) Walter and Margery Fish in the garden at East Lambrook Manor (1941?). Photographs kindly lent by Mr Henry Boyd-Carpenter (who may be seen standing in the basket on page 165).
(Page 168) Walter and Margery Fish after their wedding in 1928.

Indispensable Plants

Gardeners and nurserymen describe,
season by season, the plants they would
least like to be without.

Spring 1994

CAROL KLEIN

On one of those bleak, blustery January days, when the only noise audible above the thrashing wind is the chattering of fieldfares swept into an obligatory roost amongst the bare, black-budded ash branches, it is difficult to imagine that spring will ever come again. But there, shining out among the drab and battered leaves, is a small and perfect flower, bright blue with a little pale rim: *Omphalodes cappadocica* 'Starry Eyes'. This precocious flower, twinkling in the midst of the dun mud, is enough to reassure me that winter doesn't last forever.

By April the plant is covered with little bunches of flowers, the blue made all the brighter by the soft lilac edging. This is an 'ooh-aah' plant, quite irresistible to all who see it. It is from Ireland, found in her garden at Woodtown Park, Rathfarnham, County Dublin by Mrs Eithne Clark in about 1981 as a sport on a large clump of the normal form. She propagated it and gave some offsets to Dr E. Charles Nelson of the National Botanic Gardens, Glasnevin who in turn distributed it to a few people 'who would be able to grow it'. He first described it in *Moorea*, Volume 8 (January 1990), and named it 'Starry Eyes'.

Omphalodes cappadocica itself, blue-eyed Bet, is one of the most beautiful of all spring flowers. Shiny, pointed evergreen leaves on long stems form neat clumps. They provide a perfect foil for the clusters of azure flowers with five rounded petals and tiny sunken centres. The plant has an elegant self-possessed air. Nonetheless, it mixes well with other plants. *Primula vulgaris*, *Anemone nemorosa*, *Erythronium* 'White Beauty' and *Fritillaria pallidiflora* all make suitable companions.

Whereas *Omphalodes cappadocica* belies its family connections as part of Boraginaceae, *O. verna*, blue-eyed Mary, is easily recognisable as kin, with coarser, more comfrey-like leaves and somewhat untidy growth. She is less refined than her sister and flourishes best in mixed company; even so, an essential spring flower. Planted where the open sprays of pretty blue flowers can mingle with like-minded neighbours – among green mats of sweet woodruff (*Galium odoratum*), with its Milky Way flowers, or pierced by the elegant, arching stems of Solomon's seal (*Polygonatum × hybridum*), or the white version of bleeding heart (*Dicentra spectabilis alba*). And if there is the beautifully chalk-marked foliage of *Cyclamen hederifolium* or the striking white-ribbed leaves of *Arum italicum italicum* close by, the picture is complete.

There is another member of the family, this time an annual, which comes into its own in the late spring and continues to enchant throughout the summer – *Omphalodes linifolia*, Venus' navel wort, so called because of the characteristic centre. Although seldom seen, it has been in cultivation in Britain since 1748. It is a much more 'southern' looking plant, with long glaucous leaves and pretty white flowers in open trusses, and a wonderful mixer and softener in formal areas. Easy to raise from seed sown into trays or direct in well-drained soil in a sunny position, it is in complete contrast to the others, which need damp, woodland conditions. A clone of *O. cappadocica* with narrower leaves and bigger flowers, called 'Cherry Ingram', is purportedly hardier than the type.

My second indispensable plant also has a Collingwood Ingram connection. *Primula* 'Ingram's Blue' is another blue flower of small stature and big personality, a dark-leaved beauty with crimson stems and calyces and a crimson line delineating the tiny yellow centre from the ultramarine petal colour. Apparently this line and centre were the reason for its rejection – the aim was a completely eyeless, deep blue polyanthus – but it is precisely these features, together with the dark, shining leaves, which give the plant its magical, glowing quality.

This primula was given to Lady Anne Palmer by its breeder, her friend Collingwood Ingram, and I first saw it at Rosemoor; having admired it for years, I was given a piece by Richard Lee – Lady Anne's propagator and later the Royal Horticultural Society's Rosemoor Nursery Manager until his tragic and untimely death last June. As with many plants, it was thanks to Richard's care and attention that 'Ingram's Blue' survived.

All *Primula vulgaris* relations form hard and woody roots, and need regular division and refreshment to maintain healthy growth. They can be divided in autumn or spring, pulled apart, discarding the old hard roots, and replanted with their roots trimmed to a palm's length: primulas hate having their roots folded. They soon build up a healthy new root system, and with a reasonable mulch of good organic stuff and a feed after flowering of something potashy (tomato fertiliser is good) they should thrive. If you have something very special, or just hate throwing things away, try breaking up the rejected old roots into pieces and pushing them into a tray of compost. With a bit of luck and love they should eventually produce a few new plants, which can be detached from the old roots and potted individually.

Primula vulgaris is traditionally a plant of deciduous woodland, but here in Devon the high hedgerows are the place to appreciate them. There is a long lane close to where we live which is the only access to a friend's cottage; on a warm spring day, on one open stretch of this lane, the abundance of primrose flowers is almost overwhelming. Their perfume is singular and delicious, and I would go to almost any ends to experience the pleasure of these simple flowers.

My father had a quite different passion – for fast motor cars. When we were young, his great delight was to take us out for a jaunt on spring Sundays – often to North Wales. Home was close to Bolton – a primrose-free zone, apart from the ubiquitous *Primula* 'Wanda' in the little front gardens of the miners' terraces – but here we were, transported at breakneck speed into the centre of primrose Nirvana. Fortunately I have always had an impatient bladder, and the necessity to 'spend a penny' invariably coincided with the sight of banks of primroses. The vermilion Austin Atlantic car would screech to a halt, and the female contingent leap out. There were violets, too, and moschatel and wood anemones and real moss and rich beech leaves. My mother and I would greedily consume the moment, before being summoned abruptly with much honking of horn to return to the flight. As we clambered back down the steep slopes we giggled, one call of nature unaccomplished but another more important one fulfilled.

Our wild primrose makes a beautiful accompaniment to *Primula* 'Ingram's Blue', as does the pale polyanthus 'Lady Greer'. There is a change of scale, too: 'Lady Greer' is dainty and diminutive, but the plant builds quickly into large mats. White flowers would also look well; 'Schneekissen' and 'White Wands' are two good carpeting vari-

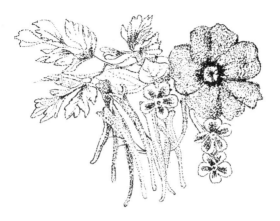

eties of primula, while *Cardamine trifolia* or the more select *Epimedium grandiflorum nanum* would also make good bedfellows, as would any of the dainty white narcissi. 'Petrel' is exceptional, a triandrus hybrid with two or three flowers on each stem and a lot of green mixed with its white.

Yellow surely is the colour of spring and warmth, light and spirituality. However, all three of my chosen flowers are blue, and the third one is three different blues. During the last three years much mention has been made of *Corydalis flexuosa* – not surprisingly, since this must be one of the most valuable perennial introductions we have been privileged to meet for a long time, in terms of garden-worthiness, great beauty and ease of cultivation. The men we have to thank for this glorious and important addition to our gardens are those intrepid plant hunters, Messrs Compton, D'Arcy and Rix (CD&R), who in 1989 brought back three distinct clones of the plant from high, wet woodland in West Sichuan, China. In April 1992 they put on an educational exhibition, at a Royal Horticultural Society Westminster Show, of plants collected on this 1989 China expedition. Glebe Cottage Plants was exhibiting there too, and I had climbed onto my table top to get to grips with an unruly log, just as a particularly noisy trolley was being manoeuvred past. Turning to survey the squeaky offender, I almost fell off the table with sheer amazement and delight. The bed of the trolley was a waving mass of blue – the flowers of *Corydalis flexuosa*. Pulling the trolley was John D'Arcy, a small man in a small brown warehouseman's coat, and pushing the other end was Martyn Rix, a tall man in a much longer brown warehouseman's coat. Their display was enthralling, packed with exciting and subtly beautiful plants – *Epimedium davidii* and *E. acuminatum*, dryopteris and adiantums – but the star of the show was the corydalis. If the plant caused such a sensation in the concrete vaults of the Horticultural Halls, imagine the thrill of climbing up steep wooded slopes in central West China to discover it carpeting the woodland floor amid the unfolding shuttlecocks of matteuccia.

The three corydalis clones collected are all in cultivation now. 'Père David' (CD&R 528B) is the one most widely grown; it has fresh green, much divided ferny leaves with that lovely poppy succulence, and panicles of brilliant cerulean flowers. The plant spreads fast by fleshy stolons and soon forms a good clump. Although Martyn Rix describes it as being dormant in summer, with ample moisture it seems to grow continuously throughout the year, and to produce some flowers in every month. *Corydalis flexuosa* 'Purple Leaf' (CD&R 528A) is the form which gained an RHS Award of Merit in 1993. It is a neater, more compact plant than 'Père David', with distinctive bronze-purple foliage marked symmetrically with red and with closer, denser flowers of a warmer blue.

The third clone, and my favourite, is *Corydalis flexuosa* 'China Blue' (CD&R 585). Forget any inference of Spode: this is a blue of blues, electric and startling. The foliage is taller and a more olive green, with a hint of pink, especially in dry conditions. The blue flowers look particularly well with the fresh green of young leaves and it is in spring, at this time of the great unfurling, that *C. flexuosa* is at its most floriferous, smothered in its sky blue, long-spurred flowers. Of course, it looks wonderful with yellow – in March and April with daffodils, in April and May with trollius and *Hemerocallis lilio-asphodelus* (some yellow after all, although the trollius with which these blue corydalis look best is *T.* 'Alabaster').

Drawing by Carol Klein

Gardens in Fiction
The Gardens of Beatrix Potter
PETER PARKER

One of the first gardens I ever loved never really existed. Like many of the better things in life, it was encountered not in reality, but in fiction. It was an extremely neat kitchen garden, in which were grown lettuces, French beans, radishes, cabbages, gooseberries, peas, onions and blackcurrants. All these are mentioned in the text of the book, and in the illustrations one can discern holly, nasturtiums, geraniums (i.e., zonal pelargoniums), water-lilies, irises and pots of what look like chrysanthemum cuttings. One assumes that cucumbers are grown, since mention is made of a cucumber-frame, and it may be that parsley is to be found – though not by the book's hero, who is interrupted in his quest for this herb. The garden is presided over by an irascible old man called Mr McGregor, who looks rather like an elderly Lytton Strachey.

Part of the attraction of Beatrix Potter's *The Tale of Peter Rabbit* (1901) is that the protagonist behaves rather as any small child might, disobeying the sensible advice of his parent, entering forbidden territory, overeating, getting chased by an irate adult, managing to escape, losing articles of clothing, being fed nasty medicine and sent to bed early without supper. It all sounds horribly familiar. And do we learn from our mistakes? Not a bit of it. Shortly afterwards, tempted by his equally disobedient cousin Benjamin Bunny, Peter returns to Mr McGregor's garden, ostensibly to retrieve his jacket, which is being used to drape a scarecrow. On the grounds that crawling under gates 'spoils people's clothes', Benjamin suggests they climb down a pear-tree into the garden.

> Peter fell down head first; but it was of no consequence, as the bed below was newly raked and quite soft.
> It had been sown with lettuces.
> They left a great many odd little foot-marks all over the bed, especially little Benjamin, who was wearing clogs.

As with a lot of good books, what is going on *between* the lines here is quite as important as the explicit narrative. We do not need to be told that a rabbit tumbling onto a newly-sown seedbed is certainly of consequence to the poor gardener, particularly if that rabbit goes on, with his cousin, to tread all over the freshly raked soil. Beatrix Potter (1866–1943) is one of the best prose stylists of the century and for this reason, if for no other, an ideal author for children to meet at an early age. The sheer economy of her writing is a lesson to us all, and her dry wit nicely seasons tales that might otherwise be mistaken as artless. There are those – usually those who have never read her – who believe that because she dresses up her animal characters in clothes, her stories are whimsical. In fact, she was an amateur naturalist, who had spent much of her isolated London childhood studying the pets she smuggled into the nursery and dead specimens brought back from summer holidays in the country. She was quite aware of what really goes on in the animal kingdom, and in that dangerous no-man's-land where animals and humans meet. The principal reason that Peter is warned not to go into Mr McGregor's garden is bluntly stated: 'your father had an accident there; he was put in a pie by Mrs McGregor'. Potter originally intended to illustrate this unhappy piece of information by a picture of the elderly, apple-cheeked Mrs McGregor serving the pie, fresh from the oven, to her husband – off-camera, as it were, except for a knife and fork held in eager readiness – and an equally expectant dog. This was eventually dropped, but chiefly because Potter, a brilliant draughtswoman when depicting animals, was not very good at drawing human beings.

Potter herself stated that Mr McGregor's garden was a composite affair: 'If the vegetable garden and wicket gate were anywhere it was at Lingholm near Keswick,' she wrote in 1942; 'but it would be vain to look for it there, as a firm of landscape gardeners did away with it, and laid it out anew with paved walks etc.' The lily pond, she said, was at Tenby in Pembrokeshire, another place she had spent childhood holidays. If Mr McGregor's garden seems somewhat different when Peter returns there in *The Tale of Benjamin Bunny* (1904), this is partly because the illustrations are altogether finer, and partly because they are based upon another Lake District location, Fawe Park, where the book was written. Potter made a series of background sketches of the gardens there, which she worked up into illustrations, adding in the animal characters, when she returned to London. The new garden has a patch of parsley in the lettuce-bed and there are some superbly-realised onions, which Benjamin decides to steal. One must assume that he has also stolen a pink, since he is suddenly sporting one

Beatrix Potter's illustration for *The Tale of the Flopsy Bunnies*, 1909

(*Dianthus* 'Gran's Favourite'?) in his buttonhole as he strolls through the garden, nonchalantly chewing a lettuce leaf. Some rather straggly carnations are shown in another illustration, while near the cold-frames a fuchsia is growing in a sizeable terracotta pot. The large cat they encounter lies on a path edged with ferns and behind her are what might be red lupins, or possibly valerian. The Fawe Park studies show that Potter simplified the wall, along the top of which Benjamin's father, old Mr Bouncer – switch in hand, smoking a pipe of 'rabbit tobacco' (or lavender) – comes looking for the juvenile delinquents. So that he can make his progress unhindered, she has removed a climbing rose and a brick holding protective netting in place over some sort of fruit tree.

The third of the rabbit books is *The Tale of the Flopsy Bunnies* (1909), which deals with the offspring of Peter's sister, Flopsy, now married to Benjamin. Peter himself has set up a gardening business – 'Peter Rabbit & Mother. Florists. Gardens Neatly Razed. Borders Devastated By The Night Or Year' – and is depicted in one illustration, spade in hand, amongst some knobbly stalks, explaining that he has 'no cabbages to spare'. Although this story also takes place in 'Mr McGregor's garden', the illustrations are based upon Gwaynynog, a garden just outside Denbigh in North Wales. Now restored and spelled 'Gwaenynog', this garden is open under the National Gardens Scheme, and visitors may attempt to discern the spot where the Flopsy Bunnies fell asleep having been made 'soporific' by eating bolted lettuces. (That 'soporific', incidentally, is characteristic. 'Children like a fine word occasionally,' Potter quite rightly wrote to her publisher, who sometimes queried her use of them.) The Flopsy Bunnies, now numbering seven 'and all of them twins', reappear in Potter's dark masterpiece, *The Tale of Mr Tod* (1912). This is a positively Gothic novel about 'two disagreeable people, called Tommy Brock and Mr Tod'. No gardens appear in this book, since Mr Tod is a fox, and his squalid demesne is described by Potter with palpable relish: 'There were many unpleasant things lying about, that had much better have been buried; rabbit bones and skulls, and chickens' legs and other horrors.' Mr Tod does, however, also have a more attractive dwelling: a 'stick house' topped with a pail chimney, rather like the huts constructed by charcoal-burners, which is set amid oak stumps in 'a sea of blue hyacinths'. (In one of her marvellous letters, Potter described bluebells in Westmorland as being 'like a bit of the sky come down'.)

Another fox, never actually described as such, appears in *The Tale of Jemima Puddle-Duck* (1908). One of the jokes of the book is that poor, foolish Jemima never recognises that the person she meets in the wood *is* a fox. He is first introduced as 'an elegantly dressed gentleman reading a newspaper'. Although he has 'black prick ears and sandy coloured whiskers' and 'a long bushy tail', Jemima never cottons on to the fact that he is a cousin of Mr Tod: she thinks him 'mighty civil and handsome'. As Potter informs us, Jemima is 'a simpleton', never even made suspicious when 'the hospitable gentleman with sandy whiskers' suggests they have a dinner party. 'May I ask you to bring up some herbs from the farm-garden to make a savoury omelette?' he asks her. 'Sage and thyme, and mint and two onions, and some parsley. I will provide lard for the stuff – lard for the omelette'. On the following page, Jemima is depicted in a well-stocked herb garden 'nibbling off snippets of all the different sorts of herbs that are used for stuffing roast duck'. The reader, of course, immediately sees through the gentleman's elegant tweed knickerbocker suit and cherry-coloured waistcoat – even before they are shockingly discarded when, undisguisedly vulpine, he secretly inspects the eggs Jemima has laid. A further, punning clue to his identity is that he is discovered seated on a tree-stump 'amongst some tall fox-gloves', beautifully painted by Potter, who had been making highly accomplished sketches of *Digitalis pupurea* since the age of nine.

Wild flowers usually feature in those books which take place away from human habitation, and were occasionally used by Potter in order to bribe her publisher, F. Warne & Co., to accept stories. 'I'm afraid you don't like *frogs*,' she wrote to Norman Warne in February 1905, enclosing a draft text of *The Tale of Jeremy Fisher*, 'but it would make pretty pictures with water-forget-me-nots, lilies etc.' Warne was evidently won over by this promise and the story was published the following year: forget-me-nots and some luxuriantly flowering water-lilies feature prominently in the illustrations, along with violets, cowslips, ranunculus, water-plantains and assorted reeds and rushes. The entrance to Mr John Dormouse's home in *Ginger and Pickles* (1909) is wreathed in pink oxalis, while the protagonist of *The Tale of Mrs Tittlemouse* (1910), who lives 'in a bank under a hedge', stands in a doorway surrounded by pennywort.

The respective merits of urban and rural dwelling, derived from Aesop, are debated in *The Tale of Johnny Town-Mouse* (1918). Timmy Willie, a country mouse who was 'born in a garden', falls asleep in a hamper of vegetables and is carried to town, where he quite literally falls in (through the skirting board) with Johnny Town-Mouse, a most elegant personage who sports a high-necked Regency shirt and cravat and (what else?) a blue tailcoat. Johnny is quite sure that his unexpected guest will be converted to urban life – 'It sounds rather a dull place?' he says of the garden. 'What do you do when it rains?' – but Timmy Willie wants to return to his 'roses and pinks and pansies' and his vegetarian diet (the breakfast bacon disagrees with him). Johnny thinks equally little of the country when he visits Timmy Willie: he is frightened by the noise of cows and a lawn-mower (propelled across the back of one illustration by someone looking suspiciously like Mr McGregor). Johnny returns to the town, waved off by Timmy Willie, who brandishes an ox-eye daisy. 'One place suits one person, another place suits another person,' Potter concludes. 'For my part I prefer to live in the country, like Timmy Willie' – who is depicted on the final page nibbling a large and luscious strawberry.

Potter had always preferred the country and eventually went to live there, buying a farmhouse at Sawrey, a village tucked between Esthwaite Water and Lake Windermere. Sawrey and its gardens had featured prominently in *The Pie and the Patty-pan* (1905), another story about friends with dissimilar tastes. The plot is rather complicated and concerns a tabby cat called Ribby who invites a black Pomeranian dog called Duchess to tea. Fearful that she will be served mouse pie, Duchess attempts to substitute one of her own veal-and-ham pies, surreptitiously placing it in Ribby's oven while her hostess goes shopping. The book was produced in a new, larger format and Duchess has the most spectacular garden in all Potter's work – based in fact upon two gardens in Sawrey. Duchess receives her invitation standing in the crammed front garden of a house called Buckle Yeat, with – and here scholars may disagree, since the effect is decoratively impressionistic rather than botanically detailed – its antirrhinums and linaria, yellow Welsh poppies, calendula, helichrysum, centaurea, mallows, a pink standard rose, sweet williams and turks'-cap lilies. When she sets out from her house, however, the garden is that belonging to a building on the other side of the road, the same one that served as a model for the shop kept by Ginger and Pickles (it was in fact the Post Office). The garden path, leading to a beautiful Georgian door, is flanked by enormously tall tiger-lilies, among which are some (no doubt self-sown) opium poppies. The lilies are underplanted with what looks like *Malva moschata alba*, but might be some sort of cranesbill geranium or oenothera. Ribby's front garden is that of nearby Lakefield Cottage, copied by Potter down to the smallest detail, including the *Clematis* 'Jackmanii' and *Tropaeolum speciosum* scrambling over the porch and the slate shelves with their pots of scarlet geraniums. Duchess carries a large bouquet, clearly gathered from her own garden.

It was while Potter was working on *The Pie and the Patty-pan* that she finally decided to have her own personal stake in the Lake District, and she bought Hill Top Farm in the summer of 1905, asking the current tenant to stay on as manager. The following year she set about improving the small house and reclaiming its garden. She hired the services of a quarryman to make paths and walks, but was rather alarmed at how new it all looked when next she visited. Worse still, her instructions about the lawn had been misunderstood:

> I started a man filling up one corner in the garden to make a flat lawn. I believe the word 'tennis' *was* mentioned but I have never played it, so it conveyed nothing particular to my mind. I could not think why he was taking such a time & now discover a thing big enough to play football!

Since she was fond of old walls, she spent much time planting up her own, rescuing 'some pretty wall-rue fern' from a nearby bridge that was being demolished, and collecting assorted rock plants from nurseries and neighbours. The effect of this scheme may be seen in *The Tale of Tom Kitten* (1907), which is 'Dedicated to all Pickles – especially to those that get upon my garden wall'. 'Pickle' has nothing to do with chutney, but comes from the old word for a mischievous child. Potter applied it to kittens. She had borrowed one from a mason to use as a model, describing it as 'very young & pretty and a most fearful pickle'. Tom not only is, but gets *into*, a fearful pickle, as do his sisters, Moppet and Mittens. Chasing butterflies amid the violas and pinks of their mother's garden, Moppet and Mittens get 'green smears' all over their pinafores, and drop their tuckers into the road as they scramble up through ferns and rhododendrons onto the well-planted wall. Tom fares equally badly:

> He came up the rockery by degrees, breaking the ferns, and shedding buttons right and left.
> He was all in pieces when he reached the top of the wall.
> Moppet and Mittens tried to pull him together; his hat fell off, and the rest of his buttons burst.

Three members of the Puddle-Duck family (including Jemima) happen to be passing and steal the clothes. The kittens' mother, Mrs Tabitha Twitchett, is depicted spanking them in a garden well stocked with peonies and irises before leading them back to the house and sending them to bed. A year later, Tom gets into even worse trouble in *The Roly-Poly Pudding*, an alarming tale in which he is kidnapped by a pair of rats, Mr Samuel Whiskers and his wife Anna Maria. No gardens feature in this book, but there is a view of the countryside, with trees in full blossom, seen from the chimney-tops – 'put in,' Potter said, 'because there was such a string of sooty inside pictures'.

Beatrix Potter's frontispiece for
Peter Rabbit's Almanac, 1929

The garden at Hill Top Farm took up a great deal of Potter's time and money. Like most authors, she was occasionally obliged to chase her publishers for money owing, and wrote to Warne in August 1908:

I do not in the least mind waiting for money, *if* I know beforehand. I should like to know what I have, to spend this autumn, without being rash.

The place is not at all expensive to keep going, but there is still ample opportunity to lay out the garden & surroundings.

She was an astute businesswoman and soon began buying other properties in the area. In 1909 she acquired Castle Farm, Sawrey, and in 1913 married William Heelis, the solicitor who had handled the deal for her and subsequently advised her on installing a water supply there. They moved into the farm's spacious cottage, which became her home for the remainder of her life. In July 1924 she wrote about Castle Cottage to Dulcie, an unidentified correspondent:

Yes I have lots of flowers, I am very fond of my garden, it is a regular old fashioned farm garden, with a box hedge round the flower bed, and moss roses and pansies and black currants & strawberries and peas – and big sage bushes for Jemima, but onions always do badly. I have tall white bell flowers I am fond of, they are just going over, next there will be phlox; and last come the michaelmas daisies & chrysanthemums. Then soon after Christmas we have snowdrops, they grow wild and come up all over the garden & orchard, and some in the woods.

Potter's animal characters continued to be keen gardeners, notably the guinea-pigs in *Cecily Parsley's Nursery Rhymes* (1922), whose well-tended beds contain blue lupins, (moss?) roses, white lilies with prominent brown anthers, and what looks like *Linaria dalmatica*. The illustrations were reworked from ones she had made in the 1890s, when she had also made an exquisite drawing of 'The Rabbits' Potting Shed', which depicted a pair of rabbits potting-up pelargonium and fuchsia cuttings.

By the 1920s, however, her eyesight had been worrying her for some time, and she was much more interested in breeding and showing Herdwick sheep than in providing the importunate Warne with more of what she referred to with exasperation as 'these d——d little books'. The last of them, *The Tale of Little Pig Robinson* (1930), was in fact an early story, inspired by childhood holidays on the Devon coast and first drafted in 1893, which she revised 'when I had left off writing and was scraping together something to appease my publishers', as she characteristically put it. In spite of her reservations, the book sold well both in America (its original intended market) and in England. Royalties from the books and other 'merchandising' (decorated china, handkerchiefs, soft toys, wallpaper and friezes and so on) allowed her to buy further properties. The last of these, acquired in 1939 at the age of eighty-one, was Belmount Hall near Hawkshead. The American owner had gone to live in Italy and died there, and Potter set about reclaiming the garden.

> The old fan-trained fruit trees are in the last stage of old age [she reported to her cousin, Caroline Clark, mother of the dedicatee of *The Tale of Mr Tod*]. I have planted some clematis against them, and some shrubs, such as ceanothus, between, to gradually grow into their place. Is chimonanthus fragrans a bush that would grow? I have witch hazel, and shrubby spireas, and syringas. I remember you said you were going in for shrubs – and for the same reason. I should like to plant some bushes that might grow on at Belmount Hall without much attention? The garden is not seriously weedy. It is carpetted [sic] with jonquils & spring flowers. The house is scarcely

habitable, though it seems a pity to let it fall in – fall *down* it will not. Georgian building stone. Perhaps some time it might be repaired for a hostel . . . I have had over a ton of good leaf mould removed from the roof & gutters and the rain no longer runs downstairs; but it is in a mess. [The owner] went away suddenly because her Italian chauffeur knew what was coming; he was in a fever to get back to Italy last August. She admitted that he belonged to a fascist organization – she was a horrid old fascist herself, in spite of being R.C. . . . There is her shroud in a cardboard box; presumably blessed by the Pope. I did not post it after her as I thought it seemed like 'carrying coals to Newcastle'. Father Taylor has obligingly buried some remains of the early Christians in consecrated ground.

It must have been a relief to find Father Taylor a good deal tidier than Mr Tod.

Over half a century later, the 'd——d little books' are still on sale, their illustrations reproduced from new transparencies of the original watercolours and enhanced by 'the most modern electronic scanning methods'. No doubt Potter would have approved of this. What she would have made of the rest of the ever-expanding Beatrix Potter Industry is another matter. While she might have regarded Wedgewood pottery and Crabtree & Evelyn soaps as a legitimate extension of her own shrewd merchandising, she would hardly have approved of the large-format omnibus editions of her books, since she designed them to be the correct size for small hands to hold. The less said about editions illustrated by others – including the recent ones using pictures derived from a cartoon vulgarisation of the works – the better. Potter was a true artist, who took pains to match text and illustration so that they are not only complementary but often provide commentaries one upon the other, as in *The Tale of Jemima Puddle-Duck*. One result of the success of her books was that at her death Potter left several thousand acres of land to the National Trust, including Hill Top, which is now a much-visited shrine. Tourists throng the streets of Sawrey in search of original locations, but the real gardens are to be found in the books, which celebrate modest country plots, where fruit, flowers and vegetables thrive in happy profusion throughout the long, drowsy Edwardian summer.

Le Rouge et Le Noir . . . et Le Vert

DEREK TOMS

Leafing through magazines or glancing into the windows of horticultural suppliers, I have been made aware that there is a fashion in
powered garden machinery for it to be finished in red and black,
the most aggressive colour combination imaginable – coloration
which in nature advertises venomous spiders and unpalatable cater-
pillars. Hand implements have for some time now been coated with
Teflon and metallic flaked silver, while their designers have borrowed heavily from current trends in hand-held weaponry. Even
hosepipes may be fitted with a pistol grip – are they intended for
irrigating, or quelling riots? Whatever happened to the garden
equipment we grew up with, with the metalwork painted an in-
conspicuous green and handles of comfortable hickory or ash?

One can understand (though not necessarily sympathise with) the
business executive's need to assert himself in a cut-throat world by
driving a saloon styled like a streamlined clenched fist and armoured
in battleship grey. Others seek to shield their private anxieties by
cocooning themselves in massive 'off-road' vehicles with wide
wheels which announce their intention to crush any living thing in
their path. (How fortunate that they are rarely driven off the road.)
Product design must inevitably respond to the mentality of the
consumer; if the newspapers are to be believed, we are living in a
paradoxical peacetime where violence is endemic in our society.
Videos now offer vicarious enjoyment of bloodshed of the most
gruesome kind, such as was once provided by gladiatorial combats
and Christians fed to the lions. Technology may have advanced
considerably since Roman times but mankind, it appears, has not
changed one iota.

Yet surely gardeners are exempt from this condemnation? Is not
the garden a refuge for those of us who wish to dissociate ourselves
from the barbarians? I would like to think that this were so, but
reason insists that aggressive styling would not be employed to
market horticultural implements unless it has been shown to enhance

sales. The conclusion is uncomfortable but inescapable: gardeners (or at least some of them) are no better than the rest.

This leads me to pose the question: to what extent is gardening an aggressive activity? Now, aggression in nature is limited and functional; it serves to ensure that an animal gets its share of the grub, or a suitable mate. The compulsive or gratuitous aggression which typifies human behaviour is largely the result of the psycho-pathological condition euphemistically known as civilisation. Nowhere is the difference between 'civilised' and 'primitive' societies more pronounced than in their attitudes to nature around them. What seems an untamed wilderness to 'civilised' man is to the hunter–gatherer (on the evidence of the few palaeolithic peoples who have survived into the present century) a bountiful earth. Even dangerous animals are not automatically to be feared – only respected. And fear is the mainspring of aggression.

Once we begin to cultivate the land something in our relationship with nature starts to go horribly wrong. As the stockades are erected around the village huts (to be followed at a later date by solid city walls) we cut ourselves off from the environment of which we were formerly a part. We lose our intimate familiarity with things, and the ensuing ignorance breeds fear. Like any other caged animal we display symptoms of misdirected aggression – to each other and towards ourselves. We project our fears onto the natural world outside, seeing savage beasts where in fact there are only animals going about their daily business and conducting themselves better than we usually do. At a more sophisticated stage in our development we map the unknown with warnings that 'Here be Dragons'.

All this is not an irrelevant digression. I only wish it were. The hysterical reactions of gardeners to the wildlife which attempts to take up residence among their precious plants never ceases to amaze me. Animals of every phylum are variously labelled 'enemies', 'pests', 'nasties', and other epithets which I would prefer not to record here. I have known mature adults not normally given to manic outbursts who will swear profusely and exhibit malicious glee while stamping on snails – it is rather like watching someone possessed by a malevolent djinn. Has it never occurred to anyone that these creatures existed long before we took up gardening, and that by precedence they have more right to wander around than we do? For my own part, I feel that in the well-tempered garden the little damage they do is more than compensated for by the pleasure of their company; and that a garden bereft of wildlife is, however tastefully laid out, as dead as a graveyard.

If control is necessary, it usually only needs to be minimal and selective, but if all gardeners were to follow this approach the agrochemical producers would face a ruinous drop in sales. What sustains the industry is the irrational overkill practised by gardeners who feel threatened by every creature which flies, walks or crawls. The industry is well aware of this and plays upon the public imagination with advertisements in which 'Molehills become mountains and the ant/Appears a mighty elephant'. A similar situation applies where weeds – habitually referred to as 'noxious weeds' – are concerned. To hear some people talk, you could be forgiven for assuming that their gardens were being invaded by triffids, so het up do they get about a few wild flowers.

While we are on the subject, 'Consider [yet again] the lilies of the field. They toil not . . .' This, I have to say, is arrant anthropocentric nonsense: in their own quiet way lilies are toiling twenty-four hours a day to promote the survival of the species – we just happen to be blind to cellular biology. The above well-worn quotation further implies the moral superiority of man's labours, which accounts for its popularity with exponents of the Puritan work ethic. But surveying the mess we have made of the living tissue of this planet by our intrusive efforts, it is difficult to see how such values can be defended. Coming back to the need for pesticides and herbicides, it is worth noting that a high proportion of the more prevalent pests, weeds and diseases would not now plague us if only we had left well alone. Hubris does not go unpunished.

One form of labour which has traditionally been regarded as highly commendable is the bringing of virgin land into cultivation. It has been the favourite exhortation of European colonists confronted by idle natives – a basic ingredient of the pioneering spirit. But you cannot make an omelette without breaking eggs, and you cannot clear land for cultivation without the wholesale destruction of ecosystems. If this is not aggression, then I don't know what is. In the case of gardens, our collections of plants uprooted from their distant habitats are likely to be far poorer in terms of species diversity than what we destroy. Whether they represent an aesthetic improvement is also open to doubt. Having rambled happily throughout my life over moor and mountain, salt-marsh and sea-cliff, woodland and wetland, and having been constantly delighted by the gardens of nature, I am inclined to feel that our own attempts score rather as the paintings of a chimpanzee when compared to Velazquez.

It is not difficult to find instances of blatant aggression in the annals of garden history, from the great parks whose construction involved the razing of villages and the diverting of rivers, to the Villa Lante where unsuspecting garden visitors were drenched by hidden fountains. But such examples, though they serve to put us on our guard against the generally accepted view that gardening is a wholly benign pastime, are not really representative. On the other hand, countless gardens (including mine and, probably, yours) demonstrate the aggressive imposition of straight lines (and other geometric elements) on nature.

I realise that geometric shapes are encountered in natural objects and living organisms, but the formal garden is an overweening assertion of man's intellectual vanity in the face of the natural order of things. If you are convinced that art can triumph over nature, then *parterres* and *pattes d'oie* will satisfy you. An alternative view is that imposed formalism is an expression of human braggadocio at its most pathetic. Unfortunately for those of us who have to make gardens within small rectangular sites bounded by adjacent properties, the geometry is imposed on us from the outset, and unless we have a touch of genius at our disposal the wild garden in a built-up area is scarcely distinguishable from a derelict plot, more likely to provoke a vague feeling of sadness than 'happiness and repose of mind'. A poignant reminder of paradise lost.

As more and more of life becomes computer programmed, the future comfortingly pre-set and even reality itself replaced by electronic simulation safely regulated by the remote control button, the anarchic tendencies of the garden stand out as ever more in need of subjugation. Even plants of the same species have a distressing habit of growing in quite individualistic and unpredictable ways, not to mention their predisposition to react to the changing seasons by periodically dropping dead leaves everywhere, necessitating the purchase of a large red-and-black vacuum cleaner to restore order. This no doubt explains the popularity of Disney-tinted conifers of regular shape and size which have the merit of appearing to be manufactured from synthetic material. Another solution is to phase out the plants and replace them with low-maintenance plastic garden (*sic*) objects of every description.

All things considered, it is hardly surprising that garden imple- ments in the ·regimental livery of the Guards should find a ready market. What next? Possibly camouflage-painted mowers with the manufacturer's name stencilled in white? At least then, when the closet Rambo next door emerges clad in flak jacket and combat boots to rev up his multi-purpose tractor to cut the lawn, or dons gauntlets to take a chainsaw to the lilac suckers, the noise will be just as irritating but the visual impact less obtrusive.

Mercifully there is another kind of gardener. She respects and cares, seeks always to understand though knowing that when the day comes for *her* to be composted there will still be more to learn. She welcomes the self-sown violet and counts it a privilege to be visited by butterflies. There is no creature in her garden so insig- nificant, no patch of lichen so small that it passes unnoticed. Her plants thrive and cohabit easily. Be it well-appointed or ever so humble – and maybe just a little untidy – her garden will inspire you with an exquisite pleasure; though, try as you may, you will never extract a neat formula for its success. Such gardens, and such gardeners, are to be cherished.

It was six years ago that a copy of HORTUS first fell into my hands, and that particular issue carried a review of Mirabel Osler's *A Gentle Plea for Chaos*. Note well the adjective.

A Time There Was, at Sissinghurst

ANTONY KING-DEACON

There is a claim to fame that I believe is mine and mine alone: I am probably the only man who has slept regularly in the bed of Vita Sackville-West. For three years I slipped nightly between her crisp and scented linen sheets, pulled her silken eiderdown up around my ears, and communed with her. The experience made me the man that I am.

She was dead, of course. Her ashes, in a small pink marble sarcophagus, had been placed in the Sackville crypt at Withyham a year or so earlier. Her husband, Sir Harold Nicolson, had insisted that her bedroom in the South Cottage at Sissinghurst Castle should remain exactly as it was. His grief was monumental, and shattered every corner of his life, causing a stroke. Fate determined that I was to look after him. He was, he said, 'ga-ga': his stick-supported walk was no more than a shuffle, his words a jumble of sounds. I went to him as his nurse/companion and we became inseparable, literally, my arm through his through all our days together. At night I tucked him into bed in his room next to mine – Vita's. The door was left ajar in case I should be needed in the night.

Sissinghurst has been perhaps the most famous garden in the world for more than thirty years, visited by nearly a million people annually. Vita and Harold began its creation in 1931 and she died, still working amid the loveliness she had made, in 1962.

When I went to look after Harold and live with him in the South Cottage, it was still very much a private family garden – and one still in the making, evolving all the while. Vita spent her life experimenting with plant associations. She was obsessed with colour, and made riots of it everywhere she could, although the White Garden she created is today one of the cornerstones of modern gardening, emulated throughout the world. There was as much gypsy in her soul as there was, many years before her birth, in her lineage. To live in that garden where the roseate, domestic Elizabethan tower dominated the days and perfumes were the soul of each season was a profound privilege. Come with me to Sissinghurst as it was when I was there.

This garden of many gardens, each with its own distinct personality yet all singing the same song, covers about seven acres. It is named 'castle' but it presents no defence, there are no battlements, no crenellations. It has a gentle face of mellow brick and beckons, welcomes, embraces.

You enter through a wide arch, as would Harold and I after having been away, passing from its echoing gloom into a spacious courtyard wide with daisy-enamelled lawns. Vita would never let her 'wildlings' be killed. A path divides the lawn – it was of weathered York stone in my time – and leads to the waiting tower ahead, its twin turrets topped with glinting grey slates. Two bulging, funereal Irish yews stand sentinel beside the path, today bound to restrain their waywardness, formerly given the freedom to be shaggy.

Under the tower's arch, on the left, is a rickety door opening on steps leading to the room in which Vita wrote, about gardening as well as her poetry and novels, and letters every day to Harold in London. It too has been held in the amber of the years, preserved exactly as she left it. On her desk to the left of the door her diary is open, framed photographs of Harold and her close friend Virginia Woolf murmur their shared memories, and there are her secateurs. A tuzzy-muzzy – her name for a nosegay of flowers – in a small vase, whatever is in season every day of the year, keeps the gardener's flame alight. In my day a sensual mustiness mingled with the scent of the tuzzy-muzzy. I know not what the room smells of today.

Through the tower's arch we moved, to the top of a flight of steps overlooking another daisy-encrusted lawn peppered also with buttercups. Here Harold would pause, because the steps presented a difficult physical effort. He might lean against the wall of the tower; often he would weep, often, often, his body shaking with his sobs, his face made ugly by pain, his tie, the front of his shirt, wet with his tears. I would gently squeeze his arm, in encouragement and in deep sympathy. Then down the steps, across the lawn,

Sir Harold Nicolson

through a gap in the yew hedge, and along the uneven brick path to the door of the South Cottage. Two steps, and we are home, to a nap if it was afternoon, Harold in his armchair beside the fireplace, a rug across his lap, I upstairs in Vita's room.

Here I was the ghost, the spectre incapable of moving any object. Vita's presence, her scent, her very breath on the air were tangible. On the bedside table were the medicine bottles from her final illness, a book of Elizabethan poetry with a plant label as a marker, and framed photographs of Harold and their sons Nigel and Benedict. The table under the window was strewn with the paraphernalia of a gardener: a small bundle of raffia, Boot's the Chemist notebooks filled with hasty jottings, seed catalogues, and a wooden dibber, so poignant, polished by seasons of handling, of dibbing. My own clothes I folded over the back of a chair because the wardrobe was filled with hers, leather riding boots toppling out should I open it.

Despite the emotions it must stir, Harold then always wanted a turn round the garden. It was as though he expected Vita to be waiting for him out among her roses, or in the greened gloom of the nuttery. Since it was unsafe for him to go alone, I would take his arm, as usual. Standing on the threshold of the cottage we would wonder which way to go, this late in the afternoon, hesitating under the confetti of falling petals of the climbing rose 'Mme Alfred Carrière'. We might go forward across the Cottage Garden and around the huge ancient copper, mossy and patina'd, filled with a heart's-tug of flowers, a bonfire of colours, reds and ochres, oranges and yellows, through to the Lime Walk; or left, through a bower and down the Moat Walk with its massed azaleas, larger and fiercer bonfires, down to the moat and its mysteries, especially evocative on later autumn afternoons when it gave off a swirling mist like a visible sigh.

In my day there were four full-time staff, the two lady gardeners whom Vita had indoctrinated with her own style, Copper the odd-job man and chauffeur, and Mrs Staples the homely cook/house-keeper. Ursula Codrington was the part-time secretary, with an office in the entrance arch. The domestic arrangements were, to put it kindly, peculiar. Meals were taken in the Priest's House, which

South Cottage, from a photograph taken by the author in the early 1960s.

stands at the edge of the White Garden. Here Nigel and his then wife Philippa, any guest staying in the main body of the house, Harold and I would meet for lunch and dinner, and for afternoon tea on Sundays, when dinner was a cold buffet. It was in this dining room that we watched the assassination of President Kennedy and its aftermath, Harold sobbing at the black-and-white television images.

Some evenings Bunny Drummond would cycle over from her home nearby at Sissinghurst Place for an hour or so before dinner, for a few drinks and, refreshingly, a few laughs. She was an old family friend, and a most welcome gin-and-tonic for Harold, outrageously funny, with a strident ass's laugh, a hee-haw of gaity. She was also harmlessly though perceptibly indiscreet, and made us laugh till we cried, begging her to stop. It was heartening to see tears of mirth rather than sorrow dampening dear Harold's cheeks.

He was generous with his drinks measures, and Bunny was usually well away on cooking sherry before she arrived. As seven ticked nearer, drowned by our shrieks of laughter, she would begin to gird her loins, as she would say, and prepare to mount her 'trusty steed'. After she had cheerily stumbled off into the gathering darkness we sometimes, as we prepared to make the journey across the garden to dinner, heard little moans, outraged squeaks, childish giggles and gurgles. And just outside we would find her on her back in a flower border, her trousered legs kicking the air. I would run for Copper, to haul her and her steed into the car and drive them safely home.

It was Bunny, dear, funny Bunny, who died in 1981, whom Nigel asked to perform a very special favour. Among the treasures Vita had on her desk in the Tower was a pink Italian marble sarcophagus. It was solid, but when Vita died Nigel asked Bunny to hollow it out to take Vita's ashes.

Autumnal journeys, before the first frost, from the South Cottage through the White Garden to dinner, my arm through Harold's, are the essence of my memories of Sissinghurst. In the darkening dusk we turn right at the cottage door and slip through the yew hedge, a-dance with midges, out onto the tower lawn. If the day has been balmy the heat is now rising in eddies waist-high. The tower clock chimes seven, each mournful note clinging to the echoes of the last before subsiding into silent rumour. Under the catalpa and its folds of shadows we pass the benches where we spend our mornings reading, chatting, or simply watching the garden grow around us, those who have paid a shilling to walk around the garden sometimes slipping quietly by.

I must release Harold's arm as we pass through the Bishop's Gate into the solemn beauty of the White Garden, an almond tree at its heart, as the gate is too narrow for two abreast. But quickly I reclaim it. I carry a torch, of course. It will be needed against the hazards of the return journey in the dark. But now, in the half-light, in the misty glow of greys and off-whites and dulled greens that nudge as we pass, its little beam of yellow is paltry. The perfumes are almost indecent, invading and confusing in a foreign fashion, an Eastern medley like a forbidden drug. We duck the swags of 'Iceberg' roses. Shrubs heavy with rising dew brush and dampen our knees. If there is a moon, its pale limpid light suffuses the garden with an eerie and luminous texture that the perfumes seem to absorb as part of themselves.

I most ardently believe that during my time at Sissinghurst, my arm always through the grieving Harold's, our thoughts ever of her, Vita's soul stayed on, was there with us. It was as though it had become snagged in the gossamer of the magical web that was the atmosphere of this profoundly haunting garden.

Before we lived permanently at Sissinghurst, Harold and I commuted between his chambers at Albany in London during the week (where I had the servant's room high above the Rope Walk) and the South Cottage at weekends. This arrangement lasted only about a year, but while it did there was a Sunday afternoon ritual of picking flowers to take back with us on the train.

Again, as in our turns around the garden arm-in-arm, I was taking Vita's place in a little Sissinghurst ceremony. Harold would point his stick and I would cut the stems with the secateurs exactly where he indicated. Not there, nor there, but *there* – just above an eye. I ferried armfuls of old roses – drowned among them, stifled by their perfumes, bloodied by their thorns, showered by raindrops from them, the deep red-velvet 'Souvenir du Docteur Jamain' that Vita personally saved from extinction, the salmony- orangey- ruddy confusion that is 'Léontine Gervais', the blushing 'Ophelia', all bouncing in my arms noiselessly – sheaves of acanthus, mists of gypsophila, wands of the pink and yellow linaria 'Canon Went', joyous burdens to be plonked onto the bench in the flower room at the rear of the South Cottage.

In another household, in yours or mine, this would have been a boot room a-jostle with drunken wellies and hung with swinging dogs' leads. Here at Sissinghurst it was, it must have been, The Flower Room. It had the smell of wet tweed and home-made compost, all bound together with dusty, ancient cobwebs (and the spiders thereon must have been enormous). The small windows gloomed it and even, it seemed, muffled sound itself. It was, had been, Vita's half-way house for plants on their way to the garden. Here too was a wooden tomato box, which was 'The Box of the Dead', wherein were thrown (and many a time my finger pushed around among the myriad despairs) the labels and tags of plants that had died, had defied Vita's love.

After wadding the stems of our cut flowers, destined for an alien death in Piccadilly, with damp newspaper and packing them into the long, purpose-made wicker baskets which travelled ever to and fro, we would have one of Mrs Staples' teas before Copper drove us to Staplehurst and the London train.

And such a tea! The lady's cheeks flushed as we walked to it through her kitchen domain: sponge-cake the shades of amber of a Russian sea skeined with the tangy flavour of almonds; scones that whispered and oozed local butter and pippy raspberry jam; still-warm crusted white bread from the oven whose heat made its maker's gentle face run. And at the end, magicked into the pockets of our macs, little rock-cakes, wrapped in noisy greaseproof paper, for the journey. The good-byes at the kitchen door afterwards were strangely solemn. As if . . . as if pleasure contains some guilt.

Drawing by Simon Dorrell

Young Stoneface

TIM LONGVILLE

Do you ever rebel against the unstructured flower-power of many English gardens, yet feel equally unhappy with those in which plants become just green geometry, statues simply decorative punctuation? Ronnie Duncan's garden in Wharfedale, North Yorkshire, is an elegant example of one which avoids those competing pitfalls since, though it's one in which plants are clearly subordinate and stonework very much in command, this is stonework with attitude – and meaning. (House and garden are nameless: an advance warning that conventional expectations are about to be challenged.) Poker-faced, its creator insists he knows nothing about plants and was only encouraged to make a garden by reading an interview with Geoffrey Jellicoe in which Jellicoe claimed to be not at all a gardener – but it didn't matter, because 'Landscape architecture doesn't really require a great knowledge of horticulture.'

Thus provoked and inspired, Ronnie Duncan set about making a garden which would be a modern re-interpretation not of one ancient gardening model but of two: the garden which comments on life and the garden which acts as a showcase for a collection.

Throughout a long life, Ronnie Duncan has always been a collector, both of paintings (particularly by Roger Hilton and others associated with St Ives) and of sculpture. He's also always been passionately interested in words and particularly in poetry. His garden combines all those passions (nods to favourite painters, works by favourite sculptors, quotations from favourite writers) and adds to them an equally passionate interest in the way gardens have been interpreted by different people and cultures at different times. In fact, it's eclectic almost on principle: an anthology of people and places he's admired and been inspired by. So its 'cast-list' includes, in fact or by implied reference, painters from Spain and Belgium (Miró and Magritte), sculptors from England and Ireland (Ian Judd, Keith Bailey, Breon O'Casey), a performance artist from France (Sophie Calle), a landscape artist from England (Andy Goldsworthy), writers from England, France, Ireland and ancient Greece ('Anon', Simone Weil, Samuel Beckett, Epicurus), a man-about-the-arts from Scotland (Ian Hamilton Finlay, whose word-and-image-rich garden at Stonypath has clearly been a strong influence), and it refers to gardening or architectural styles from Africa (the garden contains an African-style *Machan* or viewing platform), Japan (a proposed stretch of path is to be constructed in a style inspired by Japanese models) and ancient Greece (the entrance to a structure in it called The Oracle is modelled on that at Cumae).

Of course, there's nothing new about the idea of a garden containing sculptural pieces which combine to imply some overall meaning. Mostly, though, such gardens were (and, in the case of Ian Finlay's, are) concerned with public affairs, about which they make semi- or pseudo-political statements. Ronnie Duncan's garden makes no political statement and has no public face. Rather than a manifesto, it's a lyric poem. But one of a particular, mildly surrealist sort, in which straight-faced jokes make serious points and serious points are made with stylish wit.

It's different in other ways as well. In its scale, for instance. Sculptural gardens suggesting grand meanings are usually made on an equally grand scale. However, Ronnie's house began life as a row of working-men's cottages and the present garden simply amalgamates their original miniscule garden plots. The whole resulting area is no more than thirty feet deep by ninety long.

Also, although Ronnie has owned the cottages for more than forty years and though a couple of the outside works have been in position for more than twenty, the main project has been undertaken and largely completed only in the last three or four: speed is one of the advantages this form of gardening has over a conventional garden built round a framework of trees and shrubs, and it's an advantage likely to be particularly felt by those who, like Ronnie himself, only come to garden-making late in life.

If it's an encouragement for those short of time, it's also a garden to cheer those short of cash. No expensive designer has fattened his bank balance by working here and, though some sculptures have certainly been bought or commissioned, many more have been made by Ronnie himself or by local craftsmen Andy Lang and Fred Agar, working to his designs. The stone for such sculptures has often been 'second-hand': local stone, previously used and then discarded, which in this stone garden is recycled, reinterpreted, as it were reborn. Partly, no doubt, this has been done out of native Yorkshire thrift; but partly, too, from the feeling that in a thing's apparent end is its possible re-beginning: a feeling that amounts to one of this garden's half-hidden but recurrent themes. Hence its impressive list of recycled materials, including granite kerbs, sea-formed granite 'eggs', blocks, plinths, setts, gate-posts, slates, flags, gravel. Such an accumulation of stony impedimenta may make the place sound more like a quarry than a garden, but in the context both of the larger stone-filled Wharfedale landscape and of the more immediate setting of stone house, stone garden walls, stone farm buildings beyond, it simply echoes, emphasises and adds point to what surrounds it.

In some senses this is obviously a very formal garden, but in terms of its layout it isn't formal at all. Once you've passed through the gate from the lane, with its attention-concentrating sign BEWARE OF THE GOD (Ronnie once gleefully overheard a passing walker harrumph to his companion 'Huh, another dyslexic'), what you find is a wandering irregular circuit of paths: a single one to your left, hugging the equally irregular line of the house and leading eventually to a stone-flagged terrace; a miniature maze of them to your right. All take you sooner or later to the far wall of the garden, where your little journey ends in ways which simultaneously suggest absolute conclusions, contemplations of the past, and possibilities of new starts. For a garden which aims to comment on that equally meandering item, life, such a layout has an obvious point. It's also tactfully in tune with the place's unpretentious cottage-y past. Equally, this was consciously not a garden begun according to a single grand plan. It was deliberately allowed to grow and develop, step by step, stage by stage. 'Certain dispositions suggested others,' says Ronnie. 'The hope was and is to achieve an organic whole.'

That perhaps sounds rather solemn, as explanations of intentions often do, but this isn't at all a solemn garden. The reverse. Gardens aren't usually places which make you laugh. (Snigger dismissively, perhaps, or gasp with astonishment. But laugh? Rarely.) Here, though, laughs begin at the entrance and go on to the exit, though it's true that much of the humour is black (at one point, literally as well as metaphorically so). Much – but not all. Some of it is simply fun: wry, throwaway, little squibs. For instance, the garden includes a telegraph pole, as ugly as any other. At least, it *was* a telegraph pole, and it *was* ugly. Now it's no longer a telegraph pole, but, hey presto! a work of art. Yorkshire Electricity told Ronnie it would cost at least £7000 to have it removed. Appalled, our thrifty Yorkshire hero instead surrounded it with a simple but elegant metal grille (to give 'protection against animals and engineers') and fixed to it what he calls his Magritte Plaque, a piece of stone lettered by Ian Judd which parodies Magritte by proclaiming sternly *Ceci n'est pas un poteau*. Elsewhere in the garden, other visual cattle-prods provide similar wake-up calls to any visitor with conventional responses. Two of those jokes feature that ultimate gardener's adjunct, the spade. One is an unmodified and rusting old spade-head, simply thrust between two terrace flagstones, and labelled *Homage To Miró*. The other is Breon O'Casey's elegant piece of recycling, his sculpture named *Spade-Bird*. Of course, these are jokes intended to make us think. Are objects confined to one function? Does a label make a work of art? Does labelling something as a work of art make it beautiful? Many of this garden's pleasures come from such teasing games with expectations and boundaries. Where does art end and nonsense begin? Where does craft end and art begin? Even, where does life end and death begin, where does death end and life begin?

Other works have an equally stylish wit but with undercurrents of the Stoic melancholy of those last two questions. A bowl in simulated stone, made by Ian Judd, stands on an asymetrical stone plinth; in it, an assemblage of Cornish granite 'eggs'. Ronnie Duncan finds what he describes as 'deep romance' in the evolution of these 'eggs': made by the sea, destroyed by the sea (which had eaten away the cliff in which they were embedded), then rescued and reused in this inland garden far away in the north. The granite 'eggs' beautifully change colour, as light shifts across them or when rain falls, and the changes produced by water and light, the thoughts they provoke on mutability, are also central to one of Ronnie's own recycled 'constructions'. In that, a trio of stone troughs has been arranged vertically so that a miniature solar-powered fountain is able to throw water into the topmost. The fountain turns on and off unpredictably as the sun comes or (more often, in Wharfedale) goes, and the constantly recycled water trickles equally unpredictably from topmost to lowest level.

Wit and style with a dressing of discreet melancholy aren't all this garden has to offer, though. Sometimes the melancholy becomes the main ingredient, the wit merely sweetens the pill. Consider perhaps its most imposing section, a promenade along the lowest path, the one furthest from the house, leading erratically from garden-entrance to end-wall. It opens as you pass through The Henge, two massive blocks of stone topped by a horizontal third. Already ritual memories, if not precisely religious or at least Christian ones, are being invoked. Beyond The Henge is a narrow pathway, The Colonnade, lined with and enclosed by recycled, upright, head-high, pierced stone stoups, which appears to come to a dead-end in two more-than-head-high upright slabs, set obliquely one

behind the other. As you draw nearer, you see that each of these slabs, which Ronnie calls The Stelae, carries an inscription, elegantly carved by Ian Judd. The inscriptions are sentences by Samuel Beckett. On the nearer slab, I CAN'T GO ON. On the further – and as you peer to see what it says you realise that it is after all possible, with difficulty, to squeeze between them – I GO ON. A triumphant surmounting of difficulties? A Samuel-Smiles-like encouragement to strive and strive again? Hardly. 'Going on' only brings you to the garden's darkest and most serious joke, in its furthest corner, which until now has almost been hidden by a forest of stone uprights. The joke is (and is contained in) a converted privy. What it's been converted into, via the introduction of massive stone slabs to make an entrance imitating that at Cumae, is The Oracle. (The privy-oracle is not, of course, in this context, altogether a joke. Not *just* a joke . . .) And what does The Oracle say? Since the doorless entrance leads to a windowless interior, at first it says – and you see, like Milton's Samson – only 'Dark, dark, dark'. Then, as your eyes become accustomed to it, you pick up on the back wall a single glowing flickering word, the ultimate Yorkshire monosyllable: NOWT. (It's in fact a solar-powered fibre-optic piece by Peter Freeman.) If, instead of gulping, flinching and passing on as quickly as possible, you stay to explore the tiny interior, you'll also discover a stone tablet on a side wall. Its gilded lettering (by intention, barely visible) spells out a sentence from Epicurus, which may or may not be seen as marginally more consoling: 'For there is nothing terrible in life for the man who has truly comprehended that there is nothing terrible in not living.'

The Oracle is in the garden's lower corner. In its upper corner, on the wall which ends the stone terrace, past a towering pencil-thin gnomon for an as-yet-unfinished sundial, are two recently in-stalled stone plaques. Each is carved with a single foreign word and its English translation. They sum up, I think, much of what is going on here. On the first is carved the French word *L'Enracinement*, its English translation, *Rootedness*, and an attribution to the philosopher Simone Weil. On the second, the German words, *Die Entfernung*, their English translation, *Detachment*, and an attribution to the French performance-artist Sophie Calle (German words for a French artist because of her book about the Berlin Wall, originally pub-lished bilingually in German and English). A garden rooted in local materials yet detached from them by its references across time and space? A gardener rooted in his time and place yet attempting intellectually and emotionally to be detached from both? Perhaps. Or perhaps not. The aim, after all, is clearly to provoke questions rather than to provide answers.

A point proved again at the garden's physical and perhaps emo-tional heart, where its largest single structure is also – to me, at least – its most enigmatic. Ronnie Duncan calls it The People Pound. It's a substantial, circular, drystone-walled, animal-pound-

or-sheepfold-like shape, beautifully crafted by Andy Lang and Fred
Agar and reminiscent of those recently restored in the Lake District
under the direction of the landscape artist Andy Goldsworthy. At
first, you – I, at least – merely think, What a handsome object.
Then the questions begin. Why does it have three exit-entrances?
Why are two difficult and one easy to pass through? Why does the
easy one lead towards The Oracle? Why does The People Pound's
floor of stone setts include a central white south-pointing triangle,
echoing the shape of the gnomon of the unfinished sundial on the
terrace behind it? (Sundials and their ancient suggestions of awe
and terror in the face of time passing play a more than incidental
part in this garden, which also contains a small but monumental
one designed by Ian Hamilton Finlay and sculpted by Keith Bailey.)
Why do none of the entrance-exits quite align with the points at
which they seem to be aimed? Is there any deliberate intention
behind the 'echo-inversion' between the shapes of those entrance-
exits and the shape of the entrance to The Oracle? All that Ronnie
Duncan will say, in response to questions about the garden's whole
extensive repertoire of teasing games with almost-alignments, its
anthology of geometrical near-misses, is simply: 'I hate rectan-
gulitis.' Which may be true so far as it goes, but is less than totally
helpful. And that, though the comment was made with the sweetest
and gentlest of smiles, was no doubt what was intended: teasing,
provocative less-than-total-helpfulness. The Germans ought to have
a word for it . . . Though I am indeed provoked and teased, and
though I still have no answers to my questions, I don't mind.
Instead, I'm reminded of a consoling line by William Carlos Williams
which asserts that 'A poem must not mean, but be'. It would be a
characteristically dark and serious joke if at the heart of this poem-
garden's labyrinth of meanings lay a piece with no (definable)
meaning at all.

   As well as meanings, jokes and games, it does also, you may by
now be mildly surprised to learn, contain plants. All the same, and
though Ronnie Duncan says of it that 'If the architecture is the
bones, horticulture is the flesh', it's clear that the horticultural flesh
has to know its place – which, in his own words, is to show 'Nature

and its seasons constantly interacting with the garden's structure, concealing, revealing, overlaying . . .' 'Not to shout against the stone', as he puts it, he's used a very restricted palette – simply green, white and soft blue – and much of the planting consists of the simplest staples, such as grass, lady's mantle, foxgloves and lavender, though room is allowed for individual specimens with a marked presence (a white-flowered *Deutzia pulchra*, a white camellia) and for plants which effectively become part of their sculptural neighbours. For example, young holly specimens have been planted to grow into a dense hedge on both sides of the path leading from The Stelae to The Oracle. When mature, the hedge will help to emphasise the claustrophobic but to an extent illusory feeling of enclosure, of dead-end-edness. And rustling clumps of bamboo (*Phyllostachys nigra* and *P. vivax* 'Aureocaulis') stand close to The Oracle's entrance, so that their unsteady rustling presence helps intensify the feeling of imminent (and perhaps less than trustworthy) speech, of the existence of barriers (not just physical) which it *might* be possible to pierce.

In the centre of that far wall, between The Oracle's single essential word ('Nowt!') and the single essential words of each of the twin plaques ('Rootedness!' 'Detachment!'), is The Machan, or viewing platform, from whose height you have a range of options for looking, remembering, contemplating. Look directly to left or right and you encounter those ultimate (and opposing? or complementary?) monosyllabic meanings. Look straight ahead and you can re-experience your journey to this final position, whether on the left having arrived through The Colonnade and The Stelae, or to the right having travelled along the terrace past the unfinished Gnomon, the *Homage to Miró* spade-head, the Finlay-designed and Bailey-sculpted sundial, and a massive and imposing dry-stone 'egg' (massive and imposing despite being no more than three feet tall) crafted by Andy Lang and Fred Agar as a reduced version of one by Andy Goldsworthy. Look almost directly downwards and you will find yourself peering into the continuing mystery – no: mysteries – of The People Pound. Yet the meaning-rich space you survey, this ninety foot by thirty pocket-handkerchief of North Yorkshire, can be taken in in a single glance, walked in a matter of moments.

Letters from Ronnie Duncan always come adorned at the foot of the page with a hand-stamped or 'printed' quotation, one from a continually changing repertoire of favourites. Two among them seem particularly relevant. The first, a comment by Louise Nevelson: 'I never feel age . . . If you have creative work you don't have age or time.' The second, two lines by the American poet James Broughton, which go a long way towards summing up the idiosyncratic attractions of both the man and his garden:

> *Crazy old men are essential to society,*
> *Otherwise young men have no suitable models.*

Oh, yes. My title. The nickname of the great comedian Buster Keaton was Old Stoneface. An ideal phrase to describe this stone garden of poker-faced jokes and its venerable, equally poker-faced creator? No, not quite. The garden may have been made by one who is chronologically old, but both he and it feel defiantly, triumphantly, youthful. Hence the revision. Some of us do try to be helpful and to provide answers . . .

Drawings by Simon Dorrell.

The Gardens of War

ANNE POWELL

Weary soldiers found occasional solace in the world of nature as they struggled against the relentless slaughter and destruction in Northern France and Flanders during the First World War. In their prose and poetry there are many memories of gardens known and loved at home, references to gardens and orchards discovered by chance in the grounds of deserted châteaux and demolished houses, and to gardens created from the chaos of war as sanctuaries of order and peace.

Two months after the outbreak of war Rupert Brooke, serving as a sub-lieutenant with the Royal Naval Division, took part in the retreat from Antwerp. In the terrible confusion of troops, refugees, machinery and equipment, his battalion was suddenly ordered into the garden of a deserted château in the town of Vieux Dieu. Later he wrote to the actress Cathleen Nesbitt:

> The rather dirty and wild-looking sailors trudged over lawns, through orchards and across pleasaunces. Little pools glimmered through the trees, and deserted fountains; and round corners one saw, faintly, occasional Cupids and Venuses – a scattered company of rather bad statues – gleaming quietly. The sailors dug their latrines in the various rose-gardens and lay down to sleep – but it was bitter cold – under the shrubs. It seemed infinitely peaceful and remote . . .

Second Lieutenant Alexander Gillespie, a classicist educated at Winchester and Oxford, arrived in France with the 2nd Battalion, The Argyll and Sutherland Highlanders in February 1915. His letters home, vividly describing the seven months spent in trenches and billets, are enriched with his accounts of shell-torn orchards in blossom, birds defying the sniper's rifle, wild flowers found in desolate places, and his delight in the garden he made in a trench outside his dug-out in the grounds of a shattered farmhouse. At the end of March it was still too cold to sow nasturtium seeds, but the following month cabbages and leeks were growing in among the barbed wire, and he planted a clump of sweet violets gathered from the bank of an old flooded trench. In May marigold, poppy and stock seeds were sown, and Madonna lilies transplanted. On 5 May he wrote:

> The afternoon I spent in getting plants from a ruined village for our trench gardens – wallflowers, paeonies, pansies, and many others; rather cruel to transplant them perhaps, but there are plenty left. The village is a terrible sight, for what the shells have left standing has been wrecked in the search for wood, for burning and making dug-outs in the cold wet weather last winter, and you notice the contrast more now that the fruit trees are all in blossom, and the garden beds have all their spring flowers . . . There are graves everywhere in the little gardens behind the houses . . .

Two months later Gillespie was tending the Madonna lilies which 'glowed in the half-light of morning or evening' and watering his trench garden in the early hours of the morning:

> . . . a long and muddy business, for I had to jump half the way down our wall to fill the watering-can, and stand on a slippery cask . . . We have mignonette and corn-flowers coming on well now, with a lot of nasturtiums and canariensis to follow . . .

Robert Graves, a captain in the 2nd Battalion, The Royal Welch Fusiliers, discovered deserted gardens in Vermelles in the summer of 1915:

> There is one garden with currant bushes in it. I and the company sergeant-major started eating along the line towards each other without noticing each other. When we did, we both remembered our dignity, he as a company sergeant-major and I as an officer.

He saluted, I acknowledged the salute, we both walked away. After a minute or two we both came back hoping the coast was clear and again, after an exchange of salutes, had to leave the currants and pretend that we were merely admiring the flowers . . . Anyhow, along came a couple of privates and stripped the bushes clean . . .

Siegfried Sassoon also served with The Royal Welch Fusiliers. On the evening of 21 May 1916 he arrived with his battalion at the village of Morlancourt, and woke the following morning to find a 'tangled garden' behind his billet:

. . . chirping of birds among the fruit-trees, sunshine on the vine-covered plaster walls of the house, a few pink roses, and some red peonies; the horse-chestnut in flower . . .

Later that morning, operational orders and a battle plan were circulated for a raid on German trenches. In *Memoirs of an Infantry Officer* Sassoon recalled the Arcadian associations of the first objectives which were to be taken by his raiding party, and thought that Rose Trench, Orchard Alley, Apple Alley and Willow Avenue did not look 'aggressively unpleasant on paper'. In the raid three days later, Sassoon won the Military Cross for 'conspicuous gallantry'; out of the twenty-eight men who took part, two were killed and eleven wounded.

In April 1917, as a relief from the front-line trenches, the 2nd Battalion, The Scots Guards was sent to build a railway at Péronne, five miles east of the devastated town of Cartigny. The battalion arrived in snow and pitched its tents in mud. Stephen Graham, a private in the battalion, later wrote of Armstrong, an expert wrestler and one of the strongest and kindest men in the battalion, who had been a gardener on a Scottish estate before the war. Armstrong inspired the men to become gardeners, and to rescue plants and shrubs from the ruined town. 'He finds narcissus, pheasant-eyed narcissus, and tiger lilies. He never calls the latter tiger lilies, but always "tigrum lilium" – by that you may know he is a gardener.'

The commanding officer put up a prize for the best garden, and every tent created one, in a variety of impressive floral designs: a replica of the clock in Princes Street Gardens in Edinburgh; the regimental crest; a box-hedge heart.

Each man has found or improvised trowel and basket, shovel or hoe. The bayonet is forever in use, cutting lumps of chalk to right sizes, making holes in the earth, cutting and slicing wood. Petrol-tins with holes in the bottom serve as watering-cans . . . Primroses and daffodils and narcissi are soon blossoming in plenty. Lilies followed, arums and Solomon's seal, and then forget-me-nots, pansies and violas . . . Armstrong's rockeries become the wonder not only of the battalion but of our many visitors and guests in this time of qualified rest . . . Those who made the floral clock get first prize . . .

'The voice of nature cries in many ways where violence savages', wrote Edmund Blunden, a lieutenant in the 11th Battalion, The Royal Sussex Regiment. Immediately after an abortive British attack on Beaumont Ridge during the Battle of the Somme, Blunden wrote a poem with the ironic title 'Preparations for Victory':

> . . . *Look, here are gardens, there mossed boughs are hung*
> *With apples whose bright cheeks none might excel,*
> *And there's a house as yet unshattered by a shell . . .*

In the grounds of Vlamertinghe Château, before the Battle of Passchendaele, Blunden found 'a gorgeous and careless multitude of poppies and sorrels and bull-daisies'. The previous year, outside company headquarters in the village of Festubert, he discovered a garden with 'flowering shrubs . . . gooseberry bushes and walks between evergreen hedges'.

The word 'gooseberries' was also army slang for the thick balls of barbed wire used to block trenches or fill gaps in wire entangle-ments. The humorous and irreverent trench magazine *The B.E.F.*

Times, published from various water-logged cellars and rat-infested dug-outs, parodied *Country Life*'s weekly column 'In my Garden' in December 1917:

> Where the soil is damp and heavy, an early planting of goose-berries is attended with some risk. This hardy perennial, being a strong grower, will quickly cover an unsightly patch of waste ground. The best crops of this luscious fruit have been obtained when some support has been given by stakes . . .

Homesickness was an emotion shared by almost every fighting man. Edward Wyndham Tennant, eldest son of Lord Glenconner, was the youngest Wykehamist to enlist, at the age of seventeen in August 1914. He was commissioned in the 4th Battalion, The Grenadier Guards and sent to France a year later. After two weeks' leave at the end of November 1915 he rejoined his battalion in the trenches, returning every six days to billets in the small town of Laventie between Ypres and Arras. From here, nostalgic for Wils-ford, his Wiltshire home, he wrote the much anthologised poem 'Home Thoughts in Laventie'. He and his company found a neg-lected garden belonging to some ruined houses near the church:

> *So all among the vivid blades*
> *Of soft and tender grass*
> *We lay, nor heard the limber wheels*
> *That pass and ever pass,*
> *In noisy continuity, until their stony rattle*
> *Seems in itself a battle . . .*

> *The fairest and most fragrant*
> *Of the many sweets we found*
> *Was a little bush of Daphne flower,*
> *Upon a grassy mound,*
> *And so thick were the blossoms set, and so divine the scent*
> *That we were well content.*

Hungry for Spring I bent my head,
The perfume fanned my face,
And all my soul was dancing
In that little lovely place,
Dancing with measured step from wrecked and shattered towns
Away . . . upon the Downs . . .

He was killed in September 1916, shortly after his nineteenth birthday.

In a letter written to the Headmaster of Winchester three months before he was killed leading his company in the Battle of Loos, Alexander Gillespie outlined his idea for a future memorial, in the form of one long avenue from La Bassée to Ypres.

The ground is so pitted, and scarred, and torn with shells, and tangled with wire, that it will take years to bring it back to use again; but I would make a fine broad road in the No Man's Land between the lines, with paths for pilgrims on foot, and plant trees for shade, and fruit trees, so that the soil should not be altogether waste. Some of the shattered farms and houses might be left as evidence, and the regiments might put up their records beside the trenches which they held all through the winter. Then I would like to send every man, woman, and child in Western Europe on pilgrimage along that Via Sacra, so that they might think and learn what war means from the silent witnesses on either side . . .

Although the memorial is not entirely as Alexander Gillespie visualised it in June 1915, many trench systems have been preserved and plaques and memorials commemorating particular actions stand in their appropriate place. Roads and avenues are once again tree-lined, and the fields of battle are now sacred areas of pilgrimage. Alexander Gillespie the gardener would admire the beautiful gardens of rest created by the Commonwealth War Graves Commission on land given in perpetuity to Great Britain by the people of France and Belgium. Over half a million Commonwealth and foreign dead are buried in more than two thousand Commission cemeteries, and more than 300,000 names are commemorated on twenty-six Memorials to the Missing in northern France and Flanders. Sir Edwin Lutyens, one of the principal architects for the original Imperial War Graves Commission, believed there was '. . . no need for the cemeteries to be gloomy or even sad-looking places. Good use should be made of the best and most beautiful flowering plants and shrubs . . .' The Commission, in the face of much opposition, insisted that there should be no distinction between the graves of officers and of men, and that each headstone must be of identical design. Here the equality bestowed by death has broken down all class, cultural and religious barriers, and very often those who fought against each other share the same burial ground.

Magnificent trees are grouped according to the size and shape of the cemetery. There are grassed paths between the rows of graves, and the earth in front of the headstones is planted with bulbs, flowers and small shrubs, planned for each season of the year. There is a profusion of colour and scent during the summer months and warm rich shades in the autumn. Over four hundred Commission gardeners care all the year round for this 'mass multitude of silent witnesses' on the Western Front. Many of these grave gardens are near or part of a battlefield, now hallowed sanctuaries where 'pilgrims on foot', reverently treading Alexander Gillespie's Via Sacra, experience an intangible sense of tranquillity and permanence.

LETTER
FROM
ORKNEY

Katherine Swift

We left Scotland in *haar*, the cold sea-mist of this most northern coast of the British Isles, with the noise of the engines thudding back at us from the enclosing wall of fog, and the waters of the Pentland Firth as greasily calm as if flooded with diesel oil. For once the great churning salt-mill beneath the Pentland Firth was still. On board people breakfasted, played cards, slept, gazed at the fog through blank grey windows. The west coast of Hoy was already close before the *haar* began to lift. The saloons and the shops emptied then as people spilled onto the decks, chattering, crowding the rails for a view of the Old Man – an isolated sea stack 450 feet tall and Orkney's most famous picture-postcard landmark – only to fall silent as the gigantic curtain of red rock behind the Old Man slowly revealed itself through the mist, mile upon mile of towering red sandstone cliffs, striped and banded like the surface of the Red Planet itself, nearly three times as tall as the Old Man and dropping sheer into the sea – 1,136 feet high with another 300 feet or so below water – dwarfing the white car-ferry to bobbing seagull size.

Hoy is The High Island, from the old Norse *Haey*, a brooding presence seen from everywhere on the Orkney Mainland. Its dark acid hills wreathed with shreds of cloud have more in common with the Highlands of Scotland than with the low green islands of Orkney. Its upland flora is sub-arctic tundra, its birds peregrine falcon, merlin, kestrel and raven. The mountain hare lives here, alone among the Orkney islands, changing his brown summer coat each year for winter white. A single road runs the length of Hoy, hugging the sea's rim on the east coast before swinging west between the inhospitable mountains of the island's interior. The roadside is lined with the airy globes of wild angelica and devil's-bit scabious, gay against the dark hills, then broadens across the valley bottom at Rackwick to saxifrage and cinquefoil, low turf sheared by the wind, and spikes of soft rush where the fresh-water burn runs off the hills and joins the sea. Rackwick is the only chink in the island's sea defences: a green valley framed on either side by the massive crags of Moor Fea and Mel Fea. Once a thriving crofting community, Rackwick is now largely abandoned to the wind and the birds, a place of tumbled stone walls and the noise of breakers. Here the banded red sandstone of the cliffs is ground into huge striped boulders by the pounding of the sea, each one unique, as big as dolphins or a school of beached porpoises – pink-banded and grainy, striped with sunset colours, like the rings of Saturn – each one a planetary system in microcosm.

We were to spend our first night in Orkney at Melsetter, following the road south now in mist and driving rain, past the lonely grave of Betty Corigall – seduced and betrayed in life, shunned in death – buried out on the moor. It was an old fantasy of mine to arrive at an unknown house by night, travelling through unfamiliar countryside, dark shapes of trees briefly silhouetted against paler sky, ribbon of road unspooling, smell of rain and wet earth, water glimpsed through an avenue of trees, the changed note of a car engine suddenly bounced back by the walls of a courtyard, then silence and the smell of the sea. And to rise in the dawn and lean from the casement windows and see the garden for the first time. I had first come to Melsetter by night two years ago, and ever since that time Melsetter had been for me the lost domain, my own Les Sablonnières, to which I had found my way by accident, and to which I might never find my way again. And now, as I awoke in the narrow bed high under the eaves, with the pale sea-light filtering under the curtain, it was as if I had just arrived there for the first time, by chance, the previous night; and as I crept from the house to find again the secret door in the wall, hidden by the ancient thickets of fuchsia, it was as if I had never been away. I bent down beneath the curtain of crimson and purple blossom, the trailing stamens brushing pollen dust into my hair, and there between the peeling cinnamon-coloured trunks I found again the door to Elsie's secret garden.

Melsetter is a place of secrets. The house and chapel are enclosed by the gardens, each garden itself an enclosure of high walls or trees, themselves enclosed by stone walls and more trees, and they in turn by the fold of the land and the grid of stone-walled fields beyond. At the centre is a high inward-facing white courtyard made by the angle of house and chapel, and indeed there is something almost Moorish here, as if the tall narrow windows squinted against the sun and the inhabitants sought shade beneath the high walls of the courtyard – a place of sunning cats and lines of washing, of worn flights of steps leading down from the house and from the chapel court through tall narrow doorways onto flagstones beneath, of huge old terracotta pots coloured yellow and silver with lichens. But here the enemy is not the sun but the wind. The sense of enclosure was carried through in Lethaby's original designs into intricate patterns of parterres and closed knots under the outward-facing windows of the house, and in the three walled gardens with their symmetrical arrangements of beds – the old kitchen garden, divided into squares and rectangles; the new rose garden made by Lethaby on the site of the old farmstead, quartered and quartered and quartered again; and the largest of the three, perhaps the pleasure garden of the old house, where Lethaby made a two-storey tea-house in the south-east angle of the walls. I climbed the long flight of stone steps up to the door, overhung now with the branches of the great sycamores in the avenue, the room on a level with the trees outside like a tree house – mullioned windows and dark wood panelling within, a stone fireplace on the slant across a corner, benches upholstered in faded red.

But always there is the glint of the sea beyond, at the end of a drive or across a field, through the groves of venerable sycamores which protect the house, low-branching and multi-stemmed, lining the avenue up from the road, clustering in Lethaby's Rookery beyond the tea-house garden, surrounding the great open space of the south lawn which lies before the long windows of the house. And that morning, with the grass silvered from the previous night's rain, and the massive limbs of the encircling trees crusted with grey sea ivory, the expanse of the south lawn seemed to me a dancing floor for fairies, with the great trees providing entrances and exits, and a fringe of poppies – blood-red, crimson and plum – across the front of the house like footlights across a stage.

The parterres and the rose beds and the acres of fruit and vegetables are long gone: Lethaby's was a different world. But the walled gardens are gradually coming back to a different sort of life. Elsie's secret garden is the old kitchen garden, now a beautiful tangle of meadow and head-high garden-gone-wild, with tiny pockets of newly planted flowers – Elsie's 'bits of beauty, to gladden the heart' – sweet peas, marguerites, the old blue double *Geranium pratense*, among the thickets of honeysuckle and willow and rugosa rose. There are great mounds of grey artemisia and red valerian in the foundations of the demolished greenhouses, clouds of self-seeded blue borage, the remains of yellow tea roses on the high south-facing wall. Elsie's niece Inez has reclaimed two beds of good black soil in the former rose garden, one for flowers, the other for vegetables, her tall aconitums and old-fashioned climbing peas bearing witness to the efficacy of the sheltering walls. And in one corner of the tea-house garden someone had planted potatoes.

Melsetter is uniquely favoured on Hoy both by its natural position and by Lethaby's complex system of walled gardens. The gardeners on South Walls have no such advantages. South Walls is a small green almost-island joined to the great gloomy bulk of Hoy by the Ayre, one of those looping bars of sand so characteristic of Orkney. The Ayre now carries the road south of Melsetter, curving round the bay to Longhope and out to David Stevenson's lighthouse at Cantick Head, built in 1858 to mark the southern entrance to Scapa Flow. In contrast to the uplands of Hoy, the soil on South Walls is good, anciently cultivated, but the shallow treeless dome of the land gives no shelter from the salt-laden gales which rake Orkney. In May a Force 10 gale had blown for a week, scorching the gardens and frosting the windows of the houses with salt. Rowena and Alan Lord are English – Rowena formerly a mathematician, Alan a chemist – who before their retirement worked at the Agricultural Research Station at Rothampstead. When they retired they moved first to Dorset, but in their eight years there it quickly grew too suburban for them, and ten years ago they moved to South Walls. They soon realised that this was no Inverewe. There was no pos-sibility here of growing trees for shelter – and in any case the wind came not from one prevailing direction but from all points of the compass. They were told that you couldn't grow trees or shrubs here, only things that died down in the winter. And even among the herbaceous plants, they were told, no tall things would survive: only low mound-forming types. But Rowena says of Alan with a certain amount of pride that 'he likes to try and do things people say you can't'; and he counters with 'Never believe anything you are told in gardening here.' Almost everything in their garden has been grown from seed, including the sapling ash, beech, silver birch,

oak and laburnum growing in the deep-sided gulley Alan excavated
to mimic in miniature the conditions in which he noticed trees surviving elsewhere in the north. And taking his cue from the chambered burial cairns built by the prehistoric inhabitants of the islands,
Alan has also contrived small pockets of shelter in the garden by
using the natural stone flags of Orkney upright on their ends to
make little three-sided enclosures for individual plants. He uses
them all over the garden, and at intervals along his pride and joy:
a steeply raked double-sided bank, sixty feet in length, which was
constructed with rubble stone from a collapsed wall. The purpose
of the bank is to make the most of the sunlight at either end of the
season when the angle of the sun is very low. Here Alan grows his
collections of sedums, sempervivums, saxifrages and alpine willows
– things with waxed, hard leaves which stand desiccation – together
with more delicate things like low conifers (very vulnerable here to
wind scorch), dwarf campanulas and a ravishing double white campion which I long to beg a bit of, all protected by his 'chambered
cairns'. I had never before felt the appeal of alpine gardening, but
suddenly I began to see why people become obsessed with these
plants: the intricacy of them, their textures and complexity – the
whorls of the sedums, the green- and red-flushed rosettes of the
sempervivums erupting here and there into fat fleshy plum-coloured
flower stalks, the tufts and spikes of the saxifrages – all with their
brilliant band-box-smart flowers in primary colours, yellow, blue,
white and red, here set off by the tiny grey-green leaves of the alpine
willows, the dark needles of the conifers, the silver-lichened stones
of the raised bank.

'Doing things other people say you can't' was to be a common
theme in the conversations I held with English gardeners making
gardens in Orkney: as Peter Ford, Secretary of the Hoy Garden
Society, told me, 'Here on Hoy we try to make a garden *in spite* of
everything.' I was interested in how and why these people garden,
in the detail and the motivation of their battle against the climate
and the terrain, but what interested me more was the idea of gardening *with* everything – the extent to which one might bring the
natural flora into the garden or extend the idea of the garden beyond

the garden walls to embrace the landscape and the flora beyond. In 1987 Alan and Rowena's daughter Mary Jones and her partner Roy Harris set up the Loft and Hill of White Hamars Grazing Project on South Walls. The coastal heaths and grasslands are among the glories of Orkney; the combination of salt spray, wind and grazing by animals combines to produce a jewel-box of flowers in short turf close to the cliffs' edge which gradually merges, further back from the shore, into maritime heath, a densely-textured tapestry of flowering shrubs dwarfed to shin-height by the extremity of the conditions. This is the habitat of the rare *Primula scotica* – found only in Orkney and parts of North Sutherland and Caithness – which grows here in colonies numbering thousands of plants, each of its amethyst flowers so tiny that two would fit inside a wedding ring.

Roy and Mary, recognising the need of local communities to produce from land such as this a commercial crop of milk, butter, wool and meat, wanted to show that it was possible to develop a management regime that would foster the bio-diversity of these habitats while still allowing farmers a living wage. 'Overgrazing' is a term much used in conservation circles, often with the implicit message that any level of grazing is bound to be detrimental to these species-rich grasslands and heaths – that the two activities of conservation and farming are mutually exclusive. But without some degree of grazing, the rarest flowers (including *Primula scotica*) would soon disappear, crowded out by taller-growing species. Roy and Mary believe that grazing can be used creatively for shaping and developing the natural habitat, as well as to rescue previously 'improved' land – land enriched with fertilisers to promote vigorous grass growth at the expense of other species. They have 126 hectares of sheep pasture, roughly half of it at the Loft, their own traditional croft holding, and the other half owned by the Scottish Wildlife Trust at the Hill of White Hamars. Instead of following the usual crofting pattern of low stocking of large areas over long periods, where the resulting vegetation would be dictated by the preferences of the grazing animals, they set up clearly defined objectives for many small parcels of land, on each of which the intensity, selectivity, duration and timing of grazing are all carefully controlled in order to produce the desired mix of vegetation for that area. The project demands a lot of good fencing, and very precise timing.

The result is that Roy and Mary's land is breathtakingly beautiful as well as productive. The cliff-top fields, carpeted in spring with blue sea squill and primroses, in summer with the purple flowers of wild thyme, the candy-pink pincushions of thrift, the veined white butterflies of grass-of-Parnassus, with gentians and orchids and devil's-bit scabious, have also now been recolonised by the tall globes of wild angelica with its hollow pink-flushed stems, and by the yellows and orange of yellow rattle and kidney vetch. Further back from the sea the rich mosaic of grasses and sedges, bell heather and ling, crowberry and heath is also now threaded with the ethereal silver fronds of the fragile reindeer moss. Their wetlands are vivid with great green and gold clumps of marsh-marigold, the purple spikes of marsh orchid, the pink tracery of ragged robin, and the succulent amber, rose and viridian of sphagnum and the other bog mosses. If this is not gardening, it only differs in that the aesthetic considerations came second to botanical and ecological ones. Does that matter? The same may be said – at the two extremes – of many a 'plantsman's' or wild garden. Is it only intention that defines a garden? Many of the best effects in my garden are accidents of self-seeding, from plants outside as well as within the garden. But to some extent I choose what shall stay: there is an element of selection, and therefore of intervention. Must we then intervene in order to call this activity 'gardening'? When photographers intervene to remove less-than-perfect leaves or blooms which would otherwise

mar their composition, they too call it gardening. Is there no more to it than that? Or is there less? – can a garden be a garden simply because I choose it? Perhaps all that is necessary is the seeing eye.

We dined that evening on salt cod and turnips in the big kitchen at Melsetter. And then in the gathering dusk, as the gas flare at the oil refinery on Flotta flamed a vivid orange across the sound, Elsie drove us back across the Ayre to see her friend Judith Hudson. Judith is a painter who has gardened for twenty-one years on South Walls. Her first house was Snelsetter on the rocky south coast overlooking the sea-stack known as The Candle, where she gardened for ten years exposed to the full force of the weather blowing in from the Pentland Firth. The last eleven years she has gardened a scarcely less exposed hilltop at Newbigging. This is not a landscape of villages: the names are the old settlement names, referring as elsewhere on Orkney to isolated farms or 'steadings'. At night the neighbours' lights glimmer across the fields like glow-worms. We followed the coast road around the northern shore of the peninsula before swinging south to Judith's hilltop, poised above the harbour of Osmondwall which, as Asmundavagr, once echoed with the clamour of Viking warships bearing the raven-symbol of the god Odin. It was here that in 955 King Olaf Tryggvason with characteristic Viking clarity offered Earl Sigurd the Stout the choice between Christian baptism and instant decapitation; Earl Sigurd chose baptism.

It was almost dark when we arrived, the garden glimmering white around us on top of the brae. This was not a garden of brilliantly coloured low-growing alpines, nor a grassy carpet of wild flowers. Despite its position, totally exposed to the four winds, this was a Margery Fish dream of softly billowing herbaceous flowers, of hardy geraniums and *Viola cornuta*, tall spires of pale foxglove and blue sea-holly, huge soft grey leaves of cardoons. There was even an ornamental potager, with red and green lettuces planted alternately around the edges, and nursery beds of seedling trees. That night Judith was still working with the salmon at the fish farm below, but later she explained her garden strategy. The secret is dense planting. 'It's nonsense that you can't grow tall things – you just need to plant them tightly together.' Spring and summer gales may cause some plants to lose exposed shoots and flower buds, but this makes the herbaceous plants more bushy and self-supporting, and in a good season – with the abundant Orkney light – can have the effect of encouraging a second or even a third flowering. The downside is the long Orkney winter, when the herbaceous plants retreat underground and the garden is devoid of interest. Judith came to Hoy from England without preconceptions, prepared to do and try anything. She admits now to a string of failures, but over twenty-one years has grown more confident as she has discovered plantings that do work. The basics of good gardening were there for the taking: seaweed, shell sand, peat, manure, stone. She discovered that hard structures like the four-foot stone field-wall which surrounded the garden were useless as a shelter against the wind, which bounced off it in even more destructive rips and eddies – 'like throwing a bucket of water against it' – and that the wall had to be padded inside with a thicket of low-growing shrubs to act as a filter. Even so, the herbaceous plants took six or seven years to grow together and begin to support one another, before the taller plants could be introduced.

This same mutual support is apparent too among the members of the Hoy Garden Club, who visit gardens together and exchange plants and information. By definition, seeds or plants offered by one of the members have a proven track record on Hoy and are there-fore likely to do well – many of the original plantings in Judith's first garden, for example, came from Elsie at Melsetter – whereas things expensively bought in from nurseries further south all too often fail. This is not simply a question of species – of choosing whichever species within a genus has proved to be best adapted to conditions on Hoy – but also of clone, where plants even of an apparently less suitable species, if raised locally and grown 'hard', will survive when plants of the same species but a different clone, grown elsewhere and bought in, will not. And vice versa: Alan Lord had already told me that even totally hardy plants brought from the south need at least a year's acclimatisation in their pots before planting out. Orkney is, as Peter Ford said, 'a place of contradictions – all the hardy stuff we should be able to grow, we can't – and all the tender stuff everyone thinks we can't possibly grow, we grow beautifully.'

We left Hoy by ferry the next morning, heading out across Scapa Flow with the oil flare on Flotta pale now in the early morning light, and the encircling bowl of hills peat-dark on the sky-pale surface of the water. Haven and graveyard, nowhere encapsulates the shifting wateriness of Orkney so much as this huge drowned lake which curls around the southern shores of the Mainland and the southern isles, making islands of hills and sea lochs of valleys, lapping at the back door of Kirkwall on its precarious isthmus, fingering the stone walls and jetties of the harbour at Stromness in the south, filtering at last through the narrow silty channel of Waithe to merge its salt waters with the reedy network of freshwater lochs in the great dished heart of Mainland Orkney. On the sea-bed of Scapa Flow lie the rusting hulks of the German Fleet, scuttled in defeat in 1919 after one World War, and the carcasses of British block-ships sunk to defend the British Fleet in the next, their masts and rigging still visible at certain stages of the tide. Here too lie HMS *Royal Oak*, torpedoed by a German U-boat on the night of 14 October 1939 with the loss of hundreds of lives, and a forest of smaller vessels, from Viking longship to modern trawler, engulfed within sight of land by the vicious squalls that can blow up out of nowhere in this part of the world. Even today, in a dead calm, the surface of the water belies the tranquillity of the air above, its restlessness show-ing itself as whirlpools like colloidal fracture lines on pitch, and dimpled silver patches minutely roughened like hammered pewter, and smooth narrow roads like polished basalt snaking across the surface (leading where? to deep water or treacherous shallows?), the watery equivalent of will-o'-the-wisps – with the wake of the ferry spreading out behind like ripples of black moiré silk, and in the distance the Churchill barriers – built in the aftermath of the *Royal Oak* – like angular white wings.

We were heading for the East Mainland to visit another pair of gardeners, but one whose mutual support system was about to be severely tested. I knew Pat Doughty from an article she had written about gardening in Orkney which had appeared in *The Hardy Plant*, the journal of The Hardy Plant Society. But now I had learned that, recently widowed, she had sold her house and garden, and at the end of the week was moving back to England after seventeen years on Orkney. Alan Bremner is Orcadian born and bred, a cattle farmer on the family steading of Bendigo, south of Kirkwall. He is also an accomplished plant breeder, raising a string of hardy geraniums and potentillas bred within sight of Scapa Flow and now widely dis-seminated in Britain and further afield. Many of Alan's plants are named after people and places in Orkney. 'Westray', the latest geranium to be released, is named after the island home of his father's family. 'Nora Bremner' is named for his mother, 'St Ola' for the parish where he lives. *Geranium* 'Patricia' (a cross between *G. endressii* and *G. psilostemon*) is named after Pat Doughty. They met in the month that Pat arrived in Orkney. Alan had been a keen plantsman since his teens, nurtured by the redoubtable Miss Bullard, the botanical recorder for Orkney, but before he met Pat there was no one he could talk to about his dreams of creating new plants. As a schoolboy he used to walk down the lanes and wonder why there was nothing between a daisy and a buttercup. He learned to love gardening 'by trailing after my mother' and began to work in the greenhouse as something he could do when the weather – as so often in Orkney – was too bad for gardening out of doors. Now all his experimental work is done under glass: 24,000 crosses made over a period of fifteen years, each meticulously documented. From Miss Bullard he had already gained an encyclopaedic knowledge of plants and their habitats. Then in 1985 came Peter Yeo's book *Hardy Geraniums*, which explained the technique of controlled pollination of geraniums. And then Pat provided the final piece of the jigsaw – the concept of 'garden-worthiness', that novelty or botanical interest was not enough, and that to be successful a new plant also had to have a good constitution and a useful habit of growth.

Pat came to Orkney in order to paint, and their first house was bought by her husband over the telephone from England sight unseen, 'on a whim.' The land around it was bare moorland, 'innocent of shelter or fencing of any kind', totally exposed to the salt winds. But she had not come here to garden: she had already resigned her membership of the Royal Horticultural Society and intended to live on her memories of thirty years' gardening in Surrey and Hampshire. She had come because she was captivated by the Orkney sky, by the changing patterns of Orkney light – what George Mackay Brown calls the endless ballet of the weather. But gardening is such an entrenched instinct – to a gardener, such a fundamental part of one's response to the world – that she found herself making a garden in spite of herself. Five years later they moved again, to Quoylanks,

her present house. She was, she said, 'absolutely appalled' by the
site, which was if anything even worse than that of her first Orkney
garden. The dilapidated steading was surrounded by concrete yards
and tin-roofed outbuildings, utterly windswept and without a shred
of shelter, the land itself heavy clay sub-soil over rock, on top of
which the water in winter lay 'in pools'. But again she set to work.
Some of the concrete was dug out and fifty tons of topsoil were imported; elsewhere raised beds of old lichened stones were built on
top of the concrete, shelter belts of tough shrubs were planted and
lawns made, the tin roofs and abandoned sheds rebuilt as studio and
conservatory. And gradually she found that there were after all
advantages to Orkney's notoriously difficult climate. 'Once you've
got the shelter, a lot of things do better here than in the south –
alpines keep their character because of the cooler climate, and
primulas grow like weeds – anything in fact that likes the damp.
Shade-loving plants do well here too, out in the full sun, because
there is not enough sun to scorch them.' When I visited on a damp
grey August day, the garden was alive with borrowed sunshine:
Alan's potentillas in shades of butter and cream, primrose and egg-
yolk yellow; dozens of gold- and silver-variegated plants – the
quilted leaves of hostas, the sword-like leaves of sisyrinchium; drifts
of yellow monkey-flower with throats of spotted orange (*Mimulus
guttatus*, which naturalises all over Orkney), flame-coloured kniphofias and great stands of amber primulas almost a yard tall; achilleas
like great yellow platters and tall grasses with bleached-blonde
stems (Pat makes great use of many different grasses, their leaf form
making them perfect for a windy environment) – all partnered with
the cool blues of monkshood and agapanthus (grown in the open
here), *Eryngium alpinum*, *Campanula lactiflora* and the old blue double
Geranium pratense, which grows so well in Orkney.

Alan calls the potentilla 'the rose of Orkney' because of its range
of colours – the hybrids range from cream and yellow through
apricot and terracotta to pink and red – and indeed in their habit
and the form of their flowers the potentillas have much in common
with mound-forming roses like the *Pimpinellifoliae*, especially the pale
cream Dunwich rose, and with some of the taller species roses like

'Canary Bird' (*R. xanthina spontanea*) or *R. hugonis*, the pink *R. willmottiae* or the slightly salmon-tinged *R. farreri persetosa*, few of which will flower reliably in the Orkney climate. The potentillas also have the advantage over the species roses of a much longer period of flowering – many will remain in bloom from late May to autumn – and keep their colour here, not bleaching in the sun. Roses on the whole do not do well in Orkney: even the *Pimpinellifoliae*, native as far north as Caithness and perfectly hardy here, ideally need a better-drained site than many Orkney gardens can provide. Among the garden hybrids, only the Albas (the hardiest of our European roses) seem to thrive: in almost every one of the old gardens I visited here I saw the same lovely old double white scented Alba – albeit with its beautiful healthy blue-grey foliage often pruned by the wind to the height of the surrounding shelter. Among the species, *R. glauca* (syn. *rubrifolia*) – usually grown for its foliage in any case – does well, and there are spectacular examples of *R. moyesii* and *R. sweginzowii*. But it is the Rugosa roses that really do well. They seem immune to the wind. Both the species and its cultivars are found everywhere in Orkney as a mainstay of those indispensible shelter belts that surround every garden. The species is indigenous to Japan. I wonder who it was who first introduced them here? Suckering madly, their strong prickly growth and brilliant crinkled green leaves instantly recognisable, they seem to shrug off everything the Orkney climate can throw at them.

But grass is what Orkney grows best. The cool moist summers, abundant light and deep rich soil were the key to the Orcadians' financial success as cattle breeders – until BSE came along. Although the animals raised here are virtually organic, living on the rich hay meadows of lowland Orkney, all cattle breeders in the UK were tarred with the same brush. Times are hard. But Alan will survive, as Alan's father survived when dairying collapsed after the war. There were 60,000 wartime troops stationed here then, and nearly 150 milk producers. Now there are 27.

It was through dairying that Alan met Elaine Bullard. She came north from England fifty years ago to work for the Claymore

Creamery on the outskirts of Kirkwall. Her house, Toftwood, is down in the valley below Bendigo. At this latitude, position and aspect are vitally important. Alan's land up on the brae is almost frost free but it also has the wind; Miss Bullard down in the valley has shelter but she also has the frost. When I visited her earlier in the day before climbing up to Bendigo to see Alan, she explained how Roy and Mary's land on South Walls, for example, was favoured by its south-west slope despite its extreme exposure to wind and salt spray, demonstrating for me the importance of the angle of the sun by pointing to the shadow of her walking-stick, already far longer in late August than it would be in my garden at home in Shropshire.

Trees are Miss Bullard's great love, especially the native trees of Orkney. She fights a fierce battle on behalf of all Orkney's native plants, now under twin attack not only from new farming practices – such as the 'improvement' of grassland, or the replacement of oats by barley which smothers the native weeds of cultivation like corn marigold and poppy – but also from the growth of garden centres. They have been responsible, for example, for the widespread use of a single imported hybrid willow (*Salix* × *calodendron*) for windbreaks all over Orkney, in place of the much more interesting and diverse native species. All the native species – which range from the grey willow (*S. cinerea* ssp. *oleifolia*), the largest of the Orkney species, with shiny dark green oval leaves, grey beneath, through the eared willow (*S. aurita*) with lovely yellow male pompoms and the tea-leaved willow (*S. phylicifolia*) with its shiny brown bark to the creeping willow (*S. repens*) with its trailing branches of silvery leaves, and the tiny dwarf willow (*S. herbacea*), hardly even a shrub, with neat reddish catkins held above the leaves – have round or oblong leaves, never the long narrow ones of the hybrid. When the Scottish natives are included, like the dwarf woolly willow (*S. lanata*), the downy willow (*S. lapponum*) and the distinctive net-leaved willow (*S. reticulata*) with its dark green netted leaves, the choice of willows hardy in Orkney runs to more than two dozen. But the garden centres do have their uses: only one female plant is known in the wild of the very rare Orkney alpine willow *S. alpina*, but both male and female plants are now available commercially and make good plants for the larger rock garden. Miss Bullard is by no means against the use of non-native plants in Orkney gardens, but given that many Orcadians have never even seen the native tree species, so long is it since they disappeared from most of the Orkney habitat, she wants to encourage gardeners here at least to consider them as an option. In such terrain, gardens can be a refuge for plants as well as people.

At Toftwood she has made a woodland garden on a patch of ground near the house where she grows all the tree species native to Orkney in a wonderful tangle with introduced species which she is trialling for use in Orkney gardens. She uses the garden to teach people about trees: 'I can't go about as much as I used to,' she says, 'so they have to come to me now.' She emphasises once again how important it is to grow things from seed using local clones which will be better adapted to the conditions here. And she explains how trees are pack animals – forest species which need to grow in large numbers, especially here on Orkney where they can give one another shelter from the wind. Over the years she has been the inspiration for many plantations around the island, following in a well-established but little acknowledged nineteenth-century tradition: she tells me about the very old plantation of European larch on Eday, its massive trunks lying against the hill almost like huge shrubs; the Balfour wood planted on Shapinsay in 1847, planned to include one of every known north European tree, the horse chestnuts now the largest in Orkney; the upper and lower wood at Binscarth, planted between 1850 and 1865; the numerous plantations in Harray.

'And they say we can't grow trees!' she says scornfully.

That night, as I stood with Alan on top of the brae at Bendigo, look-ing down the black waters of Scapa Flow towards Hoy, I reflected again on the importance of gardening friends – Judith and Elsie and the members of the Hoy Garden Society; Rowena and Alan, one of the few gardening couples I met on Orkney; Murray Sinclair and John Hawgood whom I was to visit the next day; Pat and Alan and

Miss Bullard – and how we are all sheltered and nourished by the encouragement and support of our gardening friends. I thought about the different things each had brought to the relationship and how the cross-fertilisation made for something new and good: Judith bringing an innocent eye and lack of preconceptions, Elsie a source of good plants and accumulated wisdom; Pat with the sophistication of the English gardening tradition, Alan with his desire to create something new and tailor-made for Orkney. And I thought about the 'laying-on of hands': the way a single individual like Miss Bullard can affect the way dozens of others respond to their environment, each one of those in turn affecting dozens of others, until a whole generation looks at things in a new way. I was learning a lot in Orkney, and not all of it about gardening.

Drawings of plasterwork at Melsetter (pp. 216 and 217), doorway at Melsetter (p. 219), *Primula scotica* (p. 223), devil's-bit scabious (p. 224), grass-of-Parnassus (p. 225) and Orkney landscape (above) by Simon Dorell.

Myosotis

FERGUS GARRETT

The genus name, *Myosotis*, is derived from the Greek words for mouse and ear and refers to the soft erect leaves, resembling the ears of a mouse. The origin of the common name forget-me-not is not so clear. Many of us, sentimental in nature, would like to link it to the tragic tale of a chivalrous knight, clad in heavy armour, slipping into the torrents of a violent stream while picking a few of the gem-like blooms growing along the water's edge. As he is carried away he casts a handful of flowers onto the bank, crying 'Forget me not!' to his helpless lady. This tale is well-known in German folklore, and Coleridge popularised the name in his poem 'The Keepsake' in the early nineteenth century:

> …Nor can I find, amid my lonely walk
> By rivulet, or spring, or wet roadside
> That blue and bright-eyed flowerlet of the brook,
> Hope's gentle gem, the sweet Forget-me-not!

Without doubt the plant described is *Myosotis scorpioides*, the water forget-me-not. A favourite of poets, this pretty little flower has in the past been regarded throughout Europe as an emblem of eternal friendship and love, supposed to have the virtue of ensuring that those wearing it will never be forgotten by their lovers. More prosaically, it could perhaps be thought that the bright azure blue flowers with their yellow eyes, once seen (especially *en masse*), are never forgotten.

The genus *Myosotis* contains about fifty mostly temperate species. All are annual or perennial herbs with alternate, hairy leaves and small salver-shaped flowers that are predominantly blue, pink, or white, though sometimes yellow or even brown in some New Zealand natives. The perennials are rather short-lived, and for garden use are usually grown as biennials.

Myosotis scorpioides is a hardy perennial European species common in Britain in wet habitats. The flowers are striking and borne over a long period from May to August, making this a valuable border plant for bedding out or permanent planting. Like many in the genus, *M. scorpioides* likes rich living and for good results needs regular splitting and renewal. The variety 'Mermaid', with deeper blue flowers on thick stems, is well known.

Common garden varieties are mostly forms of *Myosotis sylvatica*, the wood forget-me-not. A native of most of Europe through to Turkey and north-west Iran, growing in open woodland, it is popular as a biennial. Pale blue flowers (without the yellow eye) are carried in open sprays from April to June. It is excellent either as a bedding plant or when allowed to self-seed, and there are more than twenty seed strains currently on the market. Compact varieties have been developed, but sadly the grace and elegance of the parent seem to have been lost in the breeding process. Pink and white forms are useful, though not as popular as the blue.

Myosotis alpestris (*M. sylvatica* subsp. *alpestris*) is very closely related to *M. sylvatica*, and also a parent of many garden hybrids. It is now very rare in the wild in Britain, being confined to a few damp woods and meadow sites in northern England and Scotland.

Forget-me-nots are strongly associated with the English cottage garden style, to which their propensity to self-sow lends itself perfectly. They cover the bare ground in spring, but also form a unifying theme throughout the garden. The blue flowers hugging the ground make an excellent foil for other plants, like the acid-lime-green euphorbias and the rich reds and oranges of tulips such as 'Red Georgette' and 'Ballerina'. Not difficult to grow, they will thrive in any good garden soil as long as there is plenty of moisture (especially for *M. scorpioides*). Powdery mildew can be a problem in dry conditions, but in general not till the end of the flowering season. Forget-me-nots are extremely sensitive to nutrient deficiencies, and can therefore be useful as indicators of problem areas. Poor soil conditions will cause stunted growth and discoloration of the leaves to yellows and reds. Under stress the flowers often change colour from blue to pink, and this very often happens when plants have been moved while in full flower.

Propagation is simple: *M. scorpioides* comes readily from basal cuttings in early spring or in the autumn, and the rest are best from seed sown in April, May or June. For bedding purposes seed can be sown in boxes in a cold frame, pricked out, grown on in pots, and then planted in the autumn. If you already have a good seed-bank of forget-me-nots in the garden, then they are best allowed to germinate of their own accord in open ground (which they do over a long period). Seedlings must be thinned to allow individual plants to develop. A well-grown plant of *M. sylvatica* can be as large as 15 in (40 cm) in diameter when in full flower, so space between plants is essential to avoid congestion. Autumn is a good time to thin and transplant, and the best of the thinnings come in very useful for moving into bare areas. The danger always is that of leaving in too many; spacing them at about 12 in (30 cm) apart seems to work well. Transplants must be well watered-in, especially if the plants are large and leafy.

At the end of their flowering season plants can be pulled out as soon as they become tatty or mildewed. Don't worry about the seed being ripe; forget-me-nots have such a long flowering season that by the time they have lost their looks enough seed will have set for next year's stock. Easy and rewarding, these plants deserve a place in every garden.

Drawing by Simon Dorrell.

Plas Brondanw from its Gardener's Perspective

IL N'Y A POINT DE HEROS POUR
SON VALET DE CHAMBRE (Mme Cornuel, 1605–1694)

DIANA ROSS

*It was for [Plas] Brondanw's sake that I worked and stinted, for its
sake that I chiefly hoped to prosper. A cheque of ten pounds would come
in and I would order yew hedging to that extent, a cheque for twenty
and I would pave a further piece of terrace. I had indeed come to reckon
all my small earnings in terms of forestry catalogue prices...*
Sir Clough Williams Ellis, 1883–1978

By 1958 Sir Clough had been earmarking his hard-earned cash in
this fashion for almost half a century. This was the year Ron
Roberts turned up at the remote village of Llanfrothen in the heart
of Snowdonia, where Plas Brondanw is situated, because he was
courting – 'sniffing around', as he succinctly puts it – his future
wife. Twenty-one years old, about to leave the regular army that
had been his life since he was fourteen, and with little hope of
finding a job in that close-knit farming community, once married
Roberts soon found himself at a loose end. He took to wandering
aimlessly up and down the gloomy lane that makes its way past Plas
Brondanw and into the mountains beyond. As it happens, Plas
Brondanw is not a typical garden of its period, is not altogether
shut in on itself: only a low stone wall separates it from the road as
you approach the garden from the village. Which is how Roberts
spied Bowden, Sir Clough's gardener at the time, at his work, and
in due course, having got into the habit of dropping in for a chat
occasionally, took to lending the old man a hand, if only to stave off
his wretched boredom. Actions have consequences: Bowden
eventually retired, and Roberts, vague now as to the actual date,
found himself in full-time employment.

Sir Clough, he believes, wanted a dogsbody, but he must surely have spotted the man's intelligence and thought him a worthwhile investment even if he might have to wait a bit for a return on his money – because, says Roberts, 'In those days if you showed me a carrot and an asparagus I could tell you which was which. Otherwise I hadn't a clue.' Plas Brondanw is renowned for its topiary but even the word, let alone its execution, meant absolutely nothing to a man who had spent his formative years painting some things, saluting others, and – the sum total of his gardening experience in the army – digging over his Colonel's wife's garden with a table fork as a punishment for failing in either duty, if he did not find himself in the glasshouse, a term he had to explain to me: I thought it referred to the horticultural variety, which would have been useful.

Forty years on, his old boss dead these twenty years and the vegetable patch he was obliged to master (with reluctance) long since reverted to sheep pasture, Roberts is, mercifully, left largely to his own devices. He feels fortunate in this, saying he wouldn't in any case take any notice of anyone telling him what to do, a fact which made life difficult when Sir Clough was around and handing out precise orders every morning before he set off for nearby Portmeirion, his other fanciful creation. Lord Lambton, reviewing a book about the aesthete Edward James years ago, remarked of him that he was the kind of man who told his gardener what to do. Clearly, with a man like Roberts there would be little point. Interestingly, though, when it came to the baffling business of the topiary Sir Clough left Roberts to work that one out for himself, merely advising him to leave a rounded dome at the top of whatever shape he was after making so that if it didn't work he could always turn it into a column. The result is an odd assortment of forms you feel must represent something if you could only think what. Presumably Sir Clough wasn't bothered. What Sir Clough *was* 'funny' about, according to Roberts, was straight lines – he did not like them. Sir Clough liked his hedges 'dented': Roberts likes them straight. He hopes to have the straightening-out process, surreptitiously embarked upon even before Sir Clough had died, completed before he retires.

To the end of his life his boss went on ordering yew, box, beech, fir and lime trees from forestry catalogues, with the result, Roberts reckons, that if you laid the material out flat it would cover four acres. Unfortunately for Roberts, it is not laid out flat.

The garden's main axis, with a view of Cnicht.

Twenty-foot-high Italian 'cypresses', for example, are actually a type of fir pruned to simulate the pencil-slimness of the genuine article, which itself would never withstand the rigours of the Welsh mountain climate. Even the less lofty hedges pose problems because the garden is so steeply raked; to reach the centre of a two-hundred-yard-long box hedge more than five feet across and at least as high he has to lean off a ladder teetering on the brink of a ha-ha wall with a six-foot drop into the field beneath. He does it, he says, on 'a wing and a prayer'.

Roberts is used to the hair-raising aspects of his job now but there was a time when, tied to his ladder, itself tied to a 'cypress', he would be physically sick from the swaying motion as he struggled to clip its flimsy tip in a gale. To get through the work-load he must start in June, and hope he's finished by Christmas; from dawn 'til dusk every day for six months of the year Roberts sets up his Heath Robinson contraptions of apple crates and ladders, ties himself on, and gets cracking: the work can – and must, if he is to get through in time – be undertaken whatever the weather. Unfortunately, lawn maintenance cannot; when the rain holds off long enough for the grass to dry out sufficiently, Roberts has to untie himself from his ladders, and haul out the mower there and then. Annoying, but an assistant would likely be more so. An accident fourteen years ago that cost him three fingers and kept him eleven months off work meant the grass was not cut once during his time away, so when he was invited recently to do a series for Anglia TV on topiary in Tuscany he turned it down because the garden would have suffered unacceptably, and now that it is open to the public every day he dare not risk that happening. 'Who's the first one they laugh at?' he asks rhetorically – 'The bloody gardener.'

Possibly Sir Clough did not fully appreciate the extent of his gardener's pride when he first employed him: there were awesome clashes. Sir Clough hated arguments; unfortunately, Roberts loves them. They managed, mostly by keeping out of one another's way: not too many men around that isolated neck of the woods able or willing to tie themselves to trees for weeks on end for someone else's sake, and few other options open to the man who was. Nevertheless, the camel's back was almost broken on one occasion when Roberts was told by his boss he had to paint 'a dead bloody tree'. It was on the hillside outside the garden proper, in full, humiliating view of the village; Sir Clough, in the way of Roberts's previous employers, liked everything not actually alive to be painted, in Sir Clough's case his trademark colour, Portmeirion Green – actually a milky turquoise – with plenty of gold embellishment. You love it, or hate it.

Meanwhile, entirely self-taught, Roberts was turning himself into the real McCoy. I congratulated him, but he would have none of it: 'You could teach a monkey in that time. You learn, don't you? If you make a cock-up this year, you don't make it next. Plus you overhear people talking in the pub, and you listen. They'll only let on so much, but for someone who doesn't know sod all about it, getting to know the basics is something.' Anyhow, Roberts believes, 'The best way to teach someone is to let them loose. I've made some terrible mistakes, but I burnt them. I'd say someone nicked it, or I'd go to the shop and buy it.' At first he 'bloody killed' half his plants by digging in fresh manure or lime. If his boss wanted to know what had happened to something, he'd say the sheep got in. Bowden never had that problem, Sir Clough would grumble. Well, no.

Considering a Welsh mountainside must be ace slug territory and that grit and grease and eggshells don't work, Roberts's peer group at the pub gave him a particularly useful tip: coat hosta leaves with soft soap. As a matter of fact, Roberts does not use any chemicals these days, except on the paths, although once he did (once we all did), and once with potentially deadly consequences. As he tells it: 'A clump of nettles outside the kitchen door was bloody annoying me so I sprayed them with weedkiller. A few days later cook says, "She's quite bad, you know." I thought nothing of it. Next day she's worse, and cook tells me she can't understand it because she's had nothing but nettle soup.' 'She' was Sir Clough's widow, Amabel, who was cultivating the nettles for that purpose. Roberts sweated it out. Amabel recovered. He never said a word.

In due course Lady Williams Ellis became Roberts's boss, remaining at Plas Brondanw until her own death ten years after her husband's, and Roberts had a chance to make up for nearly killing her: he became her chauffeur. They got on well. For one thing, she disliked flowers to the extent that if anyone sent her any she threw them straight in the bin. Roberts doesn't care for flowers either; but then, flowers only serve to gild the lily at Plas Brondanw, where Nature Herself, at one remove, plays the Vita Sackville-West role: at the end of every yew *allée* a pair of imposing turquoise-and-gold-painted gates draws attention to the savage, incomparable beauty of the wilderness beyond, and in so doing includes it in the overall design while at the same time wittily proclaiming that the chaos outside will not gain entry. In fact, white flowers only were permitted inside the gates once upon a time, and then not many: Japanese anemones; the odd azalea; and the transient blossom on a group of cherry trees carefully planted to frame a view of Cnicht, the conical, often snow-capped, Japanese lookalike of a mountain at the end of the garden's main axis.

During the couple's lifetime, the garden was altogether private; any vegetables Roberts managed to grow were for the table, and his heroic annual work on the topiary was for their benefit alone. But that was all to change. Presciently, in his autobiography *Architect Errant*, Sir Clough observed that 'It is warming indeed to see the avenues I then planted growing so flourishingly and the whole place maturing in ever-increasing beauty ... If it is movingly beautiful also to my descendants I hope that they or one of them may be able to live there. If it is not wonderful to them, then I hope it may be enjoyed by someone else who will yet think kindly of those fore-runners who spent four hundred years, off and on, in making what they admire.' His descendants still own the property but none actually live in the ancient house, whose future is still to be settled. In the meantime, the spirit if not the letter of Sir Clough's second wish has been granted: since 1993 the gates have been opened hopefully to visitors every day at nine, and closed again at five o'clock. Sadly few, perhaps a thousand in any year, avail themselves of the opportunity because Llanfrothen is not of itself worth a detour, and to warrant those helpful signposts with the brown flower a garden must already be attracting twice that number. A Catch-22 situation: without the sign no one knows of its existence, ergo the numbers will never be up to muster to merit the sign the garden needs to get its numbers up to muster to merit the sign ...

Nor does Plas Brondanw possess any of the amenities today's average garden visitor requires: no lav, no caff, no shop, no parking; only the pub half a mile down the steep lane. Perish the thought! The thousand who do find their way there are mostly made up of faithful returnees (garden photographer Alex Ramsay, gardener and writer Sir Roy Strong, the founder and editor of this journal and this contributor all put it top of their 'favourites' list). But from Roberts's point of view, being open every day is a nuisance: it means he gets no respite. In the old days, he says, 'If I didn't get round to doing something, then I did it next year.' No longer, and we are back to his point that the 'bloody' gardener will be blamed for any perceived imperfection. 'It's professional pride, isn't it?' he explains. That, and his perfectionist streak, dare I add.

As Roberts sees it, and I would agree with him, another downside to letting the public in is the perception that a garden must have colour – at all seasons, and lots of it. Many National Trust gardens have been diminished as a result. So has Kew. Rousham, thank Heavens, is privately owned. At Plas Brondanw, Sir Clough's granddaughter Mena became Roberts's boss after Lady Williams Ellis died, and Mena, desperate for visitors, feels obliged to go along with the received wisdom. Now, a massed tangle of *Hydrangea paniculata*, phormiums and hebes flops about in a long bed running parallel with the box hedge, originally designed as a simple carpet of herbs arranged in contrasting shades of green. Roberts hates the hebes, and the way the hydrangeas fade to pink. He also hates the daffodils Mena has planted in 'his' grass, making it even harder to maintain in perfect shape. And he loathes the crocosmias spreading like wildfire along the hedges. Then there were the peacocks the family thought might do the trick, which I didn't spot when I was there. What happened? All Roberts had to say on the subject was that they didn't last long. Foxes, doubtless.

Roberts once saw a cherrypicker in operation on the topiary at Levens Hall, and felt a pang of envy. But the machine cost £8,000. Fat chance! Which is why until quite recently Roberts's topiary-clipping routine went on in the same dangerous fashion as it had for the past forty years. Until, that is, his fairy godmother waved her wand, and the Health and Safety people got to hear about the lone gardener working off dangerous ladders in the middle of nowhere, without a mobile. Ever a law unto himself, Roberts had somehow slipped through their net, and they were appalled; he should have his cherrypicker, once he had been taught how to use it, and passed a test. The instructor on the course they sent him on began by assuming everyone had heard of COSHH (COSHH is the acronym for a manual entitled *Control of Substances Hazardous to Health*).

Roberts had not, of course he hadn't. 'Cosh? What the bloody hell is cosh?' he wanted to know. Now it was the instructor's turn to be appalled. But of course Roberts passed his test.

On the day of our interview, I walked through the gates and nearly tripped over a contraption collapsed like an exhausted giraffe across the small courtyard. Roberts was there, scratching his head in disbelief: his cherrypicker, twice the expected size, already fetchingly sprayed the regulation Portmeirion Green, had arrived. It was duly replaced, but the replacement rarely gets an airing either. Roberts's only concession to COSHH is to keep the mobile handy when he's working on his ladders, because he sees the sense when he remembers how 'Many a time I've been working high up in a tree and it starts swaying around and I think I'm bloody mad: I'm here very early in the morning and very late at night. It might be days before anyone noticed.'

But how the topiary gets tackled will soon be someone else's problem: retirement beckons. What will he do then when time hangs heavy, this man who scorns to grow his own vegetables because it's cheaper to go to the shops? And who, as a natural loner, observes: 'I don't mind the odd night in the pub, but there's nothing more boring than holding a bloody pint in your hand unless you're going to have a conversation or a good argument.' Even on Sundays, his day off, he prefers to sit by himself in his refuge at Plas Brondanw, away from the noise of other people's lawnmowers, surrounded by the usual paraphernalia garden sheds accumulate, as well as some they don't – fridge, cooker, radio, filing cabinet, two armchairs filched off a skip, electric shaver, and his collection of military memorabilia. Roberts retains an affection for the institution that taught him all he needed to know to cope with life, including how to swear.

In answer to my question: he has a dream. Roberts dreams of sailing a boat alone around the British Isles. The fact that he gets seasick up a ladder and has never sailed a boat in his life is neither here nor there because, as he says, 'I haven't a clue, but I'm not stupid, I'd join a sailing club and get some training. Then I'd say bye, see you! to the wife and set off.' Unlike the errant architect, whose greatest love apart from Plas Brondanw and architecture was sailing, as it happens, but who always insisted on dragging his family with him on his excursions, and once nearly got everyone drowned in the process. The wiser, if no less romantic, Roberts insists he wouldn't go out of sight of land: 'Don't get me wrong, it would have to be something I could live with. If the weather turned bad I'd tie up somewhere for three or four days and I'd go home 'til it got better.'

And when he does at last set sail, what then at Plas Brondanw? Roberts will be hard to replace: it is unlikely any one man will be able to cope with the work-load, let alone the isolation. But gardeners cost money, and the family – all too aware that going the car park and lavatories route would destroy the *genius loci* – might yet be tempted. So long as Roberts remains its guardian, Sir Clough's spirit can rest easy at Plas Brondanw, and if sometimes in our conversation his gardener sounded less than reverential about his late employer – well, no man is a hero to his valet.

Drawing by Simon Dorrell.

The Danger of Desert Gardens

SUSAN ELDERKIN

In a public lavatory in south-west Utah there is a sign on the back of the door that reads: 'Watch out for rattlesnakes, coral snakes, whip snakes, vinegaroons, centipedes, millipedes, ticks, mites, black widows, cone-nosed kissing bugs, solpugids, tarantulas, horned toads, gila monsters, red ants, fire ants, Jerusalem crickets, chinch bugs and giant hairy desert scorpions before being seated.'

If using a lavatory is a risky business in this part of the world, gardening must be roughly equivalent to a game of Russian roulette – attempted only by the most reckless, most ardent plant-lovers. When I was researching material for my novel *Sunset over Chocolate Mountains*, which is set in the Sonoran Desert in southern Arizona, I was always being given severe talking-tos by concerned locals who had caught me indulging in such dangerous activities as sitting on the ground, or picking up pieces of dead wood, or trying to eat the prickly pear fruit. And it wasn't just the locals. Everywhere I went, the desert sent out its own blatant hands-off signals. Attack it with a spade and you hit a joint-juddering layer of cement-like caliche (solidified calcium) just beneath the surface. Wrestle with a native teddy-bear cholla and you're driven to distraction for days by the tiny, invidious prickles embedded in your skin. There's no rich, brown soil to plunge your hands into; no tender green shoots to touch. To be a gardener here, I realised, you clearly have to do one of two things: either succumb to the will of this great, fierce landscape, and humbly accept that most of the decisions concerning your garden – what plants will grow, and where – will be made by forces greater than you; or flout garden convention and think laterally.

Like most deserts, Sonora is teeming with plant life. Dotted at regular intervals over the vast desert flats are the tenacious species that have evolved to cope with their inhospitable surroundings – each jealously guarding the minimum radius necessary for survival. The knobbled outcrops of prickly pear, the spindly-legged ocotillo, clumps of chain-fruit cholla and, lording it over everything, the giant saguaro (pronounced 'suwarro'), with its cumbersome and faintly ludicrous limbs rising as much as sixty feet against the searing blue backdrop of the sky. Many of them sport scars like survival badges: shredded limbs blackened by summer lightning strikes, scabby holes where gila woodpeckers have raided the water supply. Except for a few brief weeks in spring and late summer, when waxy flowers burst open in unlikely crimsons, magentas and yellows, they remain strangely still, as if this age-old landscape has conferred on them an infinite capacity for patience. In the late afternoon, long, low shafts of sunlight transform their cornucopia of prickles and prongs into gleaming, iridescent halos. At night, the bizarre silhouettes of the saguaros look like an army of calcified men marching across the plain, captured for ever in a moment of history. It is a beautiful landscape, proud and defiant in the way that only harsh landscapes can be.

My novel features two gardens – one stolen, one created. The one I stole belongs to Billy Sol Estes of Golden in New Mexico, which lies on the old highway between Albuquerque and Sante Fe. Golden was the first mining town west of the Mississippi; when the prospectors left, it became a ghost town until the 1970s, when assorted hippies on their way to communes in the hills of Sante Fe brought it back to life. Billy was – still is – one of those hippies.

There are no plants in Billy's garden, except for untidy clumps of desiccated yellow grass, a few twisted, leafless trees and the hollow arms of dead cholla cacti, rippled with holes as if they've been used for shooting practice. Instead there are bottles, perhaps a thousand of them, heaped in piles, upturned on the ends of wooden stakes bleached white by the sun, dangling from the trees and spinning from home-made parasols. When I arrived, hot and weak-limbed from a long drive, two barefoot children, Autumn and Mikey, leapt around the garden dousing it with a powerful jet from a hose-pipe, bringing the dusty bottles and vases and broken shards to glimmering life. Everywhere you looked was the flash and gleam of coloured glass – green, blue, orange, purple, red and yellow – all of it blinking and beckoning in the reflected light of the midday sun. Bottle necks threaded like a necklace along the fence chinked and jangled like goats coming down a mountain. It was a spectacular, wonderful sight, the bottles seeming no less beautiful for their lack of roots and petals, no less out of place than the unlikely cactus flowers.

Billy Sol Estes greeted me in cowboy boots and heavy concho belt, a mass of long brown curls spilling over his headband. He shook my hand and began to talk and didn't stop till I drove away three hours later. 'I know you're gonna wanna write a book about me,' he said. 'I've had a helluva life.'

This there was no denying. He told me of the gambling house in St Louis, Missouri, that he'd inherited at the age of twenty. How there was 'no sign, no booze, no customers' until the day he defended his mother from a passing insult and from then on all the Jews in Missouri poured in for his famed double egg yolks. He told me of the boats on the Mississippi, Alabama and Arkansas rivers where he worked as a chef, playing at being Huckleberry Finn. He'd moved out here in 1974 to do the Wild West thing, and a thorough job he made of it too: getting himself arrested for cattle rustling, and bootlegging beer to pay the rent. He was given the house and garden – already with a fledgling bottle collection – and played host to the trail of spiritual seekers, artists and poets en route to Santa Fe. He showed me the coral ring given him by Dennis Hopper, the turquoise necklace from Neil Young, said that Ike and Tina Turner had taught him to dance ('and when I start dancing and kicking, I'm really good'). Everyone who came left bottles behind, and Billy started creating his garden.

By his own admission, Billy is no ordinary guy. His veins thrill with a heady mixture of Greek, Basque, Dutch and Kickapoo Indian blood – and one or two nameless substances left over from the 1970s. He called me his 'blue-eyed dude', and wanted me to come back and stay in a bottle-house he'd build at the end of the garden. But underneath it all he was as serious about his garden as any gardener I've met. 'I'm not a bad guy,' he said, watching me closely through yellow-tinted glasses, 'but don't mess with my bottles, OK?'

With Autumn and Mikey darting at our feet we made a grand tour, and I pointed to the bottles that caught my eye, this one, then that one; and, like any plantsman reeling off the Latin names of his plants, so Billy told me the place and date of origin of each of his bottles, and what they once contained. The bright blue bottles that lined the picket fence like a row of roosting blue jays were milk of magnesia bottles – 'There are a lot of bottles here that were bought by people with upset stomachs,' he explained apologetically. The clear, thick bottle dangling from a juniper branch once held an orange-flavoured soda called Dream, from Texas, *circa* 1955. There were original brown Michelob bottles from St Louis, Missouri – collectors' items now, according to Billy; and there were original Heinz ketchup bottles from Pennsylvania, dated 1916. His own favourite was the Mrs Butterworth's Pancake Syrup bottle, the glass blown into the homely curves of Mrs Butterworth herself. Billy and Mrs Butterworth have a history: when, in 1989, the manufacturers of pancake syrup switched to squeezy plastic bottles, Billy went on ABC TV to kick up a fuss, and roused enough of a public furore that they switched straight back to glass.

That's when Billy's garden got on the map. People started sending him bottles from all over the States. That very night he was expecting a truck load of fifty-year-old bottles from Colorado Springs.

Even then, I knew it wasn't Billy I wanted for my book; it was his garden. When, three years later, I sat down to write *Sunset over Chocolate Mountains*, my main character Theobald Moon and his daughter are driven there by their friend, the cowboy Jersey Kozinski. In my version, the bottle garden belongs to Jersey's father, a Polish immigrant. Like Billy, he waters his garden to bring it to life, and his visitors bring empty bottles as gifts. Jersey presents his father with a collection of green Coors beer bottles – more than one man should own up to consuming by himself. The bottles tell a story that old Mr Kozinski doesn't want to hear, but he accepts them, sadly and graciously.

I created the other garden for Theobald and his little girl, Jelly-O. Theobald is an English exile who buys himself a one-acre plot just outside Tucson with the aim of starting a new life. When he's sent a photo of his land – showing a thin line of grit along the bottom with nothing on it – he wonders if he's bought a chunk of the sky. In the first few months, painfully homesick for the damp, mulchy smells of England – rotting wood, worm casts on the lawn – he naïvely attempts to transplant seedlings from yoghurt pots on his windowsill: red-hot pokers, dahlias, sunflowers. These are no sooner in the ground than they're chomped to oblivion by a pack of wild javelinas – the wild boar-like creatures with a strong, musky odour that roam these parts – and so begins Theobald's metamorphosis. Like the cacti that have evolved spikes and water-hoarding trunks, so Theobald develops his own survival strategies. He sprays his fence with a mixture of his own urine and Tabasco sauce to ward off the javelinas (scaring the living daylights out of a neighbour's tom-cat) and, rather than trying to battle with the desert, he opens up to it, learning to love the sort of Arizona garden that nature intended.

One by one the cacti introduced themselves on to the page of my novel, bringing with them their wonderfully evocative names: the pincushion cactus, the porcupine cactus, the pancake cactus, the strawberry hedgehog, the claret-cup hedgehog, the creeping devil chirinola, the beavertail cactus. As I wrote, I threw their preferences for alluvial flats or stony, limestone hillsides out the window, became careless with flowering times and colours. Sometimes I didn't know exactly what it was I was planting in Theo's garden at all. Hell, I wanted them for their names – not their ability to perform! The novelist in me rubbed her hands in delight and shoved the garden journalist firmly to one side. I had Theo hack through the caliche with a pick-axe and plant two desert willows, one either side of his mobile home. He rakes a winding, stony pathway through the cacti and indulges in a few carefully placed Zen stones. And in the middle of the garden he clears a space in which he can practise yoga every morning, before the heat of the sun gets up.

Although Theobald Moon never gets over his fear of 'creepy-crawlies' with stings in their tails or teeth, I'm happy to say that his love of gardening doesn't kill him. But it changes him. And that, perhaps, is the biggest risk a gardener takes in this part of the world: letting a bit of the desert into your soul.

Drawing by Simon Dorrell

With Malus Aforethought

PERPETRATED BY
MARTA McDOWELL

Gardening can be murder. Mystery writers from Agatha Christie to Rex Stout have enriched their plots with horticulture's dirty little secrets. What is it about the garden that makes it a suitable spot for murder? Maybe it's the gardener's malice towards weeds, rodents and other garden undesirables? Or the mythic struggle between good and evil first played out with Eden's slithering snake and a garden backdrop?

Like all mysteries, those that are of the garden variety require a crime, a cast of suspects, and a sleuth. Many famous detectives have exhibited horticultural propensities: Brother Cadfael had his herbs [see HORTUS 29], Nero Wolfe grew prize-winning orchids, Poirot tended his *potager*.

Ask a friend to describe the traits of a detective, and they'll probably suggest 'observant', 'logical' and 'clever'. But detective fiction, and even the word 'detective' are recent inventions, products of the Industrial Age. Edgar Allan Poe's short story *Murders in the Rue Morgue* (1840) featuring French *chevalier* C. Auguste Dupin is credited with being the first mystery. Let's have a look at a few of the classic heroes and their interests in plants.

The original British sleuth and also the first with a horticultural bent is Sergeant Cuff, introduced in *The Moonstone* by Wilkie Collins. Often heard whistling 'The Last Rose of Summer', he says, 'When I have a moment's fondness to bestow, most times the roses get it. One of these days (please God) I shall retire from catching thieves, and try my hand at growing roses.' At one point in the plot, Cuff gets his wish and withdraws to the country. The narrator describes the scene: 'After ringing at the bell, I peered through the trellis-work, and saw the great Cuff's favorite flower everywhere; blooming in his garden, clustering over his door, looking in at his windows. Far from the crimes and the mysteries of the great city, the illustrious thief-taker was placidly living out the last Sybarite years of his life, smothered in roses.' At the end of the book, Cuff temporarily returns to active duty to take part in the story's denouement.

Say 'deerstalker and pipe' and any mystery buff will automatically respond 'Sherlock Holmes'. The most famous fictional detective – and, since his emergence on the scene in 1887, the most enduring – shares Sergeant Cuff's love of the genus *Rosa*. In *The Naval Treaty* Holmes waxes philosophical: 'Our highest assurance of the goodness of Providence seems to me to rest in the flowers. All other things, our powers, our desires, our food, are all really necessary for our existence in the first instance. But this rose is extra. Its smell and its colour are an embellishment of life, not a condition of it. It is only goodness which gives extras, and so I say again that we have much to hope from the flowers.'

Another hero who retires to the pleasures of the garden is Richard Hannay, brought to life in 1915 by author and later Canadian Governor-General John Buchan in *The Thirty-Nine Steps* and induced to perform his last cloak-and-dagger feats in *The Three Hostages*. After the first World War Hannay had married, bought an old manor and restored the lawns and borders: 'I felt that I was anchored at last in the pleasantest kind of harbour.' When his old Foreign Office superior asks for help with a case, his calm is disturbed. 'I lit my pipe and started on my usual tour of my domain, but nothing seemed quite the same. It was a soft, fresh morning with no frost, and the scillas along the edge of the lake were like bits of summer sky. The moor-hens were building, and the first daffodils were out in the rough grass below the clump of Scotch firs . . . But I didn't feel any more that it was really mine, only that I was looking on at a pretty picture. Something had happened to jar the harmony between it and my mind, and I cursed Bullivant and his intrusions.'

If you were to gain admission to Nero Wolfe's New York City brownstone and make your way up to the fourth floor, you would find his penthouse plant rooms with their twenty thousand orchids. Wolfe is an irascible, sedentary private investigator who works to eat and to cultivate his epiphytes. He spends at least four hours a day tending them with Theodore Horstmann, his horticulturist. Created by Rex Stout in 1935, Wolfe solves crimes and acquires knowledge from the outside world via the legwork of his sassy, street-smart sidekick Archie Goodwin. Goodwin in return, in the course of narrating the thirty-three novels and thirty-eight novellas which chronicle Wolfe's career, also describes the orchid *aficionado*'s techniques for everything from hybridisation to fumigation. Recounting a discussion of a plant disease between his 'boss' and a nurseryman, Goodwin says: 'Wolfe looked sympathetic, and he really was sympathetic. Between plant growers a fatal fungus makes a bond.'

Hercule Poirot is the only fictional detective whose death was honoured by a front-page obituary in the *New York Times* (6 August 1975). The dapper, diminutive and moustachioed Belgian speaks fondly of raising his vegetable marrows. His 'little grey cells' encompass horticultural expertise, demonstrated in such books as *Sad Cypress*, *Yellow Iris* and *How Does Your Garden Grow?* Poirot was Agatha Christie's most productive protagonist, appearing in eighty-seven works spanning five decades.

A later but equally well-known Christie creation is Miss Jane Marple. The elderly, unmarried denizen of the village of St Mary Mead is an amateur detective who in addition to being a birdwatcher and knitter is an inveterate gardener. In *They Do It With Mirrors*, Christie writes: 'Gently eluding her hostess the next morning, Miss Marple went out into the gardens. Their condition distressed her. Surveying the herbaceous border, Miss Marple clicked her tongue vexedly and pulled up a flourishing plant of groundsel.'

Dorothy Gilman gives us another geriatric sleuth with green

fingers, Mrs Emily Pollifax. In adventures recounted first in *The Unexpected Mrs Pollifax*, this widowed matron sidelines her prize-winning geraniums and gives up her New Brunswick, New Jersey Garden Club to unravel mysteries for the CIA.

In the wake of the classic heroes from the Golden Age of detective fiction a new generation of gardening mysteries has, if you'll pardon the expression, cropped up. John Sherwood, a retired BBC executive, writes a horticultural mystery series starring Celia Grant, botanist, nursery-owner and amateur sleuth, under such titles as *Green Trigger Fingers* and *Botanist at Bay*. China Bayles, a defence lawyer turned herb-shop owner, made his debut in Susan Wittig Albert's *Thyme of Death* and reappears about every other year in a new herbal title. A woman landscaper in Blossom, Oregon unearths solutions to crimes in Mary Freeman's novels which include *Deadly Nightshade*. Nathan Walpow, the real-life president of Los Angeles's Sunset Succulent Society, has invented a hero smitten with cactus, of course. Another entertaining series was launched by Colorado's Ann Ripley with *Mulch*. Ripley's heroine is a freelance garden writer who knows her Latin names, though she has been known to describe a villain as falling into the thorny arms of a *Pieris japonica*: horticulturists who enjoy uncovering bloopers could tell her that all *Pieris* are *inermis*.

The mystery genre adheres to a basic formula: motive and method are required. Typical motives for murder are greed, revenge and jealousy. Which gardener among us has not suffered from plant lust? As for method, a killer can have a field day in the garden. Poisons abound in the potting shed, alongside an armoury of sharp, heavy implements, while a typical perennial border can be a living cross-reference for a dictionary of toxicology.

It was while working as a pharmacy assistant in a hospital dispensary during the First World War that Agatha Christie got to know her poisons, and they were her favourite means of murder: victims in more than half of her novels succumb to toxins. One is done in with taxine tea, tea laced with an extract of yew berries. The pathologist, speaking to Inspector Neele, comments: 'Don't think I've heard of a case where it was used deliberately. Really most interesting and unusual. You've no idea, Neele, how tired one gets of the inevitable weed killer.' Yew makes a lovely backdrop to a perennial border, but please don't eat the *Taxus*.

Foxglove (*Digitalis purpurea*) appears frequently in deadly doses. Digitalis extracts can be used to treat heart disease, but can also be fatal when ingested indiscriminately. In one Christie short story, foxglove leaves are substituted for sage in the duck stuffing. One guest at the table was – well, a sitting duck.

Foxglove isn't the only culprit in the spectrum of botanical chicanery, and Dame Agatha isn't the only author with a penchant for poison. The castor oil plant (*Ricinus communis*) makes a statement in the garden with its bold nine-foot mound of foliage, but it can stop people in their tracks in other ways too. In one of her plots, Martha Grimes substitutes castor oil beans for espresso beans to top the after-dinner sambuca of an intended victim. It's a perfect ploy, since castor oil beans must be chewed or otherwise nicked to release their poison. Be wary if you sit down to a meal prepared by a Grimes villain: they also favour lacing saccharine and horse-

radish with monkshood (*Aconitum napellus*). In a chronicle of Brother
Cadfael by Ellis Peters, an ointment made from the ground root of
monkshood in a base of mustard and flax-seed oil is added surreptitiously to a dish of pheasant.

The potting shed, that gardener's chemical arsenal, is the source
of many bottles bearing the skull and crossbones. In one Christie
short story, Miss Marple says: 'I know that I've got wasps on the
brain. Poor things, destroyed in their thousands – and usually on
such a beautiful summer's day. But I remember thinking, when I
saw the gardener shaking up the cyanide of potassium in a bottle
with water, how like smelling salts it looks.' Poisoning with
pesticide-dipped fruit and a shower from a pesticide-laced water
tank is the *modus operandi* of a murderer in Reginald Hill's aptly-
named *Deadheads*.

The lure of the whodunnit is the chance the reader has to catch
the guilty party, since detective fiction's rules of fair play call for
clues to be as available to the reader as they are to the sleuth. The
garden provides fertile ground for plot devices. In a John Sherwood

novel, the noose tightens when a suspect uses a genetically engineered virus to treat a greenhouse full of cyclamen. In *The Estate of the Beckoning Lady*, Margery Allingham uses the language of flowers to create a trail of clues, and in *Sweet Danger* she uses another botanical device when Albert Campion, her erudite, urbane sleuth, looks for a verse said to be carved on an ancient tree. The tree is long gone, but luckily the pertinent slice of trunk, with doggerel intact, is found in the tower of the mill.

In one short story, Hercule Poirot notes with interest a suspect who has been scratched by an old garden rose, the Bourbon 'Zéphirine Drouhin', but he isn't fooled by this horticultural red herring. In another, he finds the key clue in the garden, where one bed is partly edged with shells. It seems strychnine was added to oysters, to knock off an old aunt and avert the discovery of an embezzlement. Poirot explains: 'But there remain the shells – they must not go into the bucket. The maid would see them. And so you thought of making an edging of them to a bed. But there were not enough – the edging is not complete. The effect is bad – it spoils the symmetry of the otherwise charming garden. Those few oyster shells struck an alien note – they displeased my eye on my first visit.'

Gardens are tailor-made for mysteries. They can be sinister, gothic or strangely quiet. What better place for a visit by that man with the scythe? They are perfect for the scene of a crime or as a place for hiding a body. Just consider the expression 'pushing up daisies'.

In *An Unsuitable Job for a Woman*, P. D. James uses an estate, Summertrees, and its gardener's cottage as the setting for the murder. Here are Cordelia Gray's first impressions of the grounds: 'The garden suited the house; it was formal to the point of artificiality and too well kept. Even the rock plants burgeoned like morbid excrescences at carefully planned intervals between the terrace paving stones. There were two rectangular beds in the lawn, each planted with red rose trees and edged with alternate bands of lobelia and alyssum. They looked like a patriotic display in a public park. Cordelia felt the lack of a flag pole.' Contrast this with the gardener's cottage: 'In the short time in which he had lived here Mark Callender had created a little oasis of order and beauty out of chaos and neglect. Old flower beds had been discovered and the surviving plants tended; the stone path had been scraped free of grass and moss; a minute square of lawn to the right of the cottage door had been cut and weeded.'

Flower shows also make appearances as mystery venues. In *Passing Strange*, the annual Almstone Horticultural Show is marred by inaccurate judging of the tomato category, and things get worse when a victim is found strangled with floral wire. As author Catherine Aird notes, 'The life of a Flower Show secretary had never been a bed of roses.'

Reading murder mysteries is an excellent off-season vice. I find that they are a bit like working in the garden: they start with tangled chaos and end, at least for a moment, in an ordered universe. And while the butler may have done it, I'm happy to say that, at least in fiction, the gardener rarely has.

BIBLIOGRAPHY

Catherine Aird, *Passing Strange* (1981)
Susan Wittig Albert, series beginning with *Thyme of Death* (1994)
Margery Allingham, *The Esate of the Beckoning Lady* (1955), and *Sweet Danger* (1933); later published as *The Fear Sign*
John Buchan, *The Three Hostages* (1924)

Agatha Christie, *A Pocket Full of Rye* (1953); *Appointment with Death* (1938); *The Blue Geranium* (short story, 1932); *Herb of Death* (short story, 1932); *How Does Your Garden Grow?* (short story, 1939); *Sad Cypress* (1940); *They Do It With Mirrors* (1952); *Yellow Iris* (short story, 1945)
Wilkie Collins, *The Moonstone* (1868)
Sir Arthur Conan Doyle, *The Naval Treaty* (short story, 1893)
Mary Freeman, series beginning with *Devil's Trumpet* (1999)
Dorothy Gilman, series beginning with *The Unexpected Mrs Pollifax* (1966)
Martha Grimes, *Jerusalem Inn* (1984)
Reginald Hill, *Deadheads* (1983)
P. D. James, *An Unsuitable Job for a Woman* (1972)
Ellis Peters, series beginning with *A Morbid Taste for Bones* (1977)
Ann Ripley, series beginning with *Mulch* (1994)
John Sherwood, series beginning with *Green Trigger Fingers* (1984)
Rex Stout, *Black Orchids* (1942)
Nathan Walpow, series beginning with *The Cactus Club Killings* (1999)

Illustrations taken from *Amateur Gardening*, (May 4 1929) and *The Country Gentleman's Estate Book*, (1911).

The Garden of Eden in Venice

JOHN HALL

The Garden of Eden is the largest private garden in Venice. It occupies about four acres on the Giudecca island, on the southern lagoon side, between the Redentore and the Zitelle. It is bounded to the north by the high wall of the Casa Penale Maschile del Lavoro, formerly the Convent of S. Croce, and at its eastern end by a lower wall beyond which are vegetable gardens and vineyards extending in the direction of the Cipriani hotel. The long southern side looks out over the lagoon in the direction of the island of San Clemente, formerly the Mental Hospital, opened as a de-luxe hotel in the summer of 2003. The western boundary, which includes the *palazzina* and two small buildings, is a wall down onto the Rio della Croce.

From the time of the garden's creation by Frederic Eden between 1884 and 1900 until the death of its penultimate owner, Princess Aspasia of Greece, it was a well-maintained and much-loved centre of Venice's international social scene. Badly damaged by the flood of November 1966, the garden was in decline after the death of Princess Aspasia in 1972, in spite of a rearguard attempt at restoration by Elizabeth Gardner. After being bought by its last owner, the Austrian painter Hundertwasser, in 1979 the garden turned into an uncontrolled and, after his death in 2000, an uninhabited wilderness, virtually invisible from outside: no public *vaporetti* pass its lagoon frontage, the only point from which one might see into the garden were it not for the overgrown shrubs and trees blocking any view. The garden is now owned by the Gemeinnuetzige Stiftung, a charity in Vienna endowed by Hundertwasser to encourage his social-political-artistic-ecological views, among them that Nature should be unrestrained : *Il ne faut pas jardinier mais laisser faire la nature. Pratiquer la végétation spontanée. Tout laisser pousser sans jamais couper. Il est urgent de dialoguer avec nos jardins, de signer un traité de paix.'* There is no present intention of selling the garden, nor of letting anyone in, even though in 1946 it was listed as a National Monument. It doesn't have the resident custodian who in Venice can usually be persuaded to allow discreet access to the most private places. The garden can be entered today only through the exhilarating writing of Frederic Eden, some passages in the poignantly sad autobiography of the last Queen of Yugoslavia, and the accounts of their many visitors.

A golden age of the garden was undoubtedly the era of Frederic and Caroline Eden, from whom its name derives. Frederic Eden, born in 1828, died in 1916, was a second cousin twice removed of Sir Anthony Eden, briefly Prime Minister of England in the mid 1950s; his wife was the sister of the garden designer Gertrude Jekyll. Frederic Eden came to Venice in 1880 as an invalid: 'one floated in a gondola without pain or stress that were from me exacted by Bath chair or carriage'. He was idly rich, with thwarted energies, and craved distraction. 'I'm sick of all this water. Get out and find me a garden,' he said petulantly to his gondolier, showing signs of 'some of the selfishness of chronic invalidism', as Laura Ragg, wife of the chaplain of the English Church, put it. In minutes the gondolier Eugenio was back, standing on the bridge of the Rio della Croce with Pietro 'Ortolano', who showed them into the neglected property. 'I fell in love at once.' He bought the 'garden' in 1884. In 1903 *Country Life* published his account of what he did there – *A Garden in Venice*, now a rare collector's item. The book details Eden's progress in designing and planting the garden, both the practical undertakings and the aesthetic and philosophical thinking behind them.

A recent aerial photograph of the garden

The 'estate' had for a century been in use as a fruit and vegetable garden. It was divided by axes, straight or intersecting paths, with semi-abandoned vegetable or flower plots between the lines. It reminded Eden of a favourite castle and garden in Ross-shire, with its high wall to the north, a prison in place of the castle, and water (lagoon rather than trout stream) to the south. Eden was faced with the design problem posed by such a large, flat space. He was aware of the traditional architecturally-structured gardens of Rome, the Alban Hills and Pliny – all on sloping sites, and not suitable models for Venice. He constructed a water-tank, twenty yards by five and six feet deep, bordered with red Verona marble, inspired by the Generalife at Granada – almost the only feature of his garden to survive. 'It was necessary to have tender regard for the genius of the place' – making a virtue of this necessity he tidied up the existing paths, bringing boatloads of seashells from the Lido in place of gravel, and erected pergolas to cover the paths.

After considering various materials for the pergolas – iron, sawn wood, stone – he chose the evanescent Venetian tradition of using poles of pollarded willow, in the manner of the trellises so favoured in English Arts and Crafts gardens. 'In such a garden as ours, the six or seven hundred yards of pergolas built of solid brick or stone would be utterly out of character.' The verdict of time would surely go against this missed opportunity to create a noble and lasting layout, especially since the expense would not have mattered to him. The pergolas were planted with vines. 'In a warm climate there are few things more enjoyable than a stroll, even in August, under a vine pergola. You walk in deep shade, the fierce sun held outside, the big bunches of grapes, black and purple, yellow and golden, all the promise of a rich harvest, hanging down to touch your hat, to blob your nose, feast your eye and tempt your lips.' Bordering the paths were masses of very English flowers.

Exuberance in growth and abundance in flower, scent and fruit were Eden's priorities. 'Probably the joy of a garden lies, more or less, in its health; one loves to see things grow as if they liked it. To see colour in masses, depth of shade, bloom in profusion, glorious promise and bountiful flowering – these are the characteristics that the soil . . . will give to those who ask it.' Building the momentum and crescendo of a romantic symphony, he proceeds to name with enthusiastic tenderness the plants and fruits, describing their in=dividual beauties month by month, season by season. 'If the man who makes two blades of grass grow where one grew before deserves well of his fellows, surely' he who turns plainness into beauty should be put on a pedestal for worship, and, better, for imitation.' Visitors admired particularly the massed blooms of roses, rambling and climbing in profusion, an idea inspired by a garden in Battaglia, south of Padua, and the lilies which bordered some of the pergolas. 'On some evenings they even drive us in from the garden, their scent is so overpowering . . . they grow so grandly that we often have heads of fifteen, sixteen and even twenty flowers on a single stem, of sometimes five and a half feet high.' Photographs of the pergolas and lilies were used by Gertrude Jekyll in two of her books, and in Alethea Wiel's article on the garden in *Country Life* (July 21, 1900).

Eden describes with detailed fascination how the clay walls of the traditional well in the courtyard of the *palazzina* were repaired, and with even more satisfaction the enterprise of a cunning well-maker from the Polesine whose team he brought in to sink an artesian well. After drilling through the lagoon mud, a salt water table and then hard stone, and experiencing a few gaseous explosions, they reached enough water for his garden, though its ferrous quality killed the fish and the lilies in his tank.

The only horrific episode occurred the morning he saw huge barges discharging mud and rubble beneath his lagoon-facing wall. The Municipio were making improvements in the city, piling up broken bricks and mortar from demolished houses to reclaim an expanse of mud bank for a new housing development – between the Eden garden and its lagoon view. The only solution was for Eden himself to buy or rent the *sacca*, as such reclaimed land is called. With every variation of push and pull, diplomacy, patience and tact he first obtained a three-year lease, and got it extended to nine years after he spent money covering the *sacca* with earth and planting it with vines and lucerne. Then another six years was granted, and finally he was able to buy it. 'We are deeply grateful, as I think all foreigners who live in Italy may be, for the reception given them in small things and great by the Italian authorities and people.' This new territory increased the Eden garden by a third, the old sea-wall marking the division now running diagonally from west to east between the old garden and the new *sacca*-garden.

The last two chapters of *A Garden in Venice* follow the pattern of Varro, Columella and the ancient Roman agronomists, classifying and describing the animal hierarchy of the estate, from his unsuccessful experiments with live gardeners, Italian and Scottish – in the end Eden joined the English tradition and did it himself, as Head Gardener at least – to his affectionate ownership of milk-cows – Luna, Perla, Stella, and others – on through Ligurian bees to birds, butterflies, snails, and down to the friendly earthworm. Only a careful examination of the sepia details of the two photographs of Frederic Eden extended in his deck chair reveal the six small animals sitting on his lap. Writing of his dachshunds, 'co-proprietors of the garden', he asks 'What would the garden be without them: their skins like satin, their manners of perfection, their temper,

The Palazzina

which yields each to each other, without a growl, the bone they have done with.'

Rarely does such an enthusiastic, unpretentious, observant, thoughtful and humanly-fallible character emerge from a book, as if it were a living voice, even from such a book, so beautifully papered, printed and illustrated. Occasional pleasingly unexpected and personal revelations occur. Fruits can turn his thoughts to desirable females, as when he compares greengages to their darker sisters: 'the black gage, dark blue without and golden green within, in the fullness of flavour as a brunette of the south to a flaxen-haired German'. Mulberries evoke the stained lips of young ladies. Less sensually, he compares the choosing of the willow-pole pergola to the choosing of a wife – you need to decide what you want from it/her. His *rapport* with his gardeners, with the *furlani* who maintained the pergolas, with the well-diggers, with his neighbours the monks of the Redentore, was never condescending. Of Italy and

Italians, he spoke for many of us. 'There is no country where a foreigner will meet with such kindness and civility from the people of every class – a people, too, to whom snobbishness is unknown.' He finished his book by praising gardening. 'There is no pursuit, as has been found by big men and small, that will so readily and healthily take a man out of himself and away from his pain and grief, physical and moral. God Almighty, Bacon tells us, planted a garden. What can we do better, who can so little do, than humbly yet lovingly strive to make another.'

Making the garden coincided with Eden's recovery of health, described by Charles Quest-Ritson in his book *The English Garden Abroad*. 'According to Lady Paget, Frederic Eden spent nine years in atrocious suffering, completely bedridden until the doctors gave him up. Caroline Eden then administered gout powders made by some nuns in Pistoia, and he made such a miraculous recovery within three months that Lady Paget did not recognize the "healthy, burly, red-faced man" who rushed into the room and shook her warmly by the hand.' There are many descriptions by visitors of the beauty and social accessibility of the garden, and undoubtedly part of its charm was the character of its owners. As Alethea Weil wrote of Caroline Eden, she 'seemed to be the *genius loci*, the animated creature who gave spirit and splendour to the beauties which surrounded her. Her *gentilezza* and affability in welcoming and saying goodbye to every kind of visitor, of every age and nationality, of every social position and of every temperament were such that her presence and conversation were one of the attractions for guests and were worthy of the beauty of the place.'

After Caroline's death in 1928 there is no record of alterations, developments or garden-philosophy to compare with Frederic Eden's book. Interest in the garden becomes focused on its association with members of the Greek and Yugoslavian royal families in their exile, the sad background – the bereavement of Princess Aspasia, and the increasing trauma of her daughter Alexandra – adding a sombre dimension to memories of the garden. In 1919 Aspasia, a commoner of distinguished family, had married Alexander I, King of the Hellenes, morganatically, for love. Less than a year later the king died of an infection following a monkey bite sustained as he tried to separate a favourite dog from an angry monkey in his park zoo. Aspasia, pregnant, had no desire to live, or to give birth. Alexandra never knew her father. Major James Horlick of the Coldstream Guards, who had been with the British Expeditionary Force in Salonika while Alexander was king and had met Aspasia while she was working for the Greek Red Cross in Constantinople, acquired the Eden Garden after Caroline Eden's death, and ceded it to Aspasia. James Horlick was clearly a garden enthusiast, for he became a gold medallist of the Royal Horticultural Society and creator of the Achamore gardens on the Scottish island of Gigha. The Horlick family and Aspasia and Alexandra remained close friends, and the Horlicks provide some incidental information on the garden. James inherited the Horlick baronetcy in 1958, and a nephew of his son writes: 'My uncle John [he became 5th Bt when Sir James died in 1972], who is now dead, said that he personally liberated the Eden garden (where he spent all his summer holidays) when he was a lieutenant in the Coldstream Guards in 1944. I don't think that any fighting was involved. The garden was used as a rest home for the Brigade of Guards.' He also reports that 'Aspasia had had a little house built beside the canal that you can see as you look over the wall into the garden. It is a copy of one of the gate-houses at Greywalls in Scotland, where I live. Greywalls was a Horlick house.'

Aspasia ruled the Eden garden from 1928 until her death, living in the *palazzina* from spring to autumn, often with her daughter Alexandra. A strong character, Aspasia survived her personal tragedy and invested energy and imagination in the Eden garden. She improved the *palazzina*, building a loggia over the front courtyard onto the garden and another attached to the end of the building, overlooking the canal. 'Mummy had built a real home for us in the beautiful garden in Venice, a little villa, just as I wanted. This was a home, a small, a lovely and a real home – and it was all ours,' wrote Alexandra in her autobiography *For a King's Love*. Later she describes the beautifully furnished inside of her bedroom; Frederic Eden never once mentioned the inside of the *palazzina*.

'Since I am one of Queen Victoria's great-grandchildren, I seem to be related to most of the royal families of Europe,' wrote Alexandra, touching on an issue of European power politics in the First World War period. It was the Greek monarchy's equally close family connection with the English and the German royal families that led to British intervention in Salonika – and to Major Horlick meeting Alexander and Aspasia. The chronically unstable Greek politics of the 1920s and 1930s saw abdications, republics, restorations and exiles. 'What is an exile and why are we exiles?' Alexandra asks her mother Aspasia on the first page of her autobiography. Their situation explains the list of European royal and aristocratic visitors to the Eden garden in the 1930s, recorded by Francesco Basaldella, historian and chronicler of the Giudecca, in his books _Giudecca_ and _Spinalonga_: the visitors' book took precedence over garden matters. When the Second World War came Aspasia and Alexandra had to leave Italy, entrusting the property to their gondolier and his wife, Emilio and Italia Basaldella, Francesco's parents.

In London Alexandra, highly-strung and insecure, fell in love with the young King Peter of Yugoslavia. He was just 18, she 21, and they were married on 20 March 1944. King George VI was best man. The Horlicks lent them a house near Ascot for their honeymoon, and Alexandra was shocked to find that her husband slept with a loaded gun beside the bed. 'Yes – I always have a gun with me – you'll find them littered all over the place.' His father had been assassinated in Marseilles in 1934. It was in 1944 that Britain reluctantly decided to support the Communist partisan Tito, which resulted in Yugoslavia becoming a Communist republic. In spite of the birth of a Crown Prince, Alexander (in Claridges), the marriage was doomed. Alexandra wanted love and domesticity; King Peter's priorities were his crown and his people. 'I'm a king without a job, and the only job I know is how to be a king. They've been training me for monarchy since I was born.' As he recorded in his autobiography, _A King's Heritage_, dedicated to 'my brave people of Yugoslavia', his energy and interest were devoted to the politics of a king in exile determined to return and rule. In the index of his autobiography there are no references to Venice or the garden there.

Aspasia soon returned, and noted that 'fifty AA gunners had occupied our tiny house during the war, three AA guns were still in the garden and the whole property was in a dreadful state. But our gondolier and his family were still there, safe and sound and delighted to see me.' In 1949 Alexandra too returned to Venice, desolate. 'Stateless – homeless – we didn't want you – you may be murdered – you bring danger . . .' were her frightened thoughts. 'Our Eden garden is a very lovely place. But lovely places can hurt one unbearably when one is unhappy, and Venice, more than anywhere, can tear at my heart.' The Venetian daily paper *Gazzettino* caught a moment of reconciliation in 1952, in a glamorous photograph of King Peter and Queen Alexandra, both looking elegant, happy and royally relaxed, being rowed away from the Eden garden in a gondola by Emilio Basaldella. But there was to be no happy ending. 'You don't want me to be king and I'm determined to be one' was how Peter encapsulated the dilemma they faced. Alexandra began talking to herself: 'I did not want to live any more.' She was found unconscious on the floor of her bedroom. Another picture in the *Gazzettino* of a few years later shows the *palazzina*, and marked with an arrow is the window of the bedroom where Queen Alexandra had again been found unconscious. Again she recovered, but continued to live an unhappy life with a wandering mind. She died in Eastbourne in 1993; King Peter had died in poverty in Los Angeles in 1970. Princess Aspasia died in Venice, a dignified end to a dignified life, in 1972.

In the absence of records, it may perhaps be assumed that it was Aspasia who formalised the area in front of the *palazzina*, where the Edens' superabundant plantings must in time have invaded the little courtyard. A large square space beyond the new loggia was established, with a round fountain basin in the centre and three low brick containing walls, each with a central opening marked by elegant brick piers carrying statues. Another low brick wall established an avenue from the other end of the *palazzina* leading the eye into the distances of the garden, with a pair of piers with statues marking the entrance, at a right-angle, to the avenue leading to the Water Gate in the old sea-wall onto the lagoon. In her authoritative book *Il Giardino Veneziano* Professor Mariapia Cunico says that Aspasia enriched the already extensive botanical collection in the garden, planting typically Mediterranean species – arbutus, olives, myrtles.

The Eden garden was ravaged by the great flood of November 1966 and never reinstated. Elizabeth Gardner of New York described how in 1976 she 'had the good fortune to live in the *palazzina* and to begin the restoration of the garden from the condition of abandon in which I found it'. In her book *The Gardens of Venice* Mary Jane Pool says the garden was 'brought back to its former vigour', but the Hundertwasser Foundation in Vienna commented that when Hundertwasser (a friend and neighbour of Queen Alexandra) bought the garden in 1979, it was in a ruinous state. Hundertwasser at first wanted to let it grow into a wilderness, in line with his maxim quoted earlier, but subsequently planned to restore the original state of the garden, and added numerous plants.

Professor Cunico refers to a building directly facing the internal façade of the *palazzina* which was knocked down to allow sun into the side courtyard. It is not clear whether this was done in the Edens' time, or Aspasia's. In fact, mystery surrounds the whole question of buildings being knocked down without record. Today, in addition to the *palazzina* there are the copy of the Greywalls gate-house, a larger building on the corner of the lagoon which Hundertwasser chose to inhabit, a lean-to shed against the eastern wall with some Hundertwasser ceramic tiles embedded in a column, and the remains of a greenhouse up against the prison wall. Professor Cunico writes that Aspasia eliminated the Edens' new cowshed, 'built partly within the walls of a pleasaunce house of the Patrician . . .' What pleasaunce house? What happened to 'the gardener's cottage' photographed for Eden's book, and is it the same building illustrated in Francesco Basaldella's *Spinalonga*, described there as the old *casino* of Caterina Sagredo Barbarigo? Careful scrutiny of the photographs in *A Garden in Venice* shows a building between the land entrance and the *palazzina*. It is not there now. And where is 'the Moorish kiosk set in the very heart of the luxuriant vegetation' referred to in Mary Jane Pool's *Gardens of Venice*?

With the help of a German-speaking friend and months of direct communication with Mr Harel of the Gemeinnützige Stiftung in Vienna, warming gradually from e-mail to live voice, we were allowed to visit the Garden of Eden on a sunless afternoon in February 2003. At that time of year, growth was at a standstill. A maintenance team had clearly been brought in from time to time to keep the land under control, but no plants – roses, wisteria, jasmine, honeysuckle – were visible, only trees. Many had been felled and sawn into piles of logs. One bare and forlorn trellis-pergola ran down the centre, from nowhere to nowhere. Statues remaining on their piers were not properly aligned, others lay on the ground. The old Istrian-stone Water Gate onto the lagoon, with niches and statues on each side, lay broken on the ground. Still attached to the inside of the old sea-wall were three marble plaques marking the graves of dachshunds – Cocky, Jerry, Bisetta. From the building on the lagoon corner where Hundertwasser lived, an open stone conduit leading from his WC inside ended poised over the first of a descending series of stone basins – his personal ecological sewage system. Small, enduring remnants of the past: Eden's tank and Aspasia's round fountain-basin, both dry, and Aspasia's formal arrangement of brick walls, piers and statues.

As Charles Quest-Ritson concludes, referring to English gardens abroad, 'gardens are linked to individual lives. Time and again it is the people who shape them . . .' Walking in the desolate remains of the Eden garden, one was very much in the company of Frederic and Caroline Eden, of Princess Aspasia and Queen Alexandra and their enthusiastic guests and visitors, and of the nature-loving Hundertwasser. The 'garden' is hidden and inaccessible; if not in good order, it lies fallow and in good heart. Who knows what may be its next lease of life?

Postscript
Thanks to the affectionate energy of Marie-Thérèse Weal, Frederic Eden's book *A Garden in Venice* was published in her own French translation in 2002 and a facsimile edition of the original is now available from Frances Lincoln (London, 2003).

Drawing on page 267 by Simon Dorrell. The decorations on pages 262, 272 and 274 from *A Garden in Venice*.

Ridler's Garden

ALEX DUFORT

'Box balls are two a penny,' murmurs Tony Ridler, as we survey his terraces of clipped greenery to the rear of 7 St Peter's Terrace, Swansea. Even at two a penny, there must be at least a fiver's worth strewn about the yew enclosures of this high-walled labyrinthine retreat, just a few yards from the South Wales railway line. Hundreds of feet of dark hedge, laid out in intimate courtyards, form the backdrop to a garden of deliberately limited colour range. Again and again we observe, in subtly differing seasonally dependent configurations, arrangements of yew, Portugal laurel, box, santolina, cotinus, griselinia, geraniums, hellebores, tulips and dark grasses, interspersed with sculpture and rusting cubic lead-fringed steel planters. Squares and circles abound. Sometimes the box is cut in helices, sometimes spirals, occasionally it is plucked and distorted, its stark angular tendril-like stems casting contorted shadows on matt black walls; but the shapes you notice first are balls, hundreds of box balls.

Tony's life of successive moves, from spacious apartment to tiny terrace house, has seen his ratio of living space to garden swing from infinite to negligible. A graphic designer with a flourishing business, he and his wife Caroline lived as a pair of sophisticated city dwellers with little thought for outdoor spaces until the early 1980s. Then Caroline's great-uncle died, and 7 St Peter's Terrace, one of three tiny adjacent houses, was offered to them. Caroline's father lived at Number 5, and all three had narrow strips of rough ground to the rear, making an overgrown half-acre of assorted pigsties, chicken coops, vegetable plots, and a duck pond. Tony remembers it as 'a very informal space'.

For Tony's father-in-law, the back of Number 5 was a headache, and he was content to hand it over, as were the landlords of Number 9 on the other side. Initially Tony tried a *rus in urbe* approach over the allotments, creating a 'crazy, chaotic, comfortable,

easy and natural scene, planting reeds in an organic-shaped pond and laying curvy paths.' But the 'Capability' Brown approach didn't wholly satisfy him. 'I had been reading Roy Strong's books on small formal gardens, visiting Hidcote, clocking it all up and putting it to one side. So I thought we'd just do one small formal space at the back of the garden. And that was it: I was hooked. It was straight-forward, it was easy; I was more at home planting in fours or sixes or eights, and it just went on from there, developing bit by bit, linking things together in straight lines. There was no overall ground plan as such, it just developed over a number of years.'

That initial yew courtyard measured about twenty feet square and sat oddly in the natural space that surrounded it. 'It looked so alien, in that informal setting, so it needed to be sorted out – either it's all going to go formal, or it's not – and it all went formal. I couldn't mix the two.' So Tony started planting dozens and dozens of yews. 'Yew was the easy option; any colour looked a million dollars against the yew; that gave me the confidence to carry on.

And it's still, dull and leaden, which I like, and I was keen to have a structure here during the winter as well.'

Of course, the extraordinary proliferation of hedges and terraces, narrow walks and tiny courtyards required another ingredient – the disposition to maintain as well as to create, to spend every available hour clipping and trimming, weeding and mowing. And it is the combination, in one gifted individual, of the enjoyment of creation and the love of maintenance that makes Ridler's Garden so special. Tony's graphic design work consists, in his own words, of 'shuffling papers and looking at screens all day long'. His garden is an alternative working space. He regards its development as a way of creating leisure: paradoxically, the leisure of work. 'I need to be outside, playing the garden. I need to have that interaction with real work.' And so, as he extends the hedges and develops the topiary, he creates for himself what some would regard as a Herculean task – but he sees it as an opportunity for more enjoyment. 'Weeds aren't a problem; weeds are part and parcel of "playing the garden";

I love weeding. There are no highs and lows in the garden. It's not as if I'm on a quality job today and I'm weeding tomorrow; there's no hierarchy.'

The garden has a feeling of stillness about it. Sitting under the weeping ash one has a sense of permanence, of architectural longevity. Yet one is also aware that without its creator moving quietly about, clipping here, weeding there, the garden would rapidly descend into irrecoverable chaos. 'It does take a lot to sort out, it's not at all organic, and I'm fighting all the time against nature. I'm trying to keep it under control, sort it out.'

We look up at the sky, a dark yew rectangle framing the changing colours and clouds of this perfect evening. Shafts of sunlight fringe the hedge and play on the foliage. I remark that Tony has managed, unconsciously, to create his own multiple version of James Turrell's *Airmass* (a thirty-foot cube from within which visitors gaze at the sky through a huge roof opening). 'Yes, there are no views outwards, I've made that more and more obvious. It's inward-looking. There are no landscapes to compete with.'

Tony is keen to describe his terraces as an entirely private enterprise, created and maintained to satisfy only himself. 'It's an antisocial, selfish, personal space; I garden for myself, absolutely totally for myself. And there is no compromise here. Whereas in the office there may be compromise, occasionally (and I say 'occasionally'), this is my space, I'm not here to please anybody else. I didn't say the word 'control-freak' at all, though people have called me that, with all the topiary and the hedges, and the cutting and the clipping.'

Paradoxically again, for this reclusive man, Ridler's Garden is occasionally open to the public under the National Gardens Scheme (see end of article for dates and times). 'I wanted people to say "What's going on here?" or "Why on earth do you do that?" I don't want an easy ride; I do enjoy a bit of banter. As people come round, I do have to answer a few questions; it does provoke a bit of commentary. So I'm playing to that.'

One understands him a little better as he talks about his graphic design work. He aims to make his brochures and reports look

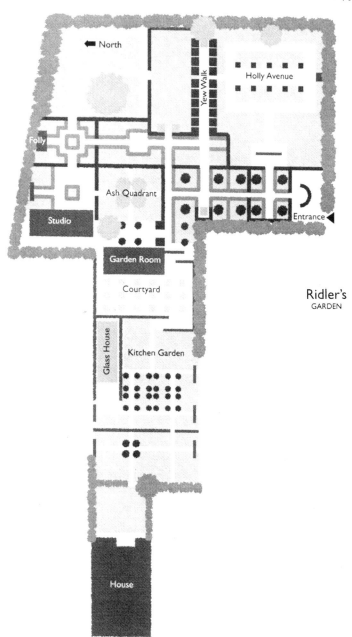

North

Yew Walk

Holly Avenue

Folly

Ash Quadrant

Studio

Entrance

Garden Room

Courtyard

Ridler's
GARDEN

Glass House

Kitchen Garden

House

undesigned. 'All the shine has gone. We are all calming down; we go matt; we go dull, we go quiet and understated; we quieten things down; we try to be seen not to be seen. There's so much clutter in the business, so I am very austere in what I do. I was always taught to convey the message from A to B as simply as possible, and it's the same with the garden. I'm clearing out now: less is certainly more comfortable. Just having that nothingness, quiet uncluttered space, is such a luxury. Not to plant is just good. You're doing so much by not planting.'

We look out at the sparse yew rectangle. The only planting is a fringe of santolina against black lily grass. 'This is full. I would prefer a more austere space. As soon as the leaves drop, I'm out here prefer a more austere space. As soon as the leaves drop, I'm out here picking them up. It just annoys me that they're filling up the rooms; I just want to pare back and simplify things.'

The intimacy of the spaces he has created reminds me of the Imperial gardens of Beijing's Forbidden City, small, close spaces where the Emperor and his family could live on a human scale, shutting out the grandeur of their formal world. These yew court-yards exert a powerful, mysterious force. Their structure is readily understandable, the planting simple, yet an enigma seems to hang over them. As Tony talks, I try to formulate my thoughts; but the more he explains, the less I seem to understand. I am reminded of *Alice in Wonderland*; his explanations, while making a kind of sense, only serve to deepen the mystery. He creates and finds it good. He is alone in his garden but shares it, he develops it for himself alone, yet with people in mind. It is a place to work when work is over. Perhaps the answer lies in his reply to my question about permanence. 'The whole garden's quite temporary, it's only good as long as I'm playing it: I tell the kids they can flatten it when I'm gone. It's a temporary blip.'

Two hours have fled by, and I make my excuses. Tony picks up his shears, and as I walk down to the house and turn to wave he is already at work on his box, clipping a faint staccato against the evening birdsong.

Drawings by Simon Dorrell.
Garden Plan by Tony Ridler.

The Age of Guano

CHARLES ELLIOTT

One warm evening in August 1830, a sea captain named Smith exhibited a small pile of brownish-yellow powder to a meeting of the Massachusetts Horticultural Society in Boston. It was, so the Society's historian later recorded, 'a kind of manure from Peru, called by the Spaniards "guano", then a novelty here.'

Guano did not remain a novelty for long. It was already being talked about, and within twenty years had come to be regarded as 'indispensable . . . like a necessary of life to us'. By then the question was no longer whether or not it was an effective fertiliser – gardeners and farmers in America, Britain and on the Continent were universally convinced of its near-magical powers. The only problem posed by guano, it seemed, was how to get more of it, preferably at an affordable price.

Today, when all manner of chemical fertilisers are readily available for our choosing in sacks and boxes and bottles lined up in long rows in every garden centre, it is difficult to imagine the enthusiasm, bordering on desperation, with which guano was received. The demand was enormous. In fact, over the relatively short course of what we may call the Age of Guano, this pungently unattractive substance was responsible for trade wars and shooting wars, the creation of monopolies, smuggling, huge profits, the passage of laws, diplomatic *contretemps*, and considerable cruelties, to say nothing of forgery and other fakery on a large scale. But it also ushered in the modern system of intensive cultivation and the use of artificial fertilisers. Not a small achievement for a pile of bird dung.

Because that's exactly what guano is. For hundreds of thousands of years, on a variety of off-shore rocks and small islands where sea birds roost and breed, their droppings built up and dried into layers sometimes hundreds of feet thick. In the case of the best guano, that found on the Chincha Islands just off Peru, all the main elements required by plants – nitrogen, phosphorus and potassium

– are present in concentrated and readily available form. Peruvian farmers had made use of guano from time immemorial, but it was not until 1804, when the explorer Alexander Humboldt took a sample back to Germany and had it tested by chemists and by a potato-growing English friend on the island of St Helena, that anyone in the outside world had an inkling of its virtues. And even then these virtues were mysterious. A basic understanding of plant chemistry was still lacking, and remained so until the German scientist Justus von Liebig finally published his *Organic Chemistry in Its Application to Agriculture and Physiology* in 1840.

What was clear to many farmers was that *something* had to be done to restore the dwindling fertility of their soil. Certain particularly voracious crops such as tobacco and cotton had reduced to practically nothing the value of many farms in the American mid-Atlantic and southern states; in the older states in the north, matters were scarcely better. In the once-rich Genesee valley of New York State, for example, average corn yields had dropped from thirty bushels an acre in 1775 to eight in 1845. In England, farmers were discovering that traditional farmyard manure was simply not adequate to boost the production of turnips, an absolutely basic crop. All sorts of fertilisers came in for trial, from salt to sawdust to bones, but with few exceptions the results were disappointing.

The first small shipments of guano, a few casks, made their way to the US and England in the 1830s. Results of tests in both countries were exciting. Before long a combine of English and Peruvian businessmen had secured a monopoly on 'mining' and shipping guano from the Chincha Islands, and the rest of the globe was being scavenged for other sources.

Everybody wanted it. In England, the Earl of Derby bought a whole shipload and was so delighted by the results that he became a propagandist for guano. In Virginia, a farmer reported growing wheat 'high enough to hide a dog' on exhausted land that had been treated with two hundred pounds of guano per acre; wheat on the neighbouring untreated field 'wouldn't hide a chicken – not even an egg'. The Prague Agricultural Society began promoting its use, and in upstate New York, the Shaker seedsmen of New Lebanon discovered that guano not only increased production but improved the quality 'of seeds of all descriptions . . . to an astonishing degree'. It did wonders for turnips and was even said to bring on repeat-flowering in roses.

Fortunately, a little guano went a long way. This meant that it could be used on fields too remote to be fertilised with bulky farmyard manure. But it had its drawbacks. It was tricky to handle – gardeners and farmers were advised to avoid breathing the dust, and at least one man died when he inadvertently swallowed some. The worst drawback, however, was the cost. In 1842 the Peruvian government nationalised its guano resources, and thereafter effectively controlled the price. Peruvian was the choicest variety – unlike competing guanos discovered elsewhere, off Africa, in the Caribbean and the Pacific, it retained a high nitrogen content thanks to the rainless climate in which it was formed. The British monopoly-holders shipped most of it to England and the Continent, making enormous profits; what little reached the United States was increasingly expensive too.

It was a recipe for trouble. In both Britain and America, frauds blossomed like chickweed as ingenious shysters pushed adulterated versions spiked with sawdust, rice, meal, chalk, sulphates of lime or magnesia, salt, sand, earth, peat or water. Low-grade guano that had never seen the Chincha Islands passed as blue-ribbon stuff, while agricultural manuals warned buyers to 'buy none but Peruvian' and offered simple tests alleged to reveal fakes. But the demand continued – according to some estimates, up to the 1850s four times as much Peruvian guano could have been sold in the United States as was available.

There were inevitable political repercussions. At one point in 1852, a Boston businessman with empty ships returning from Gold Rush California caused an international incident by attempting to load Peruvian guano, without permission, from some islands up the coast from the Chinchas (he was discouraged by a Peruvian gunboat). In the UK there were protests in Parliament about price-fixing, and year after year farm interests pressured the US government to do something to bring down the cost. It was all to little effect; neither Peru nor the monopolists had reason to make concessions when the money was flowing in at such a rate. Only brute force – a military seizure – might do the trick, and nobody was up to that. According to historian Jimmy Skaggs, by 1856 Congressional committees had investigated the guano problem no fewer than nine times. The upshot was the passage in that year of an extraordinary piece of legislation. The Guano Islands Act (which incidentally remains in effect to this day) was intended to encourage the discovery and exploitation of deposits other than Peruvian by giving any American finding one the right to it on a monopoly basis – with the claim backed up by the US Navy if necessary.

The act led to claims on dozens of islets and reefs around the world, projecting an American presence all the way across the Pacific. It also led to the production of a good deal of guano, though of a kind less desirable than the Peruvian because most of its nitrogen had been leached out by local rain. By this time, how-ever, the fertiliser world was changing. New ways of making artificial varieties and of stepping up the potency of more common substances such as rock phosphates meant that demand for high-priced prime guano was falling off. British farmers were beginning to realise that cheaper sorts were perfectly good for turnips, which didn't need the nitrogen. And it was becoming obvious that the magic powder was not the whole answer; such old-fashioned supplements as animal manure were also needed to maintain a good soil structure.

In any case, the Chinchas were running out. Vast as the original guano deposits had been ('inexhaustible', said one confident observer in 1853), over the course of thirty years more than ten million tons had been excavated and shipped abroad, often under extremely unpleasant conditions, by ill-paid or slave labourers. The trade brought vast sums into the Peruvian treasury – estimates range up to nearly twenty million pounds (over £1 billion today) during the 1850s alone – whence it was for the most part corruptly siphoned out again. In 1864 a newly bellicose Spain seized the islands from Peru and held them for two years. Finally, in 1868, shipments from the Chinchas ceased. The Age of Guano was coming to an end. By

1910 an agricultural scientist could write that 'guano is now largely a manure of the past'.

Still, it was a long time before the term 'guano' dropped out of common use among gardeners and farmers. Most early twentieth-century garden guides mention it, although the substance itself was no longer widely available. The real thing is still being produced in small quantities on the Chinchas under controlled conditions aimed at protecting the seabirds' nesting cycle, mainly for Peruvian use. Elsewhere around the world a few deposits are being worked, but most of the first-rate nitrogenous guano is gone. Some claims under the American Guano Islands Act have had exotic subsequent histories – at least one in the Caribbean ended as a secret CIA base for shipping arms into Nicaragua. As recently as 1998 a Californian entrepreneur laid claim under the Act to Navassa Island, an uninhabited rock near Haiti that was long ago the scene of a murderous uprising by guano miners; it is unclear whether he intends to excavate guano or hunt sunken treasure – possibly both. Although the deposit is distinctly marginal so far as quality goes, there's said to be a market for Navassa guano in the citrus orchards of Florida.

Lighting the Touch-paper

ELSPETH THOMPSON

PLANTS HER SPRING-FLOWERING BULBS

All around the house – on my desk, on tables, in dark cupboards and under cardboard boxes beneath the beds – are pots, jars and bowls of budding, sprouting things. Come the depths of winter, when the curtains are drawn at four o'clock and trips out into our little London garden much more rare, my gardening tends to move inside. When there are no flowers to pick, and few at the florists' worth having, I get real cheer from pots of early-flowering bulbs dotted all about the house. Some of these, such as species tulips or the rarer dwarf iris with their intricate painted faces, have much more love and attention lavished on them inside – at eye level – than they would outside in the ground. I can imagine few things more beautiful than the little pan of *Iris winowgradowii*, its palest primrose petals splashed and spotted with darker yellow and blue, that distracts me from my writing when it comes into bloom in late January.

Some organisation is needed to keep a successive supply going right through the winter months, and the groundwork begins in autumn. First off the mark are the forced bulbs that can survive without soil and will provide the earliest blooms. I always do twenty or so hyacinths in forcing jars – they still need at least eight weeks plunged in the dark to develop good root systems, so I frequently miss the chance for that elusive Christmas bloom. I have a good supply of the plain clear forcing jars but have started collecting the coloured ones, made in the 1950s in gorgeous shades of amethyst, chartreuse and dark green, which can occasionally be found for a song in unsuspecting junk shops. Though I tend to stick to white flowers rather than the ubiquitous baby pinks and blues, I've been won over by the rich jewel-like colours of recent introductions such as 'Woodstock' (purply-red) and 'Peter Stuyvesant' (indigo-blue flowers on a deep bronzy stem), which make striking combinations with my new coloured jars. These are the bulbs that are secreted in cupboards and under beds until the nub of embryonic flowers can be clearly seen between the emerging leaves. Remove them too soon and they'll be all leaf and weak, wayward flower.

'Paperwhite' narcissi are the other early treats, and need no spell of darkness to work their magic. I used to pot these up in soil, but since seeing them grown on pebbles in a stylish shop in New York many years ago I now do the same, raising them in clear glass bowls of water where I can watch their white roots snaking round the pebbles to anchor them in place. In a warm room, the bulbs can take as little as five weeks to flower, and that cloud of scented starry white blossom seems a reward quite excessive for the paltry amount of effort involved. I often give bowls of 'Paperwhites' as presents, timing the planting so the shoots are a couple of inches high (two weeks' growth) when the gift is required.

The two-hundred-odd bulbs I order every year are ranged in single layers in the dark and cool of my basement area potting shed until required. Bulbs that need soil are potted up a little later in the autumn, when I set aside an entire day for the mildly messy process, with good supplies of plant labels, sharpened pencils, hot soup and Radio 3 to hand. I love this job, but only if there are no unwelcome interruptions or inconveniences. In the absence of a greenhouse in London, I tend to work on the kitchen table unless, as happened this year, the weather is warm enough to tempt me outside. For me, there is something unfailingly cheering and hope-filled about potting up bulbs – it even helped me through the death of a much-loved dog one sad October. As the leaves of one year are yellowing and falling all around, it is heartening to be lighting the touch-paper of next spring's growth. From the minute the bulbs are placed beneath their blanket of soil and watered in, these little nuggets of concentrated life will be silently and imperceptibly stirring, working towards their moment of glory in a few months' time.

Planting bulbs in pots is a lot less tiring than setting them in open ground. There's also considerable fun to be had in matching the different types, varieties and colours to the right pot or container. I have a collection of pretty old painted Italian mugs – too

Muscari azureum

cracked or lacking in handles to be usable for their original purpose, but great for just one hyacinth bulb, or a cluster of sky-blue *Muscari azureum*. The varying blues of the different grape hyacinth varieties look particularly good in blue-and-white patterned china. Some of the containers are cracked enough to allow good drainage, but I find I can get away with using bulb compost and a layer of charcoal chippings at the bottom of the pot. You just have to check that the pots don't get waterlogged.

Though undeniably at their finest in swathes on a lawn with the low winter light shining through them, crocuses can look wonderful in little pots along shelves or on bedside tables. I try a few new varieties every year – last year it was *C. chrysanthus* 'Gipsy Girl', butter-yellow feathered with brown – which looked surprisingly good in a little brown teapot, and I'm also very fond of 'Blue Bird' (white, with aster-blue outer petals) and 'Advance' (straw-yellow with outer petals flushed lilac). Early dwarf irises are another treat for bleak January and February – I particularly love the delicate markings of 'Katharine Hodgkin', the vibrant electric purple of *I. histrioides* 'George', and the sultry charms of the green and black 'widow's iris' (*Hermodactylus tuberosus*), which flowers a little later, in April – and last winter I was thrilled by the white and pale-yellow blooms of *I. bucharica*, with its strappy, grey-green leaves.

Though they are somewhat unreliable in pots, I can never resist planting a few snake's head fritillaries (*Fritillaria meleagris*) and hoping for the best – in one favourite Chinese green-glazed pot, they come up year after year like a meadow in miniature, and I love to study their exquisite chequerboard markings at close quarters.

Closer inspection also pays dividends with species tulips, with *Tulipa turkestanica* (several creamy pointed bells to a stem), *T. humilis* 'Persian Pearl' (cyclamen-purple with a yellow base) and 'Little Beauty' (rosy-purple shading to moss-green at the centre) as perennial favourites. These I tend to plant in bog-standard plastic or terracotta pots and then plunge them into something more decorative – a purpose-made cache-pot or an old gilded soup tureen – once the buds are showing. I've found that keeping the potted bulbs outside (with a covering of chicken wire as protection from thieving squirrels) reaps the best results: bringing them inside too early again results in excessive leaf-growth at the expense of the blooms. It's easier to stagger their flowering in this way, too.

It's a lovely moment when the time comes to bring a pot of bulbs inside. Pride of place is the kitchen table – or else on the desk where I write. It feels such a privilege to witness the buds burgeoning and opening in front of my eyes. I am reminded of a passage from May Sarton's *Journal of a Solitude*, one of my favourite books: 'When I am alone the flowers are really seen; I can pay attention to them. They are felt as presence . . . They live and die in a few days; they keep me closely in touch with process, with growth, and also with dying. I am floated on their moments.'

Drawing by Simon Dorrell

The Best Teacher a Gardener can Have

GRAHAM GOUGH DESCRIBES
THE MAKING OF A MODERN GARDEN
IN THE SUSSEX COUNTRYSIDE

"A fabulous assortment of . . . plants is stitched in to this late-season tapestry: pewterlike and dark-purple sedums, tawny heleniums and rudbeckias, gold and apricot day-lilies, opalescent aconitums, pearly penstemons, lapis-blue salvias, and ember-red and orange kniphofias held like sturdy torches among the drumstick seed heads of earlier-flowering plants."

From David Wheeler's editorial in Hortus 67.

If the saying that first impressions count most held any truth, our initial visit back in 1998 to view the small Victorian cottage known as Marchants and its two-acre field would have ended much faster than it did. The problems seemed myriad. Since we – myself and my partner, textile artist Lucy Goffin – were neither of us country people, we were not familiar with the term 'poached' as referring to anything other than illicitly acquired game, but as we struggled to negotiate the desperately uneven ground underfoot its meaning in this particular context became clear. A broken drain spewed the stinking contents of the sewage tank to which it was attached into the field, and nearby a Ford Fiesta car was quietly decaying in a bower of bramble, dock and nettles. The deep thatch of neglected grass in the bottom paddock rose to knee-level, penetrated only by seed-bearing dock stems forming threatening swathes and drifts in all directions. But as we stumbled across that Sussex field something compelled us to lift our eyes towards the South Downs, some four miles away to the south, where their gentle crest formed an unbroken line from east to west without interruption or cadence. These same rolling Downs had been my playground during the school holidays, and had cast their spell on Lucy while she was living in nearby Newhaven – the town of my birth, as it happened. Standing together in this seemingly desolate field – the rendezvous-point of parallel but unshared experiences – we felt a profound sense of homecoming, and we knew that our dream of creating a beautiful garden and nursery could at last become a reality.

That reality came closer still when, two months later, Number 2 Marchants Cottages, a small Victorian labourer's cottage built in 1873, become our home. The cottage sits at the highest point of the property and the field falls away in a gentle slope to our southern-most boundary 200 yards distant, giving wide and unrestricted views of the Downs. The widest point, also at the top, is about seventy paces across, while the narrowest point, at the bottom, is thirty-five paces. To the glider pilots who fly the thermals above us Marchants must look in shape like a wedge of Cheddar cheese with the 'nose' removed.

A large empty field may not appeal to every gardener as a

starting-point but for us it was a prerequisite, enabling us to approach our project with a clear and unrestricted vision. Despite its inherent problems, there was no time at which we were daunted by the task in hand; and if no fully-formed 'grand design' emerged in the early stages we were at least equipped with a few (if basic) design principles, and day by day our confidence grew. So confident were we in fact that it was not long before I found the courage to determine the axes of the three paths that were to form the backbone of the nursery and garden. They still do. We knew that the site demanded a broad and generous visual approach and so, like the first generous sweep of an artist's brush on a large canvas, the first of these paths plunged west into the field at a right-angle to the main axis of the cottage. The second and third paths were spurs off this first one, again at right-angles, heading due south straight down the field in the direction of the Downs and joining a hundred yards away at a newly-erected gate into the bottom field. I don't mean to make gardening sound like an anatomical exercise – but with the backbone in place we had the treat of applying 'flesh' in the form of borders, hedges and windbreaks.

The 'feminine' outline of the Downs I'd observed as a young boy and the fluid and *legato* line I had tried to create as a professional singer (my first career) together stood me in good stead for the task, and the design of the borders flowed symbiotically with and sympathetically into the all-important surrounding landscape. On a site with such unrestricted views the hedges and windbreaks were above all practical measures designed to defeat the unrelenting south-westerly gales that often sweep across and batter the garden. *Carpinus* is a handsome genus well suited to our soil, and the hornbeam hedge we planted to divide the sales yard from the nursery flourished – but if we were to progress as quickly as we wanted to, we needed instant windbreaks to protect the young plants in their lee. We were determined not to use the hideously ugly woven mesh favoured by commercial growers, but we needed *some*thing. An opportune conversation with a friend revealed the methods used by Orkney Islanders to protect their crops: simple mobile latticework fences that, most importantly, *filter* the wind – function and form in tandem. Our own fixed windbreaks evolved from this, constructed by recycling the chestnut post-and-rail fences left by our predecessors, nailing on tannalised roofing battens equidistantly spaced to create wind-permeable rather than solid screens. In a moment of inspiration we decided, rather than making the fences horizontally level, to 'sculpt' them into abstract, rhythmical undulations that echo the line of the distant Downs. They may not be unique, but they are one of the garden's most commented-on design features and the wood, having aged, is now a most beautiful silver colour. As the hornbeam grows apace, the windbreak is being used as a template to define the shape of the hedges.

After all these essentials had been dealt with the time had come to turn our attention to the soil and its preparation. If at first I'd thought of this task as being the icing on the cake, it soon became plain that – to extend the metaphor – it was more the soured, heavy dough of unleavened bread. To this day I still puzzle over what lay behind the spell of ineptitude that was apparently cast on me as I analysed the soil and its structure, a procedure normally quite simple to perform: dig a spit of soil, take some in your hand, rub it between your fingers, feel the texture, squeeze some in the palm of your hand, observe how it behaves. In theory, on an early visit to Marchants armed with my trusty spade I had diligently performed this ritual, digging and sampling across the entire site – and in the process I had managed to convince myself that our soil was the equivalent of a fine Green & Black's organic chocolate.

The terrible truth of the matter was cruelly driven home when I attempted to dig the very first bit of paddock, a large rectangular area destined to become our vegetable plot. As they were rhythmically turned the cubes of earth held their shape beautifully; the side on which each spit had been cut was glistening and polished; a finger pressed into this surface left an indelible imprint; and Lucy was heard to remark how similar it looked to the clay she had thrown in pottery classes at art school. How I growled, but how right she was. We were shocked to discover that Laughton – our home village – and its environs were renowned for brick production, and insult was added to this injury when, really

keen and attempting to double dig, I was confronted with a layer
of the nastiest, palest and most impenetrable 'brick' clay I had
ever encountered.

I no longer sink, in a manner of speaking, to these depths, for as
our good friends Pam Schwerdt and Sybille Kreutzberger so succinctly commented, 'There is only one way with a soil such as
yours, Graham – upwards!' How right they were, too, having
learnt the hard way as Head Gardeners on the Wealden clay at
Sissinghurst Castle. Six years on, having incorporated ton upon ton
of coarse grit and home-made compost into the soil, together with
tons of mushroom compost as a top-dressing, we are at long last
reaping the rewards of our hard labours – and Lucy no longer has
to suffer my reiterated demands to know whether I am not worthy
of something more amenable.

If the design of our garden and nursery has slowly unfolded, the
same could be said of the range of plants that we grow. Trial and
error and rigorous self-selection have played a part, for the truth is
that many of the plants we love have not obliged us by thriving, but
above all, the dominating landscape and the mood we have
attempted to create in the garden have been most important in our
choice of plants. It follows that the plants we love and grow with
success in the garden are those we also offer for sale in our nursery
– a simple philosophy, but one that is not always easy to achieve.

Every season offers something of interest in our garden. In late
winter we don our scientists' hats for the arrival of the snowdrops
(we grow, with mixed success, over eighty forms and varieties).
Ovaries, pedicels, perianth segments (inner and outer), sinus marks,
scapes and spathes are reverentially observed. Before our sanity
becomes questionable the hellebores and pulmonarias distract us,
begging our homage. 'Spots or no spots?' – that is the question. It
applies to both genera, but we are unable to decide. March is Nose
Month: whether fat, furrowed, fleshy or fubsy, the emergence of our
herbaceous and grassy friends as they nose through the heavily
mulched soil to begin their cycle afresh never ceases to enthrall us,
and our fingers are always poised to search for late arrivals. April
invariably draws the question 'What's that yellow thing?' 'That

yellow thing' is *Thermopsis villosa*, of course; more to the point, it is lemon yellow, and every garden should have one. We enjoy opening visitors' eyes. And so it continues. We have even succumbed to planting the odd rose. Our hearts were lost to 'Buff Beauty' many years ago, and it grows well here. Two other great favourites are *Rosa* × *odorata* Sanguinea Group, discovered in France at a tiny nursery high in the Cevennes. Its copper foliage and velvety single carmine flowers are almost indistinguishable from the elusive 'Bengal Beauty'. The other rose, 'Betty Sherriff', is an extremely vigorous climber we have grown from a cutting. It has excellent foliage too, and its festoons of white-flushed-pink single flowers fill the air with almond scent.

We have been careful with our choice of shrubs – they are mostly light and airy in character, rather than dense and heavy. *Bupleurum fruticosum*, *Elaeagnus umbellata*, *Euonymus planipes* and *Ligustrum quihoui* (among others) all fit the bill admirably, and most have scented flowers. We have high hopes of a Chinese 'box', *Sarcococca saligna*, recommended to us by Roy Lancaster at a snowdrop party. It is still a young plant, but already there is a pedigree look about it. Willows flourish on our heavy wet clay and it is these – we have several forms – more than any of the other shrubby plants we grow that provide the symbiotic link with the herbaceous plants and many graceful grasses that form the nucleus of our collection. *Salix acutifolia* 'Blue Streak' takes on a ghostly appearance each spring as its stems develop a remarkable white bloom, while *S. alba* var. *britzensis* provides the antithesis to this: its glowing mahogany-red bark cheers us through the winter months with a warm glow, never better than when the light catches it against a cold grey sky. A smaller willow, *S. purpurea* 'Nancy Saunders', is the epitome of elegance, with narrow blue-grey leaves on extremely slender, whippy stems, and charcoal-grey pussies emerging from purple-mahogany buds. This plant has everything, and is admired by all who see it.

Our herbaceous plants, and the grasses in particular, are our passion, and it is difficult to know where to start. Four favourites might best sum up both our approach and our taste: *Scabiosa columbaria ochroleuca* has pale yellow flowers no bigger than a tenpence piece, but its airy and 'hovering' display lasts throughout the summer. It seeds around obligingly as well, creating an informal effect. Agapanthus hover too, if in a much more stately way, and provide true blue just when it is needed. I have been hand-pollinating and selecting agapanthus seedlings here for several years, and although it is still early days I have produced one child with very dark, slightly pendulous flowers. I would, of course, like to think it is unflawed – perhaps in my vanity I should call it 'Blue Perfection'.

Both the scabious and the agapanthus associate well with grasses, and this brings me to my last choices. The ubiquitous *Stipa gigantea* is a grass I simply cannot live without. It doesn't do particularly well here, but when it is in flower in late summer I am continually mesmerised by its ability to capture and play with the light, like no other grass. I hope one day to see it growing in the wild in its native Spain.

Miscanthus grows on the other side of the world, in Asia, but some of the best garden forms have been selected in Germany by nurseryman Ernst Pagels, now, I believe, in his late eighties. We grow a number of these majestic grasses, and while it is difficult to single out any one in particular, 'Silberspinne' is, to my mind, invested with all the qualities one expects of this genus: ruggedness and hardiness, combined with beauty and elegance. The fine foliage looks marvellous throughout the summer and provides a good foil for surrounding plants, and in late summer a mature plant will produce hundreds of flower spikes, buff at first, fading to white and gold, with a beauty that persists in winter.

Our lives and our philosophy of living, as regards both work and pleasure, are now inextricably linked to the elements and the landscape that surround us here at Marchants and, constantly humbled by the presence of the ancient and timeless Downs, we reflect on what is, in the greater scheme of things, our brief curatorship of this small plot of earth. Any personal development, like that of a young child, must of necessity involve the pains of teething and growing. Our garden will surely never be completed but, as we say to our customers in our catalogue, 'We hope . . . by sharing it with us, seeing new plants, new ideas and juxtapositions (as well as the odd mistake!) you will find it an enriching, informative and stimulating experience. That is all we ask.'

As we stand and admire our plants in relationship to the surrounding countryside and landscape we find ourselves constantly humbled, reminded of the fact that it is wise to keep an eye turned to Nature, the best teacher a gardener can have.

Water-colour sketch by Simon Dorrell.

The Winter-Flowering Algerian:
Iris unguicularis

URSULA BUCHAN

There are few plants in the garden which can really be said to thrive on brick rubble rather than soil, but the Algerian iris, bless it, is certainly one of them. Since it also has a touchingly beautiful flower, and blooms in winter and early spring, you can be sure it is a plant very dear to every gardener's heart.

Iris unguicularis (also known as *Iris stylosa*, although that is a later name and, therefore, invalid) is so-called because the bases of the flower segments are narrow and look like small claws or nails (*unguiculus* in Latin), but I should be surprised if more than one person in a thousand has ever examined it that closely. *Iris stylosa* refers to the fact that the style remains united in a distinctive way for an inch (2 cms) or so before it branches into three, and is actually a more useful name. But no matter.

This evergreen beardless iris, with branching rhizomes, is found not only in Algeria but in other countries on the Mediterranean littoral, such as Greece, as well as on islands such as Crete. The Algerian type has thin, strap-like leaves up to two feet (60 cms) in length in a clump about eighteen inches (45 cms) tall, and flowers which are up to three inches (7 cms) wide and six inches (15 cms) long. *I. unguicularis* subsp. *cretensis* is shorter and has narrower leaves still.

The flower has no stem to speak of, indeed the ovaries are to be found at ground level, but it does have a very long perianth tube, sufficiently long to render the flower suitable for putting in a water-filled sherry glass and displaying on the dining table. The trick is to pick the flowers when they are still like pale furled umbrellas and watch them open out quickly in the warmth, giving off a pleasant primrose scent in the process and lasting a couple of days before fading.

The colour of the flowers varies according to where the plant has been collected but essentially it is lavender, with a yellow stripe on the falls. This lavender is almost purple in the form 'Mary Barnard' and definitely purple in 'Abington Purple'. 'Walter Butt' is pale lavender but larger, and there are also some white forms in gardens, although I think them rather insipid. Winter is not the time for insipidity. There is considerable variability as to flowering time, too, but after a good summer you can expect to see the first flowers in November, continuing intermittently until late winter or early spring, especially in mild weather. In a bad season, you may have to wait until after the New Year.

The Algerian iris grows in rocky soil, and is often protected by low shrubs; these conditions dictate the circumstances in which it can be expected to thrive in our gardens. Mine has been planted as close to the south wall of the house as is possible, near the central heating vent, so that rain hardly touches it, and in a soil which has been deliberately impoverished by the addition of limestone rubble and stones. This is easy for me to achieve since I live on the limestone belt in central England, but elsewhere brick rubble can be used as a substitute. In old gardens, this iris was often planted against a stove greenhouse wall, so that the plant would benefit from heat at its back as well.

The great enemies of iris flowers are molluscs, which naturally do not care for rubble but thrive generally in wet autumns, making it necessary to clear away the old dead leaves (they come away quite easily) and place one or two slug pellets strategically in the centre of the clump, before the flowers are above ground. A tiny slug bite in the furled umbrella is a great big hole when the umbrella opens out.

When gardeners think of this iris, they tend to lump it with a closely-related species called *Iris lazica*, from the south-eastern border of the Black Sea. However, this has broader leaves, makes a laxer clump, has shorter flowers and, as a result of its upbringing, prefers very different conditions, being happiest in dappled shade and a moist, fertile spot, and thus perfectly able to hold its own in the open border.

As I write this, at the beginning of November, the first flower of my 'Mary Barnard' clump is fully out in the autumnal sunshine. We have been blessed with such sunny weather this summer as ideally suits the Algerian iris, which should flower really freely (and earlier than usual) in response. Enjoy it. I certainly intend to.

Drawing by Simon Dorrell

The Wild and the Gardened

NOEL KINGSBURY

There are few things that give me a greater thrill than seeing familiar garden plants 'at home', growing in the wild. Here is something we think we know and understand, but in a strange setting, albeit a setting which is in fact their real place in the world. It is a little like a friend you think you know, and then visit in a family context: you see that person in a completely different light – sometimes exuberant and 'larger' than you knew them, sometimes reduced in stature, even cowed.

Garden plants have a good time of it – they face little competition, they get watered and fed if they need it, they are pampered and cared for. Life in the wild is dramatically different, as plants are not only frequently exposed to much greater extremes of climate and environment than in the garden but are often in intense competition with other species for the same patch of ground. We tend to think we can learn something about the cultivation of a particular plant from seeing it growing wild, but are often confronted with sights that seem so counter-intuitive that doubt begins to creep in. The fact is that we know very little of the wild lives of nearly all familiar garden ornamentals. We know how to grow them in the garden, but very little about how they function as ecological beings. The way garden plants grow in the wild can sometimes seem confusing, but trying to understand how they do so can add much to our understanding of ecological as opposed to simply horticultural practices. With the increasing interest in growing plants in a 'naturalistic' or 'ecological' style, this knowledge may turn out to be more than simply theoretical.

To illustrate what can be learned with a little help from basic ecology, the forests of central Nepal are a good place to start. Dense and rich in a variety of tree species, they are the home of *Rhododendron arboreum*, so familiar from Cornish gardens, and, nearer eye level, *Daphne bholua*, a connoisseur's plant – sought-after, difficult to propagate, somewhat tender. It grows by the paths along which pass the thousands of trekkers who have become the main-stay of the local economy of this part of Nepal and often forms great thickets, with flowers in every shade from deep pink to white, sometimes scenting the air for a considerable distance. After a week of trekking the thrill of seeing it has long worn off, and I think I can remember pulling one of the innumerable seedlings out of the ground to use as a stick for some purpose or other. Indeed, it is common enough to be harvested for making the handmade paper which is one of the country's leading craft souvenir products. In Nepal the thought of all those proud gardeners saying 'do come and look at my *Daphne bholua*' seems faintly ridiculous, and the knowledge that the price of a single plant in a British nursery is equivalent to several months'-worth of a trekking porter's wages somewhat disturbing.

Looking at the daphne with an ecologist's eye, it is clear it is a good example of a 'pioneer plant', one which occupies bare ground, grows rapidly, seeds profusely and then dies relatively quickly, to be replaced by slower-growing more long-lived species – whose seedlings the pioneers have provided with a good sheltered habitat. Pioneers have a 'live fast, die young' philosophy, and a vital role in establishing new habitats: grassland or meadow on bare soil or forest on grassland. *Daphne bholua* clearly thrives on disturbance, with profuse seedlings occupying bare soil along paths, but much less within the forest. So, two lessons here perhaps for daphne growers: propagate from seed, and don't expect plants to live that long.

Of all the places to see garden plants growing wild, Slovenia is probably the best. Dutch writer and fellow enthusiast for looking at wild plants Henk Gerritsen describes the country as 'the home of the garden flower'. The reasons for this are probably historical: geological history which brought Mediterranean, Alpine and Dinaric (Balkan) floras together, and human history with its trade routes between Venice and central Europe criss-crossing the area and opening it to early botanists, gardeners and plant collectors. A Slovene woodland in spring can feel like a garden gone wild, with pulmonarias, hellebores, lily-of-the-valley, hepaticas and periwinkles thickly carpeting the ground. These are all growing more or less where we expect them, in shade, and for the most part look not dissimilar to what might be seen in the garden at home.

On a recent trip to Slovenia we visited a completely different habitat, dry limestone grassland, where a peony (*Paeonia mascula*) grows alongside a bearded iris (*I. illyricus*) and vast quantities of *Narcissus poeticus*. To see all three flowering together seems strange, but spring here is more of an event than a season, concertina'd between a cold winter and a hot summer, so plant growth is rapid and species flower together which would not do so in Britain. The landscape is of gently rolling hills exposed to a Mediterranean sun, with virtually no shade-giving trees, and hollows (known as *dolinas*) where water seeps down to underground streams and rivers. The peonies favour these hollows, where the soil is no doubt richer and moister, and the colour of their lush pink flowers seems startlingly out of place in what appears to be a harsh and unforgiving environment. We are used to the flowers of ancestral wild plants being much smaller than those of garden ones, but these peony and iris flowers are surprisingly large, more or less the equal of their garden relatives, which makes for a slightly Alice in Wonderland feeling.

In the normal course of events, wild herbaceous plants are considerably smaller in stature in the wild. In the garden we give them enough space to grow luxuriant and expansive, whereas in the wild there may be hundreds, even thousands of individual plants – and in some habitats, up to fifty species – per square metre. The result is a dense tapestry of vegetation which often can only be really appreciated on hands and knees. In Europe the most species-rich combinations are to be found in dry meadows on limestone, where the growth of grasses and vigorous species is reduced, largely from a combination of summer drought and low nutrient levels, so allowing a vast array of slower-growing plants to flourish. For the gardener there are some surprises. Solomon's seal (*Polygonatum odoratum*) and lily-of-the-valley (*Convallaria majalis*), both of which we think of as shade-loving woodlanders, clearly flourish on very hot dry slopes, their broad leaves standing out among the warp and weft of fine grasses and herbaceous wild flowers. The resolution of this apparent conundrum may be that both grow and flower during the brief spring, when soil moisture levels are good, and then die back to tubers during the hot summer; they may also benefit from the summer drought that tends to limit the growth of larger, potentially competitive plants. What can the gardener learn from such seeming anomalies? To be more adventurous perhaps, not so guided by conventional wisdom, and to think more about the various environmental factors which affect the plants we grow.

A good example of the difference between a plant in the garden and in the wild is provided by *Centaurea montana*. One of those cottage garden perennials not showy enough to have attracted the attention of the plant breeder and too vigorous for more refined borders, its energetically sprawling stems topped with big blue thistle-like flowers are ideal for wilder plantings, where there is no danger of it overwhelming smaller and choicer species. Yet in dry meadows it is a much reduced plant, even demure, each stem reaching a mere ten inches (25 cms) in length, about half the height that might be expected in cultivation, and seeming only to occur singly, in contrast to the great bunches of shoots we are used to from the herbaceous border.

Shrubs are more likely to reach the size we are accustomed to seeing in the garden, but don't always. The mahonias in the forests of Oregon puzzled me, for instead of forming upright shrubs they exist only as ground cover; I must have walked through miles of monotonously mahonia-carpeted coniferous forest, with only an occasional trillium or orchid to provide some interest. Perhaps it is deer grazing them that keeps them so low, and encourages the development of side shoots. Seeing *Cotinus coggygria* at home in Bulgaria was a similar experience. Instead of forming mounding shrubs as it does in the garden, it exists as scattered small suckering shoots, never thick enough to form a canopy. Its brilliant orange autumn colour was spectacular, and made it easy to get a good impression of its growth habit over large areas of woodland floor. I suppose the competition of the larger trees and shrubs among which it grows limits this growth, and grazing deer too, perhaps. But seeing it wild emphasised to me the potential value of the 'coppicing' (an annual or biennial cutting-back to base) approach to shrub growing, which prevents plants from becoming too large, encourages suckering and ensures that only small stems are produced, often with better quality foliage and a more elegant and upright habit than if the plants are simply allowed to grow unrestricted.

Shrubs have a habit which is best described as 'plastic', meaning that their growth is very flexible and so the shapes they develop are very much dependent on the environment. In the garden, with little competition, they generally form themselves into rather dense amorphous masses, while in the wild the habit of many is to be sparse and gappy. Many grow densely intertwined or in situations where they are stretching to reach the light, so making it impossible to appreciate what they might look like in the vastly more generous conditions of the garden. I remember finding populations of *Ribes sanguineum* along the edges of the forests in Oregon where the mahonia grew so rampantly. None looked remotely tidy enough to belong in a garden, yet of course their flowers added much to the beauty of the locality, standing out vividly amid the dark green of an overwhelmingly coniferous population. Like the daphne of Nepal, the range in colour was large, from deep pink through to almost white, a phenomenon that seems particularly to affect pink-flowered plants (blues and yellows appear to be much more consistent). Such a range is much rarer in cultivation, where colour depends so much on the selection made available by widespread commercial propagation of particular clones.

What we have in cultivation is the tip of the iceberg of the range of plants we could have in our gardens. Thinking of Slovenia, we have *Vinca minor*, *Hacquetia epipactis* and *Helleborus orientalis*, but why not *Jurinea mollis*, a deep pink-red thistle/knapweed with splendid seed heads, or *Serratula lycopifolia*, another striking member of the daisy family, both clearly tough, drought-tolerant plants? Further east, in Bulgaria and Turkey, the flora is richer still, but has been much less trawled through by those interested in garden plants, so we have even fewer of their species in cultivation. The selection made available to gardeners is, I suspect, ever more a matter of chance. Very often the genetic range in cultivation is very limited, the result of one seed collection from which a number of cultivars has been selected by nurseries over the decades in the years following its introduction. Factors such as whether the seed collection was made before or after a plant hunter's lunch may have major ramifications: was only one batch of seed collected, in a hurry, or several at different locations from plants growing in slightly different environments? It is exciting to think just how many good garden plants are actually out there, both new species and good forms of well-established ones. For the gardener who takes to the wild, there is much to see, to learn, and to gain, as well as many puzzles and surprises. The complexities and richness of the world's wild places can make the garden seem a tame and predictable place by comparison.

Acknowledgements

In Slovenia, thanks to Stane Sušnik, Dr Sonja Škornik, Dr Joze Bavcon for their guidance to good wild flower habitats, and in Oregon to Maurice Horn.

On Meeting Ian Hamilton Finlay

This year the poet and garden maker Ian Hamilton Finlay celebrated his eightieth birthday. AMBRA EDWARDS recalls meeting him at his garden near Dunsyre in Scotland.

The Pentland Hills are only an hour from Edinburgh. Yet perched on a windy hilltop, under a glowering sky, Little Sparta feels as remote as Patagonia. I turn off the road, and my little car bumps perilously up the long, stony track. Every hundred yards or so I have to stop, push open a heavy metal gate, drive through, and close it again behind me. These actions take on a ritual quality, as if I were walking the Stations of the Cross.

I abandon my car by a pile of rocks which may or may not be artwork in the making, and reverently open the garden gate. It is inscribed 'A COTTAGE – A FIELD – A PLOUGH'. On the reverse it reads 'THERE IS HAPPINESS'.

Is Ian Hamilton Finlay, I wonder, a happy man? All I have read about him has prepared me for a Jeremiah – a seer, a visionary, a man of uncompromising intellectual ferocity who delights in combat. Yet his garden suggests a Roman contentment. Will he prove to be more Pliny than Robespierre?

The house is low and modest. Along the front runs a glassed sunroom with a reassuringly scruffy muddle of battered cane chairs, fishing floats and half-dead geraniums. Outside, artworks are crammed on to the tiny patio – one of his characteristic 'wave' mosaics playing games with the Latin word UNDA, a large pink fibreglass cube, bitten away on one side, a pair of watering cans, enigmatically inscribed, all jostling for space among sweet peas and strawberry troughs.

But it is raining stair-rods, so I knock energetically.

The door is answered by a Valkyrie – tall and magnificent. She scowls at me suspiciously from under a mane of tawny hair. 'Yes?' she demands.

'I've come to see Dr Finlay.' (Mr Finlay? Dr Hamilton Finlay? Doctor Finlay's casebook?)

'He is not seeing visitors,' she barks. Her accent is as Teutonic as her demeanour.

'But I have an appointment.'

'You did not make any appointment with me,' she snaps, and makes to shut the door.

'I didn't speak to you, I spoke to him.'

'Do you know anything about this?' she demands, over her shoulder. Another beautiful young woman emerges from the shadows, later to be introduced as Ann, tamer of wild horses.

'No,' says Ann, and disappears.

The rain has long since gone through my coat, and is running down my neck. 'Why don't you go and ask him?' I suggest. 'Can I wait inside while you do?'

The Valkyrie scowls again, and shuts the door in my face.

'Unda' is a good word to contemplate in the rain. It is repeated four times on adjacent paving stones, and each time a wave-shaped printer's mark rearranges the letters. The very word has the rise and fall of the sea in the sound it makes . . .

'Hello,' says a quiet voice behind me. It is Finlay. He is tiny and soft-spoken and fragile-looking, like a small bird. But his handshake is firm, and his eyes bright as knives. He ushers me into his study. Wobbly towers of books and CDs cover the walls, the floor, and every available flat surface. There is a narrow tousled bed, and a tangle of pyjamas, an ancient typewriter and wellingtons on the floor. A single log burns in the fireplace. A length of fishing net and a fleet of model boats in the window block out all views of his garden. He points me to a high, stiff chair by the fire, perches on the bed, and we begin to talk of gardens.

He has recently been to Peto's Buscot Park, and relishes its formality, its austere magnificence. A visit to Stourhead has been less successful. His arrival coincided with preparations for the annual Fête-Champêtre: instead of a perfect Gaspard he has been greeted with chemical toilets and fat men in shorts. The smile freezes on his face as he speaks of it: the loss of dignity offends him to the point of physical pain. Is it not odd, when his own garden is so full of humour, that he should feel such need of *gravitas*?

'There is a place for jokes, and a place for not-jokes,' he says firmly. It is as if one of his heroes, a Saint-Just or a Robespierre, has revealed himself to be humanly weak and venal.

There are jokes aplenty however at Little Sparta – the raspberry canes painted in pink and green camouflage; a pair of Nazi tortoises with 'Panzer Leader' inscribed on their shells; pineapple finials on a gateway transmuted into hand-grenades; a fingerpost marked '*Zur Siegfried Linie*': of course – the washing line!

And between the jokes, there are poems – 'The wind is teaching the rowan to write,' 'Dividing the light, I disclose the hour' (a sundial). A bench round the base of a tree reads:

> THE SEA'S WAVES
> THE WAVES' SHEAVES
> THE SEA'S NAVES

So many images in so few words: the rippling of the wind through sea and corn and the surrounding grassland . . . the awesome architecture of the barrel of the wave . . . the wordplay of nave with the latin *navis*, a ship . . . the sussurating lilt of the lines, like the rise and fall of the sea . . . Finlay drops his poems into the garden like stones into a pool: ripples spread slowly out from them – ripples of emotion, intuition, understanding – establishing a dialogue between the object and its setting. Context is all: often he creates the setting around an inscription after he has placed it – stage-managing the effect and manipulating a response as meticulously as any Kent or Shenstone.

The garden, he complains, is always discussed in art terms – rarely in garden terms. Which is a pity, for this is cracking good gardening – not a rich man's garden, but one that has grown piecemeal over decades of physical and intellectual labour. When Finlay brought his family here in 1966 there was nothing – just sheep grazing on the wild moorland and a single storm-blasted ash. Bit by bit, he dug and planted. (Hardy native trees like birch and wild cherry; swathes of durable ground-cover: hardy geraniums, dicentras and ferns, great clouds of astrantias.) He diverted streams into pools and a little loch. Gradually he extended the garden out into the moorland, so that the garden offers a stirring contrast between the tight, intense, enclosed spaces surrounding the house, closely packed with sculpture and inscriptions, and wide, sweeping views over loch and hill. Bordering the pool is a tiny patch of forest, deep, dark and deliciously gloomy, criss-crossed by a maze of tiny paths that double back and forth across a stream. Beyond lies a wood of a quite different character: all sunny pools and shady groves – like a scene from Ovid, trembling with magic possibility, where anything might turn into anything else at a moment's notice. (The scene is set by cut-out figures of Apollo in pursuit of Daphne.) The latest addition is a piece of open land smoothed into a miniature eighteenth-century parkland, a gracious landscape that leads abruptly to a dinky fenced vegetable plot. Such trenchant juxtapositions make a relatively modest plot – just four acres – endlessly interesting and varied.

I step from the pillars and porticoes of the Temple Pool Garden into a patch of dripping pines. It is the embodiment of one of the poet's most resonant 'sentences': 'Superior gardens are composed of Glooms and Solitudes and not of plants and trees.'

Skipping about in the wood there appears to be some sort of fairy – a small, wet, red-haired sprite of about ten years old.

'Hello,' she says. 'Have you come to look at the garden?'

'I have.'

'It's a funny garden,' she says. 'It's full of secrets. Shall I show you?' And she points out panpipes and pyramids, and a marble bird's nest hidden in a tree, and a child's paper boat on the Temple Pool, magically turned to stone.

Her name is Rainee; she is the housekeeper's daughter. In the holidays, she comes with her mother and the garden is her play-ground. 'I'll show you the swans,' she says, and leads me suddenly into the outer garden, where three black swans sail portentously over the loch. A sombre stone column ('Nuclear Sail') looms on the bank, and a small boat lies half submerged on the shore. 'Can you keep a secret?' she whispers. 'In the summer, when it was hot, we went for a row on the loch, my mam and me. The swans all followed us.'

Rainee disappears in search of bread for the swans, and returns with an invitation to lunch. The Valkyrie does not reappear. Instead, there is a Celtic beauty with dark Rapunzel hair. This turns out to be Rainee's mother – who serves up a wonderful soup at the scrubbed kitchen table and fusses very gently till the poet has eaten it all up. Rainee chatters between mouthfuls. 'You do talk a lot,' says Finlay, coldly. (Currently on display at the Royal Botanic Garden, Edinburgh is another of his sentences: 'Chatter sprains the soul'.) His own speech is soft and slow, costing him some effort since a stroke last winter.

It has changed him, he thinks. 'Pia complains that as I have grown older I have become very peaceable.' (Pia Maria Simig is his companion and collaborator.) 'She complains I no longer like a good fight.' We talk of the glory days of the Battle of Little Sparta, his long struggle to have his garden temple accepted by the local rating authority, Strathclyde, as a religious building, and therefore rate-exempt. 'It took a lot of time and energy, but I got a lot of works out of it, so it was a good battle.'

But he has not become so dove-like, I suggest, that he would wish to temper the martial imagery that abounds in the garden – machine-guns, grenades, tanks, torpedoes and especially battle-ships?

'Lots of visitors object to the battleships,' he observes, 'but for me they are objects of great affection.'

'But as you change, and your preoccupations change, does the garden record that, becoming a kind of album of your intellectual life over the years?'

'Not really,' he says. 'My preoccupations haven't really changed at all. I certainly haven't transcended my interest in battleships.'

We go out together in the pale afternoon into the Wild Garden, where he laughs at my schoolgirl Latin, before confessing cheerily that he never learned any himself. 'I have a girl who puts things into Latin for me.' (Another girl – surprise, surprise. But his charm is immense: it is easy enough to understand why he is surrounded by adoring handmaidens.)

I am at once elated by the sheer emotional power of the garden and dismayed by my own lack of learning. The range of his allusions is so vast, from Classical mythology to the Revolutionary Calendar, from German Romantic poetry to provisions for camouflaging tanks. He must yearn to walk round with cultured folk like Sir Roy Strong, who will pick up all his quotations.

'Not at all,' he says gallantly. 'Strong knows nothing about battleships.'

We come at length to a bench by the loch, and sit looking through the skeletons of meadowsweet and iris across the water to the distant hills. The wind sends little wavelets skittering towards us. A sudden shaft of sunlight catches the hills, turning them gold between dark stains of heather and pine.

How does he want people to respond, I wonder. Does he want us to come in a spirit of humility to be taught by the garden?

'That's a leading question,' he laughs. 'I left school at fourteen, so I reckon if I know something, other people ought to know it too.'

But not everyone, surely, will understand the identification of the revolutionary Saint-Just with Apollo. Not everyone will have read the speeches of Robespierre. Why has he chosen such stern and forbidding figures for his pantheon?

'They are not stern – they are serious. It is a pity that our age lacks their seriousness, their idealism. Robespierre I really admire – he is fine.' And it becomes clear to me that for him, the French Revolution is as immediate as if it had been yesterday. 'What's important about them is that they meant what they said. You can't say that about Blair, now, can you?'

'But what about the Terror?'

'That didn't make what they said less true.'

The very things I find appalling in them – their fanaticism, their ruthlessness – is what commends them to Finlay. It is that selfsame uncompromising single-mindedness that might lead a man to battle bureaucracy over decades or to value his art above the needs of his family. What I call cruelty, he would call clarity.

'You're a very modern person,' he remarks. It is not a compliment. 'Who then would you choose for your garden god?'

Orlando Bloom?

It is not a question I have previously considered.

And therein lies the glory of this garden and its gently spoken, courteous, terrifying maker.

What does a garden mean in our time? For some of us, a plant museum. For others, a place to laze about in. But why should we laze – physically, intellectually or morally? Why shouldn't we be poked into greater perceptiveness, greater effort?

'I am very happy to be chastened by your garden,' I say.

'But I'm unhappy that you should feel chastened.' He is all embarrassment and solicitude – as if I had found a fly in my soup.

What more should we want from a new experience than that it be enlarging?

'I'm not used to being enlarging,' he declares, a naughty grin spreading over his face. 'I'm used to being just wee me . . .'

A Fragment of Italy on an Atlantic Shore

ILNACULLIN: A GARDEN BY HAROLD PETO IN COUNTY CORK

JOHN AKEROYD

In the Italian Garden

West Cork has some of the wildest and most picturesque coastal scenery in Ireland. Though comparatively unexplored, these rocky Atlantic coasts are a paradise for the botanist, and also home to some of the most remarkable gardens in these islands. Near the head of the spectacular sea-lough of Bantry Bay, Glengariff possesses one of northern Europe's best gardening climates. The village, for the most part a long street of hotels and pubs, its bay or 'harbour' and a scattering of islands – including the island garden of Ilnacullin or Garinish – are invested by the almost treeless bogs, cliffs and rocks of the scenic Caha Mountains and perfectly sculpted Sugarloaf Mountain to the south-west. By contrast, village and immediate surroundings are extravagantly lush. Cut out the fierce, salt-laden south-westerlies and anything ought to grow – if it doesn't require too much lime. Gardens and bar frontages are vivid with bedding plants, lawns are plush, all is green with subtropical shrubberies, oak and arbutus woodland, and exotic garden escapees run riot.

Glengariff is the sort of place where one barely expresses surprise at a hotel car park with a tall flowering *Luma apiculata* (*Myrtus luma*), or *Desfontainia spinosa* growing in a pub garden, or sheets of native St Patrick's cabbage (*Saxifraga spathularis*) flourishing on quayside rocks. Hedges are red with fuchsia and escallonia, roadside banks orange with crocosmia; even the invasive purple *Rhododendron ponticum* gives a magnificent show. All this exuberant vegetation and colour is set against a magnificent backdrop of mountain, moor and sea, the light constantly changing in a mosaic of rain, cloud and sunshine. It is a little bit of the Italian lakes transplanted to wild Atlantic shores. That great Irish naturalist Robert Lloyd Praeger, his no-nonsense Belfast heart clearly stirred, wrote of Glengariff: '. . . a fairyland-like island-studded bay, facing full south, very sheltered, almost frostless in winter, seldom too hot in summer (though the midges may be pesky), embowered in native oak-woods and semi-tropical shrubs.' At the mouth of this natural sheltered harbour stands the 37-acre island of Ilnacullin or Garinish, given over to a paradise garden created less than a century ago. (It should not be confused with the other Garinish, on an island just to the north in County Kerry.)

For centuries Ilnacullin was an uninhabited, heathy, rocky place, with a small bog and a few humble cabins. Then, just before Christmas 1796, the French fleet came to Bantry Bay. Richard White of Bantry House at the head of the Bay sent a messenger to alert the authorities in Cork and drew up the militia – four hundred locals against 15,000 soldiers – a gallant little show of strength for which King George III made him Lord Bantry. Luck was with the British, as for once winter winds failed to blow from the south-west and the weather turned bitterly and unusually cold. Fine Irish writer Sean O'Faolain eloquently summarised the dramatic events that followed: 'They anchored . . . under Bere Island, while the wind blew from the east with drifting snow that whitened these mountains. Ships cut their cables and blew out to sea. Days passed. Christmas went by. Still the wind was implacably their enemy. In the end the remnants of the fleet sailed before it, back to their base; neither the first nor the last time that the winds and seas saved Great Britain from her enemies.'

The invasion scare prompted the British Government to think seriously about coastal defences and extend its building programme for Martello towers to County Cork. In 1804 the very first Irish Martello tower was built on the summit of Ilnacullin, like a small castle with keep and curtain wall. These compact round forts fit well into a landscape dotted with ruined castles, tower houses and later relics of the Industrial Revolution. West Cork was more than once quite a Copper Belt – starting in the Bronze Age – and bare mine-spoil and old mine engine-houses bear witness to times well described in Daphne du Maurier's novel *Hungry Hill* (Gollancz, 1943). A century on, Ilnacullin was no longer deemed of strategic importance, and in 1910 the War Office sold it and its fort to Annan Bryce, a British MP born in Belfast. Bryce, long a visitor to Glengariff, had the inspired vision to realise the horticultural possibilities of this rocky island, then more or less treeless but presumably once wooded – hence Ilnacullin or Illaunacullin, 'Holly Island'. The formerly widespread native woods of West Cork, like those that survive around the lakes of Killarney, consisted of sessile oak with evergreen arbutus, holly and yew, the trees and red sandstone or limestone rocks covered with mosses and ferns. It is no exaggeration to call this vegetation temperate rainforest.

Bryce was also inspired to commission architect and garden designer Harold Ainsworth Peto (1854–1933), more at home in an Italian Renaissance garden than among the rocks and furze of West Cork. Undeterred by the wild scene he rose to the occasion, borrowing the island's own topography to blend charming Italianate buildings with a series of garden vignettes, woodlands and shrubberies, while incorporating natural features such as lichened rock outcrops, sandstone boulders and patches of boggy ground. The collaboration of Peto, steeped in the formal Classical garden, and Bryce, a disciple of William Robinson – a man whose informal style was eminently suited to his native Ireland – and the cult of the wild garden, was a fusion of sheer genius. The visitor is led through woodland and clearings dominated by a fine varied collection of temperate and warm-temperate trees and shrubs, geographically dominated by the southern hemisphere. Simple herbaceous plantings and more than one hundred naturally-occurring native wild flowers and ferns complete a tableau of studied informality that achieves a seamless blend of garden elements.

Old photographs show a seemingly naked island of rocks, rough grazing, furze, heather and bog, dominated at the higher, eastern end by the Martello tower. As with the Abbey Gardens on Tresco in Scilly (see HORTUS 63), the first task was to establish effective (and attractive) shelter belts. These are well matured now, apparently self-regenerating, mostly of pines, both Scots (*Pinus sylvestris*) and the mighty Monterey (*Pinus radiata*), with its great limbs, massively ridged bark and whorls of cones. Other conifers and native or long-established broadleaves such as sessile oak, holly and chestnut thicken the dense woods of the shelter-belt, with self-sown rowan (*Sorbus aucuparia*) and thickets of *Griselinia littoralis*, *Rhododendron ponticum*, bracken and, in more open spots, over-grown heather and purple moor-grass tussocks. Within this semi-natural boundary zone the garden thrives in a true Glengariff microclimate, supporting a remarkable range of plants. My own visits to Ilnacullin have, by poor luck or sheer necessity, always been from July to September, so I have always missed out on some of the great glories of the garden, the numerous rhododendrons, azaleas and camellias. But there is plenty more to see in any month.

The landscaping is developed around the central Italian-style garden, a fabulous kernel of pure Harold Peto at his best. It brings to mind the lovely garden at Peto's old home, Iford Manor near Bath, a sublime blend of stone terraces, columns and Classical ornamentation based around his magnificent eighteenth-century house. The architectural elements of Ilnacullin have cleaner lines, more Arts and Crafts than Age of Reason, but much the same spirit. Peto's love of thirteenth-century Italian Romanesque detail, which he used at about the same time in the cloisters at Iford, is an obvious stylistic link between the two gardens. The Casita and Italian Garden, together comprising one of the most iconic images of Irish gardening, are carefully welded to the surrounding garden by woody plantings and walks. From the eastern end of this central garden area, a broad path flanked by richly planted herbaceous borders bisects the walled vegetable garden and nursery. This leads through a narrow arch into an open space dominated by a lawn, once a tennis court – in pre-garden days a small peat bog that served the people of Glengariff for fuel turf – bordered to the south by natural south-facing rock outcrops planted with mesembryanthemums, to the north by a heather bed. At its western end is the Casita, apparently stolen from Italy, which looks out through an elegant Romanesque triple arch framed by trees and shrubs to a vista of islands and the Sugarloaf and Caha mountains – a northern, subdued, Celtic version of the glories of Lake Como. Comparable to the vista of the larger quartzite Sugarloaf at Powerscourt, County Wicklow, this is one of the finest views from any Irish garden.

The Casita and Italian Garden, not far from the landing stage, come early on the itinerary of most visitors. That is not to say one has seen the 'best bits' first and will thenceforth be disappointed, for they are integral to the whole Ilnacullin experience, an anchor to the wider garden, and many will have a final look at them on the way out. The landing place itself has certainly escaped from the

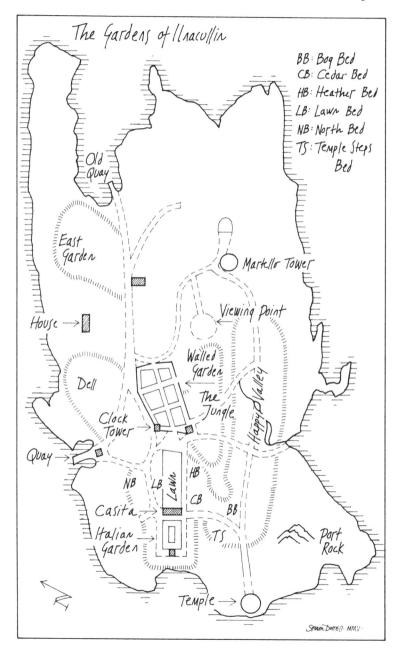

The Gardens of Ilnacullin

BB: Bog Bed
CB: Cedar Bed
HB: Heather Bed
LB: Lawn Bed
NB: North Bed
TS: Temple Steps Bed

Old Quay

East Garden

Martello Tower

House →

Viewing Point

Walled Garden

Dell

The Jungle

Happy Valley

Clock Tower

Quay →

NB LB Lawn HB

CB

BB

Casita →

TS

Port Rock

Italian Garden

Temple →

Simon Dorrell · MMV ·

Italian lakes. The sloping stone quay, at the top of which are the neatly constructed visitor reception area and excellent café, always reminds me of Como or Maggiore, even if the view on the ten-minute crossing of stout, contented harbour seals basking on rocky islets is essential West Cork, as are the mats of wrack and oarweed heaving in the swell that slaps against the stonework, and the bubbling call of a curlew from a nearby strand.

Once in through the entrance and up the steps, foliage and trees surround you and the sea somehow recedes from memory, just glimpsed dramatically from time to time as you proceed around the garden. Immediately you are indeed out of Cork and into a fantasy landscape, with an eclectic cosmopolitan assemblage of special woody plants: *Acacia pravissima*, *Azara microphylla*, *Crino-dendron hookerianum*, *Desfontainia spinosa*, *Luma apiculata*, *Magnolia grandiflora* and many others. In spring, several magnolias – not least the high-flying pink tulips of *M. campbellii* subsp. *mollicomata* – and camellias dominate this part of the garden. But this is only a taste of what lies ahead, as the path leads on to the colonnaded terrace of the Casita, festooned with wisteria and *Vitis coignetiae*. Here at the heart of the Italian Garden stone structures blend with exotic planting and the softening effect of smaller native and garden plants colonising stonework and hidden corners of borders. Italy meets Japan – some venerable bonsai in containers – and Australia, with a range of reds and pinks – *Callistemon citrinus* 'Splendens' and other cultivars and species, grevillea and cultivars of *Leptospermum scoparium*. Fuchsia and olearia rub shoulders with myrtle and another Mediterranean stalwart, Spanish broom (*Spartium junceum*), and that impressive glaucous-leaved, white-flowered California poppy-relative *Romneya coulteri*. Small ferns naturalise in the chinks and angles of damp steps.

Heading out of the Italian Garden the path winds north towards Happy Valley, the large glade that links the west and east ends of the garden with a walk through some remarkable plantings – a veritable botanic garden. The route passes along the eastern end of The Jungle, the area lying between Happy Valley and the more formal part of the garden, planted especially with a rich miscellany of larger rhododendrons, camellias, olearia and pittosporum, together with gems such as the red-flowered *Berberidopsis corallina*, *Crinodendron hookerianum* and *Embothryum coccineum* from Chile, spiky-tussocked *Puya alpestris* from the Andes and the lily-of-the-valley tree (*Clethra arborea*) from Madeira, all thriving in the mild, humid microclimate of the island. Out into the glade, up a flight of steps and you are into another Peto creation, the Grecian Temple. This viewpoint, looking westward over to the mountains, is in the form of a roofless *tholos* similar to the one at Delphi in Greece. Cypresses and more *Luma apiculata* line the way; azaleas and agapanthus fringe the steps, but there is also a real sense here of the mixed woodland shelter belt that partly surrounds the temple on its rocky promontory.

The walk through the mini-botanic garden of Happy Valley should satisfy the intellectual and aesthetic perceptions of the most demanding plantsman. Particularly impressive on my last September visit was *Eucryphia lucida* from Tasmania, covered in large white flowers and woody seed-pods, as was another Tasmanian, the Huon pine (*Dacrydium franklinii*), with its elegantly drooping twigs and branches. The walk is a parade of fascinating and beautiful trees both evergreen and deciduous, conifers and flowering plants: Kauri pine (*Agathis australis*) from New Zealand, pines as varied as *Pinus armandii*, *P. heldreichii*, *P. strobus*, *P. thunbergii* and *P. wallichiana*; mature witch-hazel (*Hamamelis mollis*), the ericaceous *Pieris formosa* and its more obscure relatives enkianthus, gaylussacia and zenobia, several species of cornus, camellia-like stewartia, and numerous azalea and rhododendron species and hybrids. The variety is remarkable, and plenty more good woody plants can be seen just to the north in The Jungle.

Half-way along Happy Valley a trickle of water through a damp hollow has been dammed into two shallow ponds, alongside which flourish dawn cypress (*Metasequoia glyptostroboides*), tree-ferns, bamboo and yellow tormentil, mauve devil's-bit scabious (that great autumn flowerer) and other native wild flowers. Boulders and low-growing conifers and a line of stepping-stones across one of the ponds complement an oriental feel that would have pleased Peto.

Here too a path cuts out through a thicket to a cobble strand littered with seaweed and eelgrass fragments. Suddenly the veil lifts, and for a few moments coastal West Cork reasserts itself. Heather, bird's-foot trefoil and kidney-vetch flower on rocks above the strand, and a very Irish rocky island juts out of the waves, even if it is crowned by great clumps of escaped New Zealand flax (*Phormium tenax*). This little area of Ilnacullin has for me a special dream-like magic.

Now the valley slopes upward and then a long but shallow flight of steps leads irresistibly up to the Martello tower for more views of the sea and across to the low hills of Whiddy Island off Bantry. Again the veil is lifted, and we are among heather, broom, rock outcrops and shattered stones. The seaward-facing curtain wall of the tower is a mass of fairy foxglove (*Erinus alpinus*), that quaint little plant that seems especially at home on ancient monuments (like Hadrian's Wall); it grows too on walls at Muckross House in Killarney to the north. The tower and its open vistas give the punch-drunk plantsman a break from sheer variety and from plants that this botanist at least couldn't always recognise (family as well as genus). But the garden's magic spell returns after the tower – itself a neat enough structure, with seemingly Mediterranean roots, to have been designed by Peto himself – and following a short diversion to a rocky knoll viewpoint just to the west, overlooking the garden itself. The path descends through trees and shade to a small damp lawn and the handsomely arched entrance to the Walled Garden. In this lawn, as on the main lawn by the Casita, grows wild chamomile, a relic of the island's original vegetation that is rather common on the coastal heaths of West Cork.

Many visitors move quickly through the Walled Garden, missing a range of obvious and hidden treasures. I love it, if only for that sense of comfort and security that a walled garden gives, but also for a wealth of familiar flowers and old friends, like the grand, stately *Cardiocrinum giganteum* – you can tell who's sniffed it by the pollen on their nose – or just the 'flore pleno' variant of red campion. The nicely weathered walls themselves support a fine collection of clematis and climbing roses. The herbaceous borders,

The Clock Tower

backed and sometimes interplanted with shrubs, are a mass of colour from summer to early autumn, with old familiars such as delphiniums, phlox and a good selection of North American daisies – aster, erigeron, helenium and rudbeckia. These plantings give this part of Ilnacullin an English feel, despite the rather exotic shrubs. The architecture, however, is distinctly Italianate: the north-western corner has a compact turret with an octagonal roof and Romanesque door, the south-western corner has a slender Romanesque clock-tower that gently dominates this semi-formal area. An alcove on the southern wall has a magnificent Roman sarcophagus in sculpted marble that echoes Peto's collection of Classical antiques at Iford. Beside it is a mature example of the choice East Himalayan *Michelia doltsopa*, magnolia-like and with attractive rusty-velvet buds. Out through another lovely arch, and the Casita is again in view.

My school art teacher always reckoned an hour and a half round a gallery, and then it's time for tea. It is hard not to feel a little overwhelmed after an afternoon in the gallery of plants that is Ilnacullin and, after a pause for thought on a bench by the lawn, still surrounded by wonderful plants, I usually head for the café. This is on a par with the garden for quality, a peaceful place (if there are not too many visitors) with excellent tea and food and some solid iron chairs on the little terrace. Perhaps a questing mouse gleans crumbs and a coal-tit, the more yellowish Irish sub-species, flits and sings in the branches above. The boat comes, and in a few minutes one is back in Glengariff for a pint or two of stout under the hanging baskets. The dream is over, but not forgotten.

Sadly, Annan Bryce didn't enjoy his dream garden for long. Nor did a planned Big House materialise – only a large cottage just east of the landing stage. Bryce died in 1923, but his wife and his son Rowland continued the project. Their splendid Scottish head gardener Murdo Mackenzie, who enabled the family to realise the dream of this island garden, retired in 1971, having assured continuity in the development of Bryce and Peto's vision. When Rowland Bryce died in 1953 he generously bequeathed the garden to the Irish people. The State has managed and maintained it since, first under the Office of Public Works and latterly, and most ably, under Dúchas, The Heritage Service of the Department of Arts, Heritage, Gaeltacht and the Islands. Ilnacullin is a national treasure – Ireland's Tresco – which combines, art, craft, science and a curious spirit of place, fusing as it does the wild and the tamed, the Irish and the exotic, and horticulture and botany.

Drawings and plan by Simon Dorrell.

In an Irish Garden

PETER DALE

Gardening and football – are they the last remaining topics of conversation in which it is still permissible to talk about England and Englishness without either causing embarrassment or committing an offence? In the case of football, the thought-police probably wouldn't dare to intervene (and anyway, the Englishness of the team is a fiction: more than half the players are imported, aren't they?). In the matter of gardens the case is probably simpler still: it is unlikely that they've even noticed the breach of discipline, but if they have, they probably aren't fussed, so insignificant is the cultural and political constituency of fine gardening (or so they think, but watch this space).

Style apart, and national temperament notwithstanding, what first makes an English garden English is the soil, the soil and then the climate. It is Nature, and not Nurture, which makes the difference in the first place. Style, attitude, character, national temperament, and so on, follow after, if they follow at all.

We English are always congratulating ourselves on having – along with Japan – the kindest climate in the world (but Japan has earthquakes). It has become a central tenet of national gardening discourse, but it is not quite true. These days, East Anglia isn't getting anything like enough rainfall to sustain its herbaceous borders, and drought-stressed trees have become an almost endemic feature of the landscape everywhere.

Nevertheless, as an idea it lives on. In fact it seems to enjoy as much currency as ever, if not even more, as if – forbidden any kind of nationalistic navel-gazing elsewhere – we still claim a climatological special place: an Isle of the Blest, without the religious or ethnic overtones, but reinstated with wellingtons, brollies, and the occasional pair of sunglasses. Long may it continue, but . . .

If it is true of mainland Britain – a uniquely favourable climate, that is – how much more true is it of Ireland? The rainfall there still comes up to scratch, on the whole. Summer there remains an idyll of soft warm days – wet sometimes, it's true, but not the sort of scorching solar acupuncture we get now. And the Gulf Stream flows past all Ireland's coasts and not just the western littoral as in the case of Britain.

As a fleeting visitor to Ireland, you could be forgiven for thinking that gardens and gardening have failed, so far, to bring out the best in the Irish. There are the big set-pieces, of course: Powerscourt, Birr Castle, Malahide, Fota, Mount Usher, and so on. But away from these hot spots what you tend to get is less a sense of gardening as an absorbing national passion, and more an abiding impression of varietal *Acer platanoides* planted in every third front garden throughout the land. Though statistically unfair, this would still be impressionistically faithful, and you'd have to wonder about what became of the real genius of place. Jekyll worked a little in Ireland (Lambay Island, Co. Dublin); Harold Peto translated the spirit of Italy and the flora of the southern hemisphere to the island of Ilnacullin in Bantry Bay and, sprinklingly, other English gardening luminaries have left their marks too, but you'd be forgiven (again) for thinking that the traffic of talent had been mostly in the other direction. To wit, at least one contemporary figure: like him or not, Diarmuid Gavin, complete with his Irish brogue, features large on English television (though actually only slightly in Ireland). You'd be forgiven too for overlooking the enormous gift to us all of plants first bred in, or first introduced through, Ireland. All those fabled dieramas and libertias (from Slieve Donard once upon a time, and now from Ballyrogan). All those escallonias. All those yellow, gold, old-gold, tawny-bronze crocosmias. All those plants from the National Botanical Gardens: *Solanum crispum* 'Glasnevin', *Cortaderia selloana, Olearia semidentata, Parthenocissus henryana, Zauschneria* 'Glasnevin' (now *Z. californica* 'Dublin'), *Tweedia caerulea* (though it's now *Oxypetalum caerulea*), and so on. Or the less-than-common and far more than ordinarily beautiful *Crinum moorei, Cymbidium mooreanum*, and so on. And forgiven also for not connecting those plant-specific names with the names of (Irish) plant hunters, and/or directors of Glasnevin: John Tweedie, Augustine Henry, David Moore, E. C. Ball.

Harder to forgive and indulge, but probably the most common oversight of all, is the fact that good old William Robinson – and the style he espoused (which, as the dust settles on the last century, seems to be emerging as the most influential of them all, doesn't it?) – was not English at all, but Irish. Once you appreciate that overlooked point, it follows really that an informed approach to his garden at Gravetye Manor in leafy Sussex would see it not as distillation of Englishness and England but as an outpost of Ireland. And that really does put the cat among the pigeons!

Gardens in Ireland are still not the widely-visited, often discussed places they are in England – staples of journalism, natural focuses of design concepts both trendy and traditional, places to lavish money on. Green space is not yet in Ireland the vanishing thing it is here, not yet deemed so precious because it is not yet so threatened. The Irish are more realistic about their climate than we are, so they don't go in much for the fiction of the outdoor room so beloved of English design gurus (and particularly those further reaches of credibility which take the form of the outdoor kitchen and dining room: the barbecue). The Irish are still a bit ambivalent about all the cultural baggage that comes with their centuries of endeavour to sever the colonial connection with Britain. Because residually they remain as symbols of alien occupation, some beautiful eighteenth-century houses are still left to rack, ruin and rot down there in the country. Because gardens and gardening belong, in the associative imagination, with that same colonial way of life – immensely cultured, but also alien, not vernacular, and therefore somehow tainted – they have yet to be 'forgiven' and absorbed into the perception, popular, scholarly and ethnographic alike, of what is legitimately Irish. Things are changing, though – very rapidly, actually. And anyway, sooner rather than later the national consciousness will recover and rediscover things about Ireland and her gardens which predate by far the English centuries – I mean the whole panoply of mythic paradises rooted so far back in pre-history as to be historically invisible: the Garden of Fand, Hy Brasil, Tir n'Og, and so on – or else the still palpable fact of the whole place, the entire island almost, being a natural garden anyway at certain times of the year. These things will legitimatise gardens and gardening in the end, and Ireland will no longer fight shy of its cultivated any more than it does now of its natural beauty.

As in England in late spring, the lanes of Queen Anne's lace are fabulous, but what happens after that? Well, in June and July, for example, consider this: 'the road verges are golden with tall buttercups, and flag irises still wave their yellow banners from bogs and ditches by West Cork roads. They stand tall amongst the deep green verdure of the damp places where they grow. Towering over them are the last of the foxgloves, thirty or more fingers and no thumbs . . . navelwort, that round-leaved plant of stone walls, seems sometimes to be almost competing with the foxgloves, which it resembles in small scale. Some years, it flowers to unprecedented heights, a metre from root to top, covered in creamy bell-like flowers . . . throughout July the procession of wild flowers goes on and on; it is a great month for the hedge scholar.' (Damien Enright: *A Place Near Heaven – A Year in West Cork*, 2004). That's one kind of Ireland-as-a-Garden, one style, if you like. Another, but much simpler and more beautiful even than that in my opinion, would be those still dampish but also sunny places a month later when meadow sweet (*Filipendula ulmaria*) and loosestrife (*Lythrum salicaria*) simultaneously blossom. Seeing the effect, you would impulsively and quite unselfconsciously call it 'drifts' and 'drifting', so right, so uncontrived and so stunning is the naturally massed combination of these two plants. A third – and this is the really famous one – is the western seaboard all summer long, where hundreds of miles of lanes are literally (and naturally) hedged by fuchsia (*F. magellanica*) and then, in late summer, hedged and edged by ruddy-gold montbretia. If that weren't enough, for connoisseurs of Lusitanian/alpine flora in spring there is the exquisite flora of the limestone trenches of the Burren in Co. Clare. In early autumn, the heaths on the mountain sides of Connemara have to be seen to be believed. And so it goes on.

That being the case, you might ask: Why bother to garden at all, when you've got all that, free on the doorstep? I sometimes wonder that myself, but not for long. Nature is a great landscaper, but only an accidental gardener. Or, rather, it is our perception of these events as 'gardens' which is actually the accident. The plants are there all right – at their numerical peak, 592 different species recorded on the islands of Roaring Water Bay off the farthest southwestern coast, the richest concentration of flora in Ireland – but not, except occasionally by accident, the associative contexts you find and expect in a garden. Gardeners cultivate not just plants but also the mind – its constructs and artifices of form, aesthetic associations and patternings, its thoughtful settlements of the competing claims of variety, on the one hand, and unity on the other; literary, mythic, cultural, even philosophical associations; and so on. Garden-like accidents do occur in Nature – I like to think that Jekyll would have given her eye-teeth for that combination in natural drifts of loosestrife and meadow sweet – and very happy accidents they are too, but that is why we notice them in the first place and then go on to remember them – as serendipities.

Had I to choose one single garden to epitomise the idea and the ideal of An Irish Garden, just one place which qualified as such, both because of its quality and because of its character, then – despite choosing from a very wide field – I would not have to ponder for all that long. Great gardens in Ireland spring readily to mind, but curiously enough they are not yet all that numerous, and not necessarily by any means particularly Irish: Ilnacullin, of course (but that's really an Italian garden – just as the travel posters say, and John Akeroyd faithfully reported in HORTUS 76); Powerscourt, to be sure (but that's Versailles-cum-the-Veneto-cum-Potsdam – and all refracted through a reactionary late-nineteenth century English-esque, and then superimposed upon the milieu of an emphatically eighteenth-century house); there's Butterstream, the darling of the pack I think (but even on its own terms, it is modelled as 'the Irish Sissinghurst'). And so it goes on. These high-profile, rightly-admired places are situated in Ireland, but you could not really argue that they are idiomatically Irish or that they set tones and patterns for any true vernacular. And now that one comes to think of it, a notional differentiation between Gardens in Ireland and Irish Gardens begins to take on the character of a very clear and virtually categorical distinction. But that's matter for another day.

So where would I go to enjoy an Irish garden on its own Irish terms, marrying Irish weather, soil and climate with a truly indigenous Irish frame of gardening-mind? The answer is Annes Grove, near Mallow in Co. Cork.

Not a lapse of the apostrophe, as it happens. The name came about as a playful (?) cross-pollination of surnames when, in 1776, one Mary Grove became the wife of a new member of the Irish peerage, the first Earl Annesley. She brought this estate with her, and left half her name attached for posterity. The playfulness continues with some of the place names in the garden itself. Parkeen (where 'park' is the English word and 'een' is the Irish diminutive), Top Inch, Skinny Inch, Upper Inch and Island (where the fun is that 'inch' comes from 'inish', the Irish noun for island, and 'island' doesn't). The house is a lovely, long-windowed, tall-roofed essay in Palladian simplicity and Wyattesque modesty. The gardens are later, so much later in fact that you can almost reach out and touch them as part of our own times and mindset, and that's part of the charm of the place: it doesn't stand upon ceremonies, nineteenth-century airs and graces, nineteenth-century affectations, or indeed upon anything pickled in the artificial aspic of the heritage industry. What we see now was begun only as recently as

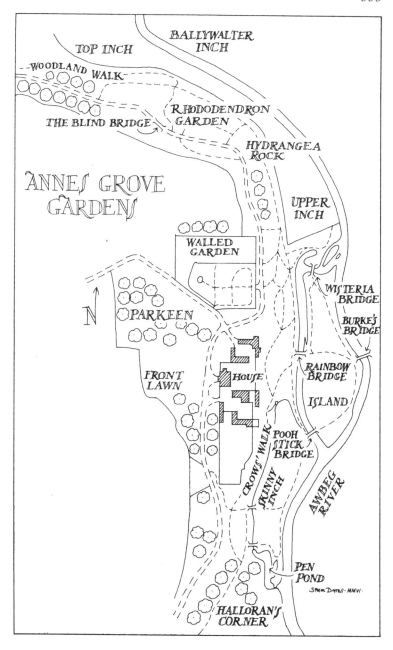

BALLYWALTER INCH

TOP INCH

WOODLAND WALK

THE BLIND BRIDGE

RHODODENDRON GARDEN

HYDRANGEA ROCK

ANNES GROVE GARDENS

WALLED GARDEN

UPPER INCH

N

PARKEEN

WISTERIA BRIDGE

BURKE'S BRIDGE

FRONT LAWN

HOUSE

RAINBOW BRIDGE

ISLAND

CROWS' WALK

POOH STICK BRIDGE

SKINNY INCH

AWBEG RIVER

PEN POND

Steve Dorrell · MMVI ·

HALLORAN'S CORNER

1900. Its begetter, Richard Grove Annesley, died only in 1966. It's all pretty well mature by now, of course. What we see, in effect, is an almost-period garden now at its probable apogee.

There are no architectural features, no sculpture. Such stone as you see is still growing in the earth, something else which makes this place essentially different and – though I think it's quite unconscious – contributes not a little to its striking but quite unforced, un-framed beauty. The house is stone and stucco, so is a pretty little lodge-gate cottage, and part of the garden is walled, but beyond that all the architecture is natural. Basically, it takes two forms, the arboreal and the riverine – fine beetling old trees on the one hand along the woodland walks which wind the length of the garden (half a mile or so – the garden itself covers something like thirty acres) and mark first its elevation, and then a steeply falling valley bottom – in part a gorge, really – which takes in most, but not all, of the rest. Together, these comprise two of the garden's three broad moods.

This is certainly not a garden of big views, but it does not by that token lack drama. Look up from the ground in the valley bottom (rodgersia, primula, hostas, lysichiton, gunnera, bamboos, all in riotous quantity and rude good health) and, over and over again, the eye will be lifted on and on upwards by carefully placed stands of coniferous trees – groups of green sky-scratchers, really. The sense of scale – vertical rather horizontal; a Sibelian tone poem rather than Wagnerian blockbuster – is terrific. The same goes for the valley floor itself. On the garden side it is spacious and meadow-like, but the paths wander over bridges, through groves of bamboo, under gunnera leaves, past promenades of stooled willows and, of course, allow the construction of a dialogue with the river itself. Its name is the Awbeg – lovely word, and not a joke this time because the word is ancient, but 'beg' means little, and it isn't, really. It flows sometimes so slowly and quietly that you could set your watch for Christmas by it. It's so clear, too. Then it speeds up, fairly chuckles on its way, but then finally shouts over the weirs. A heron gracefully beats up-stream. But on the other side, away from the path, the garden and the flat meadows, there is a cliff, a wall of rock, sheer in parts and thirty feet high, dripping with wild plants and well-behaved water.

The genius of the place is Ireland itself and Ireland's own gardener, William Robinson. There's not a straight line anywhere, except upwards in those perpendicular trees. There's almost no formal, geometrical orderliness either. There is only one lawn (in front of the house, and it's daffodil-strewn in spring), and there is not even a whisper of bedding. That's Robinson. Instead, there's a fantastically rich collection of woodlanders: rhododendrons, azaleas and magnolias punctuated from time to time by summer spots planted with hoherias, embothriums, myrtles, abutilons, azaras and – unlikely though it might seem, on steep rocky banks – hydrangeas. The health and happiness of the plants here are infectious: the heart sings with it all. The symphonic scale of the place and the planting is pretty impressive too, but not overwhelming or bombastic or grandiloquent. Here a *Magnolia obovata* or there a *Cornus controversa* 'Variegata', each of extraordinary size, share their neighbourhood with mosses and ferns, wrens and voles. The manic efflorescent clouts of *Gunnera manicata* share the space with water avens and some miniature equisetum, just as, up in the woods, the very big crinodendrons don't necessarily steal the show in spring; they share it with *Anemone nemorosa* (at least some of it *Anemone nemorosa* 'Robinsoniana', as it happens). It's all a question of balance and blend: the exotic and the native, the large and small, the showy and the modest, and almost all of it within an essentially woodland context. That's classically Robinsonian.

So far, then, two distinct zones of gardening – the woodland and the riverine – the two connecting and melding along their shared margins. But Annes Grove has a third element. That wall mentioned earlier occurs only in one part of the garden, just beyond the house. The gate is small, Gothic and irresistible. It leads straight into the Walled Garden to one of the finest double herbaceous borders you'd find anywhere in Ireland – or England, or anywhere. It is a gem. Like all of its kind, it is extremely labour-intensive; but like only the best of its kind the labour, as here, is invisible. At eye level thalictrum, helianthus, acanthus, helenium, aruncus, veratrums and golden achillea. Above and behind them *Echium pininana*, *Macleaya cordata*, and *Tropaeolum speciosum* scrambling over the yew hedges which shut in the space. Further forward and nearer you, all sorts of poppies, geraniums and evening primroses – an amazingly skilful blend of colour, height, texture and flowering times, each successive phase replacing the earlier ones but still being supported by them and set off to their best advantage by them. This is gardening indeed!

Look back and you see the wall, but only just, because it is conceding its presence to a tumbling tumult of *Actinidia kolomikta*, its dusky-hairy leaves variegated green, pink and white. Look up and your vision climbs a towering eucryphia, an enviable genus of stupendous plants that do far, far better in south-western Ireland than they ever do in England, for all the cosseting they may get here.

Then – and still within those walls – there's a water garden, and a pair of beds rippling with box hedges which fall just short of being tied in knots. Instead, they are crammed full not of high-toned penstemons, well-bred salvias and toffee-nosed kniphofias, but of lupins! And when did you last see lupins massed, mixed and unmustered, as plants worthy of attention in their own right? These beds lie along what was originally the main axis of the Walled Garden, before the herbaceous borders came about, that is. On your right is a low mount, and a Victorian summer house, too fragile to use now, but curiously twiggy in construction and decoration. On your left there are roses and wall plants. Behind you, when you return (in spring, if you can manage it), is a large plantation of *Helleborus* × *hybridus*. But only the careless would return too soon because ahead of you, though hidden behind a hedge, lies the nursery.

It has to be said that nurseries are quite rare in Ireland, and good ones rarer still. Here is one of the latter – small, quite specialised (in woodlanders, and, again therefore quite Robinsonian), and not to be missed on any account: uvularia in several varieties, likewise convallaria, maianthemum (three species), hostas (called funkias in Robinson's time), *Jeffersonia* (both *dyphylla* and *dubia*), disporums, disporopsis, polygonatums, epimediums, and much more of the same. But there are also plenty of sunny things too – half-hardy salvias, hedychiums, and special among them some varieties of *Paeonia delavayi* (*P. moutan* to Robinson), one of them probably unique to Annes Grove. Oh yes, and there's a really charming kniphofia called 'Toffee Nose'.

A few miles upstream on the Awbeg, Edmund Spenser lived and, of course, wrote. Tradition has him associated with Annes Grove. Even allowing for the slight anachronism it's possible, though he was never a gardener. He called the river the 'Mulla', which seems a pity. Be that as it may, he might have been penning an epigraph to this very spot, Annes Grove, when in *The Faerie Queen* they resort to:

> A shadie grove not far away . . .
> Whose loftie trees yclad with summers pride
> Did spread so broad . . .
> And all within were pathes and alleys wide
> With footing worne, and leading inward farre;
> Faire harbour that them seemes; so in they entered are.

Bibliography

John Akeroyd (ed.): *The Wild Plants of Sherkin, Cape Clear and Adjacent Islands of West Cork*

Brian de Breffny (ed.): *Ireland: A Cultural Encyclopedia*

Michael George and Patrick Bowe: *The Gardens of Ireland*

Charles Nelson and Eileen McCracken: *The Brightest Jewel – A History of the National Botanic Gardens, Glasnevin, Dublin*

Terence Reeves-Smith: *Irish Gardens*

Tim Richardson and Noel Kingsbury (eds): *Vista – The Culture and Politics of Gardens*

William Trevor: *A Writer's Ireland – Landscape in Literature*

Drawing and plan of garden by Simon Dorrell.

A Work to Wonder At

THE CREATION OF STOWE AS A LANDSCAPE GARDEN

CELIA FISHER

The idea of romantic, naturalistic landscape gardening is generally said to have grown up in early eighteenth-century literary circles under the influence of Alexander Pope. He started, around 1718, to lay out his own gardens by the Thames at Twickenham with lawns, winding paths and a fashionable grotto, and wrote well-known verses praising the 'opening glade' and satirising the formality of clipped evergreens and symmetrical bedding. But half a century earlier, in *Paradise Lost*, Milton had created a garden of Eden that was even more evocative: 'A happy rural seat of various view' in Book IV; 'How nature paints her colours' in Book V; 'Hill, dale and shady woods and sunny plains, and liquid lapse of murmuring streams' in Book VIII. In an unexpected parallel, Sir William Temple's influential *Essay on Chinese Gardens* (1685) explained that their inspiration derived from natural rock formations, cascades and forests, achieving a 'beauty without any order that is easily discerned', and certainly 'scorning symmetry'. Meanwhile the word 'landscape' itself was just evolving from the Dutch 'lantskip', which meant a painting of inland scenery as distinct from a seascape.

So painting and poetry were the forebears which the landscape gardening movement very consciously acknowledged from its inception. In 1712 Joseph Addison explained in an article in the *Tatler*, 'If the natural embroidery of the meadows were helped and improved by some small additions of art and the several rows of hedges set off by trees and flowers . . . a man might make a pretty *landscape* of his own possessions.' But did these innovators realise that their creations would be as artificial as any previous style of gardening, by definition perhaps more so? Artifice had already been added to the equation in 1709 when John Vanbrugh made his plea for significant garden buildings, stressing the importance of their disposition in the landscape to 'move lively and pleasing reflections'. Many great estates were transformed according to these tenets during the eighteenth century. Stowe in Buckinghamshire led the field, constantly changing and providing an example, and embodying the spirit of the age in a great array of manifestations, some ostentatious, some melancholy, some quirky.

The approaches to Stowe, previously through the Buckingham Gates and the Corinthian Arch, now over the urn-bedecked Oxford Bridge and past the Boycott Pavilions, are grandiose. But the heart of the garden lies beyond the south side of the House (and School). Here the lawns slope down to the lakes and the tree-lined vista stretches onwards between two Tuscan temples to the Corinthian Arch on the horizon. When 'Capability' Brown arrived here as a young gardener in 1740 Stowe did not look as it does now: an earlier landscaped vision lay before him, and first opened his eyes to the potential of great estates for naturalistic development. On this spot where Brown first stood gazing into the distance there had been a seventeenth-century Parlour Garden with formal beds in long strips and rectangles, lines of box pyramids, and two circular pools with fountains, for which Christopher Wren had provided advice on water pipes. Enclosing this were arbours and walls with espaliered fruit trees. In 1694 Celia Fiennes described how this formal garden descended in 'terrace walks replenished with curiosities', while beyond lay orchards and woods, and an avenue of poplars known as the Abele Walk created a vista to the fish ponds at the bottom of the valley.

Sir Richard Temple inherited Stowe in 1697 and for more than fifteen years he let well alone. He was often away campaigning in Europe as one of Marlborough's generals, or else in London involved in the political preoccupations of the Whig aristocracy. All of which earned him the reputation – necessary to anyone who wishes to remake a garden – of being a man 'who did not hate a difficulty'. He first experienced the alternative joys of gardening leave when the Tory Government dismissed him from the army in 1713. But the following year George I came to the throne and his fortunes were again reversed. The Whigs, who had supported the Hanoverian succession, regained the ascendant and Temple was

created Lord Cobham. His finances were assured by his own successful military ventures and by his wife, who was the heiress to a wealthy City brewer. In celebration of all this the garden was transformed. First the old-fashioned terraces and fruit trees of the Parlour Garden were replaced by sweeps of symmetrical lawns and larger channels of formal water, in the manner of nearby Blenheim. For the time being the surrounding walls remained, but were newly lined with niches for urns and busts. And in 1714 Bridgeman made a first shadowy appearance, receiving a payment of £1 2*s.* 6*d.* Thus the scene was set for landscaping.

Bridgeman is always associated with the introduction of the haha, and nowhere more so than at Stowe, where he laboured between 1718 and 1733 to enclose the gardens in a huge pentagonal shape reminiscent of European fortresses (the pentagon was an ancient symbol of power). Indeed, when Lord Cobham surveyed the walled embankments and grassy ditches of his haha at Stowe – which in the earliest records were referred to as the stockade ditch – they surely reminded him of fortifications seen during his European wars, especially where the corners of the pentagon were reinforced by bastions. Horace Walpole later credited Bridgeman with the invention of the haha, and thus with creating the illusion that a garden could extend uninterrupted into the wider landscape beyond. Bridgeman's early achievements at Blenheim and Stowe earned him this reputation, but the haha already existed in France, and was first described in a book translated by John James in 1712 entitled *The Theory and Practice of Gardening*. Later Bridgeman became the Royal Gardener and created the haha which runs by the river at Kew, but the enclosure and design of Stowe remained his most spectacular achievement. From the parterres of the south front Bridgeman ran straight vistas eastwards and westwards to his expansive new boundaries, enhanced by focal points, while straight ahead in the valley beneath the south front the old fish ponds were transformed into a large octagonal lake with an obelisk at the centre. By 1724 Lord Perceval could write that Stowe had 'the reputation of being the finest seat in England' and 'Bridgeman laid out the grounds and planned the whole which cannot fail of recommending him in the business'. To commemorate his work Bridgeman commissioned fifteen views of Stowe from Jaques Rigaud, which were published by his widow in 1739. They bear witness to the geometric wonderland that existed before it was blurred and lost in another wave of naturalism.

To the west, then as now, lay Lord Cobham's two monuments to Venus – such Classical deities being a necessary part of a garden in the century of the Grand Tour, when myths of the gods added meaning to every allusion, whether it was idealistic, satirical or lustful (and Venus could be all of these). First the Rotunda, with columns encircling a golden statue of Venus under a domed roof, was designed by Sir John Vanbrugh in 1720, soon after he was driven from Blenheim to Stowe by the tantrums of the Duchess of Marlborough. 'Lo in the centre of this beauteous scene / Glitters beneath her dome the Cyprian Queen' wrote Gilbert West, one of Lord Cobham's nephews, in his poem on Stowe in 1732. Maybe Venus was chosen not only as the goddess of love but for her associations with flowers, arbours, pools, and all that was fertile. Lord Cobham and the society architect Vanbrugh were friends and fellow-

members of the Kit-Cat Club, a political fraternity commemorated
in Kneller's heavily-wigged portraits. Another of these Whig drinking companions was the poet William Congreve, who has a little
island monument in the lake at Stowe, a pyramid topped by a
monkey holding 'a mirror up to nature', as Congreve did in his
plays. In 1725 Vanbrugh wrote after a visit that Stowe was 'a place
now so agreeable that I had much ado to leave it at all', and in 1728
Congreve wrote a teasing verse:

> Say Cobham what amuses thy retreat,
> Or schemes of war, or stratagems of state?
> Or dost thou give the winds afar to blow
> Each vexing thought and heart devouring woe,
> And fix thy mind alone on rural scenes
> To turn the levelled lawns to liquid plains.

Across one such rural scene of grass and water the statue of Venus
in the Rotunda still gazes towards the south-western bastion of
Bridgeman's haha, where her Temple was built by William Kent in

1731. The style is gently Classical with low arches, columns and domes, and Kent used a tawny limestone that blends softly with the trees and reflects golden in the water when the sun touches it. Venus's Temple was then embellished with busts of debauched emperors, including Nero, and temptresses such as Cleopatra. Inside it was painted with seduction scenes from Spencer's *Faery Queen* and furnished with a 'pleasuring sofa'. Time has removed these, leaving the symmetrical serenity of Kent's design untroubled by any but the calmest thoughts.

Despite these tributes to Venus, Lord Cobham's heart was not in the Classical past and Stowe has none of the numinous quality of nearby Rousham where the gods still play – Venus hovers above the lily ponds and touches her breast, Pan leers over his pipes, Bacchus leans tipsily backwards and Mercury points the way up a dark path. At Rousham Kent and Bridgeman took time off from the grandeurs of Stowe to create the perfect picturesque garden. They turned a steep riverbank into a grassy amphitheatre, presided over by a mysterious arcaded building, which they named after the Temple of Fortune at Praeneste. The waters were drawn into cascades, rills and an octagon pool (not drowned into a large lake). Serpentine paths linked these with a small, sad Temple of Echo darkened by evergreens. Even the open countryside beyond seems drawn into intimacy, and over the fields, where a cattle-shed threatened to intrude, a facade was built to transform it into a Gothic eye-catcher.

Kent's success owed much to the chameleon quality of his designs. His Classical arches and pediments rendered in rough-hewn stone could be adapted into varying sizes and uses. He could make them more exotic by incorporating a pyramid, or more stately with columns and busts, or more functional as bridges. The Hermitage that Kent created for Queen Caroline at Kew, with three arched doorways and a central pediment, was built into a mound topped with little conifers and described as 'very gothique, being a heap of stones thrown into very artful disorder and curiously embellished with shrubs to represent rude nature'. Kent's smaller Hermitage at Stowe has just one pedimented doorway for gazing over the lake, and low square towers on either side, one of which was designed to

look ruined. The fashion for building picturesque ruins (reminiscent of many paintings of Classical scenes in distant landscape
settings) was started by Kent in the 1730s, and at Stowe was also
used for the arcaded causeway between the two lakes, and for the
Temple of Modern Virtue (no longer with us) in the Elysian Fields.

While Bridgeman was still labouring on his boundaries and long
vistas, the landscaping at Stowe which especially represents Kent's
vision and skills was created in a dip in the land east of the central
parterres of the south front. Here the old road from Buckingham to
the house and church, which ran beside and over the streams that
feed the lakes, was made to vanish. Instead Kent created a sequence
of scenes by setting temples artfully among trees, like paintings
come to life. This area was called the Elysian Fields after the Greek
concept of Paradise, and it suited the mood of the times, since
naturalistic planting had to be reconciled with sophisticated literary allusions. At Stowe the stream was the centrepiece of the Elysian
Fields. In its upper level, where it flowed darkly among alders,
chestnuts and evergreens, it was renamed the Styx after the river of
the Underworld. When it reached Kent's Grotto of Contemplation
it formed a cascade and then drifted calmly through the lawns and

dappled shade where Kent's various temples were built. In 1734 the Earl of Carlisle heard from Sir Thomas Robinson of a 'new taste in gardening just arisen' and 'a general alteration of some of the most remarkable gardens in the kingdom after Mr Kent's notion of gardening viz. to lay them out and work without level or line . . . the celebrated gardens at Claremont, Chiswick and Stowe are now full of labourers.' By 1739 the hurly-burly of construction must have died down, because Alexander Pope wrote after one of his frequent visits to Stowe, 'I never saw this place in half the beauty and perfection it now has . . . the New Part is beyond description – 'tis the Elysian Fields that is the *painting* part of his gardens.' And later Horace Walpole admitted that Stowe exemplified his dictum that 'Kent leapt the fence and saw all Nature was a garden'.

The time when Kent was making himself indispensable at Stowe coincided with a second reversal in Lord Cobham's political fortunes. In 1733 he quarrelled with the Whig Prime Minister Robert Walpole (father of Horace Walpole, the arbiter of taste) over his plans to increase excise duties, which were widely seen as a sinister extension of the powers of Government as well as damaging to the commercial interests of the City, which the Whigs were supposed to nurture. Cobham spent the ensuing years in opposition, and Stowe's ruined Temple of Modern Virtue, which enshrined a headless torso, was therefore his ironic statement on the times. It was even suspected that the torso was Walpole's. To contrast with this crumbling folly in the Elysian Fields, Kent created the nearby Temple of Ancient Virtue as a symbol of Classical integrity, circular and enduring. And there was a third edifice to balance these two, a Temple of British Worthies, where a row of eclectic busts in ruffs, helmets, caps and open-necked shirts stares out with varying degrees of surprise at being included. There are no churchmen; Queen Elizabeth is the only woman; and there is much fun to be had in puzzling out what she had in common with John Hampden, or John Milton with Francis Drake; and in what way each of the sixteen chosen Worthies was considered by Lord Cobham to be politically correct. Again there was a link with the Hermitage at Kew, where Kent created niches for busts of worthy thinkers in-

cluding Robert Boyle, John Locke and Isaac Newton. The Italianate design for the Temple of Worthies was initially drawn up for Chiswick House, the home of Kent's first patron Lord Burlington, whom he had met in Italy in 1719. There was also a conceptual link with an article published by Addison in the *Tatler* in 1710, describing an allegorical wood with many paths, and with temples dedicated to virtue, honour and vanity, and effigies which also correspond closely. On its grassy slope, facing up towards the other two temples across the stream, the Temple of British Worthies forms a gentle ellipse, with shallow steps leading to the long row of arched niches in which the busts are set. The whole is rendered more monumental by a central block topped by a pyramid, where a statue of Mercury formerly pointed the way to Paradise – or where some have suggested a secret masonic message may be read. (There were more pyramids at Stowe in the early days, including a large one designed by Vanbrugh.)

One other monument in the Elysian Fields (although it arrived here after Kent's time) testifies to a personal loss. The Grenville column, decorated oddly with protruding prows of ships, was erected

in honour of Captain Thomas Grenville, one of Lord Cobham's
nephews who, since he had no children, were like sons to him. In
1747 Thomas, commanding the *Defiance* in Lord Anson's fleet, was
fatally wounded in action against the French off Cape Finisterre.
Thomas had two older brothers. Richard Temple inherited Stowe
after Lord Cobham died in 1749 and took the title Earl Temple; he
was a Whig grandee, restlessly espousing principles of liberty, even
supporting the radical journalist John Wilkes. The second brother
was George Grenville, who became Prime Minister briefly in 1763,
introducing the Stamp Tax which precipitated the revolt of the
American colonies. More illustrious by far was the husband of their
sister Hester, William Pitt, Earl Chatham, one of the great eighteenth-century wartime Prime Ministers and father of the other. In
their youth in the 1730s 'Cobham's Cubs', as they were called, were
moulded into a powerful Whig dynasty holding the patronage of
many MPs. If they could only have retained the unity that their
father-figure Lord Cobham instilled in them they might, in the
words of a contemporary, 'have governed the country for a generation'. Their symbolic meeting place at Stowe was the Temple of
Friendship, built on the south-east bastion of Bridgeman's haha in
1739 – the only folly with a kitchen and ample cellarage. That same
year Alexander Pope described a typical day during a visit to Stowe:
'At mornings we breakfast and dispute; into the garden fishing . . .
everyone takes a different way and wanders about till we meet at
noon. After dinner and at night music and harmony, no politics.'
The Temple of Friendship also celebrated a visit to Stowe, in 1737,
by Frederick Prince of Wales, son of George II and father of George
III, who led the opposition to his father's government, a Hanoverian
characteristic. The Prince's secretary was another of Lord Cobham's
politically important nephews, George Lyttelton. Frederick was
also remarkable among the gardening fraternity. At Carlton House
his garden was in the vanguard of innovative design, and at Kew
he was among the first to collect the exotic trees arriving from
America and the Far East, thus setting in motion the process which
turned Kew into a botanic garden. On the other hand, the massive
tree-planting programme initiated by Lord Cobham at Stowe relied

on native trees, mostly reared locally, but a few eighteenth-century exotics arrived to embellish the grounds including magnolia, liquidambar, ginkgo and liriodendron.

There was another garden in the Temple/Grenville/Pitt scenario: Wotton, which lies twelve miles south of Stowe, ancestral home of the Grenville brothers, where Pitt often visited, proposed to their sister Hester, and made firm friends with 'Capability' Brown as they discussed landscape theory together. During the 1740s Brown worked at both Stowe and Wotton, being appointed head gardener at Stowe by Lord Cobham in 1742 and intermittently lent to the family at Wotton. At Stowe Brown's signature work was the Grecian Valley which extends north above the Elysian Fields. He lined its banks attractively with trees, but failed to make the valley floor flood into a lake. His great innovation was the use of a horse-drawn vehicle for transporting semi-mature trees to the valley from other parts of the garden, which achieved the dual purpose of thinning and softening Bridgeman's earlier vistas. In the 1750s Richard Grenville, on inheriting Stowe, encouraged more changes, including extending the two existing lakes into a continuous sheet of water and removing the formal outlines Bridgeman had given them. It is not recorded that Brown was instrumental in this but the 'improvement' certainly reflected his style – a style so instantly recognisable and famous that it could be parodied decades later by Thomas Love Peacock in the character of Mr Milestone at Headlong Hall 'waving the wand of enchantment and inventing the noble art of picturesque gardening' – resulting in a wonderfully farcical incident with gunpowder and a ruined tower.

Meanwhile at Wotton in the 1750s 'Capability' Brown was indeed busy bringing naturalism to the garden, extending the waters to flow around islands, under bridges and over a cascade known as the five-arch bridge, which is very like a double version of Kent's bridge in the Elysian Fields at Stowe. Also reminiscent of Stowe were the two colonnaded Tuscan Temples framing the main view of the lake as it was approached from the house; and here too the circular walk around the water passed a variety of viewpoints, temples, urns, statues and follies. Lady Betty Freemantle compared the two gardens after a visit to Wotton in 1804 when she 'took the entire round of the gardens, three miles, and was much delighted with the walks which are much more natural than those at Stowe . . . there are a number of pavilions etc. about this place, the whole laid out with infinite taste.' The most appealing viewpoint at Wotton is the Octagon which, since it lies at the furthest point on the lakeside from the house, provides welcome seating from which to stare dreamily through its elegant little arches. To the right they frame nearby views of swans and water-lilies drifting on the serpentine canal that unites the lakes, and to the left, harmonised by the arches into a continuous rhythm, lies the wider stretch of water edged with other features glimpsed among the trees. Best by far is a Turkish Pavilion, the colour of mist, its peaking roof topped by a golden crescent and descending to a row of upward curving gables like ivory tusks. It is supported on dainty fluted columns linked together with delicate tracery panels. This Islamic fantasy is a rare survival of an eighteenth-century fashion – the Turkish Tent at Painshill had to be recreated, and the Mosque and Alhambra at Kew are long gone.

If one were to compare the landscape gardens of Stowe and Wotton, with their Classically-inspired embellishments, to a rich fruit cake, then the icing was provided by the follies devised in an exotic style. But the apparent frivolity of turning mosques and pagodas into garden features was not the whole story. They reflected the expansionist and commercial obsessions of the time, which led many to risk their lives and fortunes in pursuit of the Orient and its wonders. Stowe and Wotton also had a Chinoiserie feature – which they shared – a delightful little tea-house with golden fish curving their tails on the roof, latticed windows painted green, red decorative panels, and Chinese ladies posed decorously round the outside walls. The tea house started off near the Elysian Fields, apparently designed by Kent in the mid 1730s so that Lord Cobham could be in the vanguard of every garden fashion. It is the oldest Chinoiserie building in England, but it was surely out of place where the prevailing mood was so Classical, and by the 1750s the Grenvilles had moved it to Wotton, to an island site on the lake diametrically opposite the Turkish Tent, blending far more happily into a garden adorned with pleasure domes rather than temples. Alas the Chinese tea-house was later transported to Ireland, and then recently restored to Stowe where it is now hidden in a secret garden of its own.

However, the oddest and most imposing folly of which these two gardens can boast is the Gothic Temple at Stowe, another of Lord Cobham's political statements. It was designed by James Gibbs, also a leading society architect, midway through the period from 1727 to 1741 when he was responsible for a number of important buildings at Stowe including the Temple of Friendship; the corresponding Queen's Temple built for Lady Cobham and her cronies; and the Palladian Bridge crossing the head of the lake between them. Like the Gothic Temple these buildings all lie to the east of Kent's central stronghold. This area, known as the Hawkwell Field, is pastureland where sheep still roam, the grass is rough, and armies of crows add to the Gothic atmosphere of the Tower. But in the eighteenth century, before the writings of William Beckford and Edgar Allen Poe had popularised its spooky connotations, Gothic meant pertaining to all that was most noble in our Anglo-Saxon heritage, as opposed to Roman imperial tyranny. Something Tacitus had written gave the impression that the Goths were democrats as well as fighters, hence their appeal to Lord Cobham in his indignation at the increasingly corrupt and effete government of Walpole and George II. In 1748 Lady Grey wrote after a visit to Stowe, 'The gothic building, half church, half tower in appearance, is the most uncommon and best in its way.' It was indeed a spectacular forerunner of the Gothic Revival. Gibbs had drawn inspiration for the traceried windows, battlements and turrets from medieval buildings in the perpendicular style, and he used reddish iron-stone to add an impression of brute force. Another source of ideas may have been the Triangular Lodge at Rushton, some thirty miles north of Stowe, built by Lord Cobham's distant and far more eccentric ancestor Sir Thomas Tresham in 1597. Stowe's Gothic Temple also has a triangular ground-plan, three towers, and windows in sets of three, indicating that it shared the number symbolism of Tresham's trefoil-encrusted lodge. Lord Cobham's concept of trinity was based on the three Whig watch-words Liberty, Enlightenment and Constitution, in proof whereof his Gothic folly was originally known as the Temple of Liberty. Inside, the golden mosaic ceiling was decorated with the shields of imaginary Saxon ancestors and nearby stood statues of the Saxon gods who gave their names to the days of the week. As the temple was receiving these finishing touches, Walpole finally lost power in 1742 and the way was open for Cobham's 'Patriot Boys', led by Pitt, to gain the ascendant in Whig politics.

It seems unlikely that Stowe during the period of its creation was ever particularly harmonious, although several poets wrote of the 'sweet sylvan scene' and 'social Stowe'. They must have turned a blind eye to endless construction work and alterations to the landscape, as well as political fracas. Obviously the ideal was there, lulled by the lovely rural setting, and now that everything has been mellowed by time Pope's lines from the 'Epistle to Lord Burlington' are probably more apt than ever.

> Consult the genius of the place in all . . .
> Parts answering parts shall slide into a whole,
> Spontaneous beauties all around advance,
> Start ev'n from difficulty, strike from chance;
> Nature shall join you, time shall make it grow
> A work to wonder at – perhaps a Stowe.

Illustrations by Simon Dorrell.

Who's Who

JOHN AKEROYD is a freelance botanist, conservationist and writer who lives in Wiltshire. He has written extensively for HORTUS, mainly about wild flowers and garden-worthy plants found in the British and European countryside.

RONALD BLYTHE is a critic, poet, short-story writer and novelist. He is the author of *The Age of Illusion*, *Akenfield*, *The View in Winter*, *From the Headlands* and *Divine Landscapes*. He is editor of *Writing in a War* (originally published as *Components of the Scene*), *The Penguin Book of Diaries* and *Private Words: Letters and Diaries from the Second World War*. He has edited Thomas Hardy's *Far From the Madding Crowd*, Henry James's *The Awkward Age*, and *William Hazlitt: Selected Writing*. He is President of the John Clare Society and a lay preacher serving three churches on his native Essex/Suffolk border.

URSULA BUCHAN read Modern History at Cambridge and then trained as a gardener at the Royal Horticultural Society's gardens at Wisley and the Royal Botanic Gardens, Kew. She writes regularly for several newspapers and in 2006 published *The English Garden*, a comprehensive overview of horticultural trends and the work of English garden-makers past and present.

BETH CHATTO is one of Britain's foremost plantswomen, and her Essex garden has won worldwide acclaim. Her books include *The Dry Garden*, *The Damp Garden*, *The Green Tapestry*, *Beth Chatto's Gravel Garden* and *Beth Chatto's Garden Notebook*. She was a frequent exhibitor at the Chelsea Flower Show and holds the Royal Horticultural Society's highest award, the Victoria Medal of Honour.

NIGEL COLBORN is a writer and broadcaster whose many books include *This Gardening Business*, *Leisurely Gardening*, *The Container Garden*, *Short Cuts to Great Gardens* and *Great Plants for Small Gardens*. He has appeared on many television gardening programmes and is a regular panellist on BBC's *Gardeners' Question Time*.

PETER DALE is a poet, freelance writer and gardener whose contributions to HORTUS include a series on Irish gardens.

ROBERT DASH is a painter whose garden, Madoo, at Sagaponack on New York's Long Island, is now part of the US Garden Conservancy.

ALEX DUFORT is the proprietor of Brixton Pottery and an occasional columnist in several British newspapers. He is a former chairman of Mid Border Arts, a community arts programme based in the Radnorshire town of Presteigne.

AMBRA EDWARDS is a writer, campaigner and garden historian who contributes to a variety of gardening titles. In 2006 she won the Garden Writers' Guild Journalist of the Year award, her work for HORTUS being singled out for praise.

SUSAN ELDERKIN is the daughter of an architect and a concert pianist, and writes about gardens for several British newspapers and magazines. Her first novel, *Sunset Over Chocolate Mountains* was awarded a Betty Trask prize. Her second novel, *The Voices*, set in Western Australia, was shortlisted for the International IMPAC Dublin Literary Award and the Ondaatje Prize.

CHARLES ELLIOTT was until he retired a senior editor of the American publishing firm Alfred A. Knopf. He is the author of several books on gardening and garden history and a regular contributor to HORTUS.

CELIA FISHER is a freelance writer who has studied the use of plants and their appearance in art and literature, having written her Ph.D. thesis on flowers in the borders of illuminated manuscripts. Her books include *Flowers and Fruit* (for the National Gallery), *Still Life Paintings* and *Flowers in Medieval Manuscripts* (for the British Library).

JOHN FRANCIS wrote extensively in HORTUS about gardens in the novels of E. F. Benson, Guiseppi di Lampedusa, Barbara Pym, Beverley Nichols, Molly Keane, and many others.

FERGUS GARRETT worked closely with Christopher Lloyd at Great Dixter, where he is now Head Gardener.

NANCY-MARY GOODALL contributed many articles to the early issues of HORTUS, including a series of four autobiographical essays centred on her life as a gardener and gardens enthusiast.

GRAHAM GOUGH is the proprietor of Marchants Hardy Plants in East Sussex, a renowned nursery specialising in snowdrops and late-summer perennials, many of which he has collected himself on plant-hunting trips in eastern Europe and South Africa.

JIM GOULD worked as an archaeologist and historian and grew auriculas and pinks which won prizes at many horticultural shows. His essays for HORTUS ranged over such esoteric subjects as botanical cigarette cards and birdlife in the garden.

JOHN HALL lives in Italy where he manages his own vineyard, olive grove and livestock. He is the Founder-Director of the annual Pre-University Course in Venice and arranges specialised garden tours of Italy.

PENELOPE HOBHOUSE is a garden writer, garden designer, garden historian, lecturer and gardener. For fourteen years until 1993 she was in charge of the National Trust gardens at Tintinhull House in Somerset. Today she lives in Dorset and travels in Europe, Australia and the United States lecturing and designing gardens. Her many books include *Garden Style*, *Plants in Garden History*, *Penelope Hobhouse's Natural Planting*, *Gardens of Italy*, and *Colour in Your Garden*. She is a recipient of the Royal Horticultural Society's Victoria Medal of Honour.

DEBORAH KELLAWAY, who was distantly related to Viginia Woolf, began her academic career in her native Australia. She was garden columnist for the *Oldie* magazine until her death in 2006. Her books include *The Virago Book of Women Gardeners*.

JOHN KELLY contributed many humourous, controversial and thought-provoking articles to HORTUS. In 1978 he was appointed Curator of the Subtropical Gardens at Abbotsbury in Dorset. His books include *Ferns in Your Garden*. He made numerous appearances on BBC television's *Gardener's World*. He died in 1997.

ANTHONY KING-DEACON was a journalist who, in mid-career, moved with his wife to Norfolk to become a professional gardener and garden designer, and a contributor to the *Eastern Daily Press*, the *Daily Telegraph* and *The English Garden* magazine.

NOEL KINGSBURY is a freelance garden writer and former nurseryman. He takes a special interest in 'prairie' planting, involving the combined use of native perennial plants and ornamental grasses. His many books include *The New Perennial Garden*, *Designing with Plants* (with Piet Oudolf) and *Natural Gardening in Small Spaces*.

CAROL KLEIN runs a nursery in Devon, and her knowledge of and enthusiasm for plants has won her international recognition. She has made many television and radio appearances.

STEPHEN LACEY became a freelance garden writer, lecturer and designer after an early career in property investment. His books include the *The Startling Jungle* and *Scent in Your Garden*.

ANDREW LAWSON is one of Britain's leading garden photographers, contributing to books by Rosemary Verey, Penelope Hobhouse and HRH The Prince of Wales. He holds the Royal Horticultural Society's Gold Medal for Photography and was named Photographer of the Year by the Garden Writers' Guild.

AUDREY LE LIÈVRE wrote *Miss Willmott of Warley Place*, a biography of gardening plutocrat Ellen Willmott. For HORTUS she wrote about violas, poppies, irises and the genus Primula, as well as articles about plant hunters and foreign flora.

ALVILDE LEES-MILNE was a garden designer who worked in Britain and France for a list of clients including Mick Jagger and Valéry Giscard d'Estaing. With Rosemary Verey she co-edited the ground-breaking *The Englishwoman's Garden* and *The Englishman's Garden*. She also served on the National Trust gardens panel and on the council of the National Gardens Scheme.

TIM LONGVILLE is a freelance writer, translator and poet who has written extensively for HORTUS on a wide variety of topics. His home in north-west England has given him easy access to the gardens (and gardeners) of the north of England and the Scottish borders, and he is the author of *Gardens of the Lake District.*

DAWN MACLEOD designed and made several gardens and assisted Mairi Sawyer at the famous gardens of Inverewe on the west coast of Scotland. Her books include *A Book of Herbs*, *The Gardener's London* and *Down-to-Earth Women*, a series of biographical chapters on such luminaries as Jane Loudon, Mrs C. F. Leyel, Margery Fish and Vita Sackville-West.

MARTA MCDOWELL is a freelance garden writer and lecturer who has taught at the New York Botanical Garden. In HORTUS 54 she wrote about Emily Dickinson's garden and poetry.

RICHARD MABEY is a renowned author and broadcaster whose books include *Food for Free*, *The Unofficial Countryside*, a biography of Gilbert White (winner of the Whitbread Prize in 1986) and *Flora Britannica*, the definitive reference work on British wild flowers.

MIRABEL OSLER caught a generation's imagination with her book *A Gentle Plea for Chaos* (1989), about the garden she made with her husband Michael in the Shropshire countryside.

MITCHELL OWENS is a freelance writer and former Articles Editor of *Elle Decor* magazine in New York.

PETER PARKER has written extensively in HORTUS, contributing articles about (among others) Angus Wilson and Beatrix Potter in the *Gardens in Fiction* series. He has written several books, including a biography of Christopher Isherwood.

ANNE POWELL is the editor of *A Deep Cry* and *Shadows of War: British Women's Poetry of the Second World War.*

DIANA ROSS has interviewed many gardening and literary worthies for HORTUS, among them the Marchioness of Salisbury, Beth Chatto, Donald Waterer, Roy Lancaster, Geoffrey Dutton, Anne Scott-James, Hugh Johnson, Elizabeth Jane Howard, Kim Wilkie, Richard Mabey, Christian Lamb, Dan Pearson, Ronald Blythe and Professor James Lovelock.

TONY SCHILLING has been a plant hunter and was curator of the gardens at Wakehurst Place in Sussex. In conjunction with his wife he runs the Tree Register of the British Isles.

ELIZABETH SEAGER writes on plants and gardens for several magazines and newspapers, including her local Oxfordshire newspaper. In 1984 she compiled and edited *Gardens & Gardeners*, an Oxford University Press pocket anthology.

YVONNE SKARGON is an internationally-known wood-engraver who has contributed many fine illustrations to HORTUS.

ROY STRONG is an historian and garden writer, critic, columnist and regular contributor to programmes on radio and television. He was Director of the National Portrait Gallery from 1967 to 1973 and of the Victoria and Albert Museum from 1974 to 1987. His many books include *The Story of Britain*, *Feast: A History of Grand Eating*, his diaries, and *The Laskett: The Story of a Garden*.

KATHERINE SWIFT is the author of *The Morville Hours*, initiated by a four-part series about her own Shropshire garden in HORTUS. She has also written about hyacinths and her horticultural and botanical wanderings in Orkney.

JUDITH TANKARD lives near Boston, Massachusetts, and is a frequent contributor to HORTUS. She is founding editor of the *Journal* of the New England Garden History Society and an acknowledged commentator on Gertrude Jekyll and the British Arts & Crafts garden tradition.

ELSPETH THOMPSON is a regular newspaper columnist whose impeccable hands-on urban gardening credentials made her the ideal author of *The London Gardener*.

DEREK TOMS was a leading light of the Mediterranean Garden Society. He lived in Greece for several years before settling with his family in Turkey. He died in 2003, and his ashes were partly scattered in the MGS's garden in Sparoza; 'the rest have been given to the winds of Turkish mountain'.

CATHERINE UMPHREY is a gardener who writes, designs gardens and works as a grower of perennial plants for an old nursery near her Maryland (USA) home.

JOHN VERNEY was a sometime soldier, autobiographer, writer, editor, painter and illustrator. After living for many years in Farnham, Surrey, he settled with his wife in Suffolk.

Garsington Manor (see page 140)
Drawing by Simon Dorrell.

Index

Numerous trees, shrubs, herbaceous plants and bulbs are mentioned throughout the book; only those with more than a passing reference have been included in the index.

Numbers in *italics* refer to illustrations.

The Editor's Desk
Drawing by Simon Dorrell.